OTHER PEOPLE'S MONEY

THE INSIDE STORY OF THE S&L MESS

PAUL ZANE PILZER with ROBERT DEITZ

SIMON AND SCHUSTER New York London Toronto Sydney Tokyo

Simon and Schuster
Simon & Schuster Building
Rockefeller Center
1230 Avenue of the Americas
New York, New York 10020

Designed by Laurie Jewell
Manufactured in the United States of America

10   9   8   7   6   5   4   3   2   1

Library of Congress Cataloging in Publication Data
Pilzer, Paul Zane.
    Other people's money: the inside story of the S&L mess/Paul Zane Pilzer with
Robert Deitz.
        p.   cm.
    1. Savings and loan associations—United States—Corrupt practices.   I. Deitz,
Robert.   II. Title.
HG2151.P55   1989
332.3′2′0973—dc20

89-21667
CIP

ISBN 0-671-68101-X

CONTENTS

TO MY FATHER

ACKNOWLEDGMENTS

There are many people who need to be thanked for helping to bring this book to fruition.

First, there is my agent, Jan Miller, known as "the dreammaker" to the many aspiring writers on whom she was the first one to take a chance. Second, there is my editor, Allan Mayer, whose knowledge of the world and mastery of the language has humbled me throughout this project. Third, there is Bob Deitz, whose journalistic skill in conducting original research and organizing information gave the book a broader dimension than I had originally envisioned; Bob's wife Sharon; and his researchers Margaret Mall and Deborah Shores. And finally, but perhaps most important, there are my students at New York University and my research assistants Jeremy Ofseyer, Aaron Hauser, and Brandon Williams, whose faith in me is perhaps the most sacred trust I have.

"Daddy, what's a *goniff*?"

"It's a dishonest person."

"Daddy," I said again, getting my father's attention off his newspaper, "are there many dishonest persons in this country?"

"No, son," he replied. "Let me explain. In America, everyone trusts everyone else. We help each other out. It's what the whole country's built on. For example, when we get an order at the place for bedspreads from, say, Ezra Cohen—you know Ezra, on Essex at Delancey— we'll ship him the goods but we don't expect payment from his store for sixty days. It's called 'net sixty' terms. That gives Ezra time to sell the bedspreads. But he knows that he's got to pay us in sixty days even if he hasn't sold any of them. Similarly, when Izzy the converter sells us the fabric to make the goods, he gives us sixty-day terms, sometimes more when I need it, to pay him. And he gets similar terms from the mill. And so on and so on."

"Daddy, I don't get it. Why does that mean that everyone is honest?"

"Because if as few as one percent of the people in business in this country were dishonest, the whole system would collapse. If Ezra didn't pay me, I couldn't pay Izzy, and Izzy couldn't pay the mill, and so on and so on. Then no one would trust anyone else. And people like us could never start a business. We wouldn't stand a chance. It would be like it was back in Eastern Europe."

. . .

My father arrived in the United States in 1914 and, like a twentieth-century Alexis de Tocqueville, he never ceased to be amazed by America. But where Tocqueville marveled at the prosperity of the American economy, my father marveled at the American behavioral system of trust in one's fellow man—a system that he felt was ultimately responsible for the nation's prosperity.

As a child growing up in New York in the 1950s, I would hang on my father's hand as we entered both our synagogue on the Sabbath and the Bowery Savings Bank in the Empire State Building on deposit day. To him, the two institutions were almost one and the same. Just as he evidenced his dedication to his religion by making weekly visits to the synagogue, he evidenced his devotion to his children by making weekly deposits to the custodian savings accounts he had established for our education.

His faith in the American banking system was as absolute as his faith in his religion. I remember him shaking his head in disbelief when the Franklin National Bank went under in 1974, at the time the largest bank failure in U.S. history. And even though he died ten years ago, I felt his agony from the grave in the early 1980s when, as a real estate developer in Texas, I began to uncover the S&L story. It was his agony that led me to testify in 1985 before the House of Representatives that the S&L mess was potentially a $200 billion disaster.

PZP
Dallas, Texas
June 1989

PROLOGUE

It was a muggy and overcast mid-August day in Washington, the sultry summer humidity hanging over the Potomac like a damp cloth. At their mall-like headquarters just a block from the White House, the top officials of the Federal Home Loan Bank Board were gathering for their regular monthly conference. As far as Ed Gray knew, the meeting was to be routine. Gray was the chairman of the FHLBB, having been appointed to the post just three months earlier, in May 1983, by his political patron, Ronald Reagan. It wasn't a difficult job. Being head of the FHLBB was more ceremonial than anything else—a fact that suited Gray, who was basically a public relations man, not a banker.

The main item on the agenda that day, as it was at every monthly meeting, was the chairman's briefing, a presentation by the bank board's senior executives designed to bring Gray up to date on what was going on in the nation's $900 billion savings and loan industry, the supervision of which was the FHLBB's main responsibility. Conducting the briefing were David Maxwell, the executive director of the Federal Savings and Loan Insurance Corporation (FSLIC), and Jim Croft, director of the FHLBB's Office of Examinations and Enforcement.

Gray went into the meeting with no hint that anything was amiss. But his tranquil mood was not to last very long. For the central focus of Maxwell and Croft's briefing was a troubling development whose implications

Gray and his aides could only guess at. Later, years later, Gray would realize that the August 1983 briefing had provided him with his first glimpse of the ghostly outline of what would become the most severe financial crisis the nation had seen since the banking catastrophe of the Great Depression. At the time, however, it wasn't at all clear what was going on. That was the first of the tragedies of the S&L debacle: No one in a position to do anything about the crisis had any idea what was happening.

What Maxwell and Croft told Gray was that billions of dollars in brokered funds—"hot money," in the language of regulators—were flowing into S&Ls at an unprecedented rate. Quick to seize the opportunities created by the Reagan administration's penchant for deregulation —specifically, the recent relaxation of restrictions on the kind of accounts and interest rates S&Ls could offer— Merrill Lynch and the other big brokerage houses had been putting clients into investment packages of $100,000 or less, which they then turned around and shopped to the thrifts in the form of high-interest money market deposit accounts (MMDAs). It was a great deal for the brokers and their clients. Not only were the S&Ls offering unprecedentedly high interest rates in order to compete with commercial banks, but the money market deposit accounts were virtually risk-free. After all, the FSLIC insured all S&L accounts up to $100,000, which just happened to be the maximum size of the investment packages.

By the end of the year, Gray was told, there would be no less than $34 billion worth of such brokered funds parked in the nation's S&Ls. And every penny of it would be covered by federal deposit insurance. The problem was —*one* problem was—that the federal insurance fund that was supposed to protect these and most other S&L deposits totaled less than $15 billion—not nearly enough to cover the potential obligations that were pouring into the thrift industry's vaults.

Another problem was that the funds in the brokered accounts weren't being used to finance home mortgages, the thrift industry's traditional role. Instead, the hot money was flowing into an ever-widening array of investments that until passage of the 1982 Garn–St Germain deregulation act had long been off-limits to S&Ls. These investments included loan participations to acquire and develop raw land, equity holdings in businesses ranging from barbecue stands to ski resorts, and trading in such sophisticated financial instruments as interest futures and junk bonds. All were highly risky, and all were totally new to S&Ls.

But Gray's initial concern wasn't so much where the thrifts were investing the hot money. Indeed, at that point, Gray and his fellow regulators had no idea how the funds were being used. Rather, he was mainly worried about the potential liability being shoveled onto the FSLIC. If the thrifts' investments didn't pan out—and many of the S&Ls getting the lion's share of the brokered funds were already seeing loans go bad—the insurance fund could be drained dry. Or worse. If the influx of brokered deposits continued at the current rate, Maxwell and Croft predicted, the $15 billion insurance fund could find itself saddled with an additional liability of $380 billion by the end of 1985.

What Ed Gray glimpsed that day was the tip of an iceberg. It was an iceberg whose dimensions have yet to be completely revealed. Indeed, unless action is taken to cut the losses immediately, they probably won't be fully seen until sometime early in the twenty-first century.

The somber fact is this. The savings and loan calamity

of the 1980s is the most costly financial debacle in the peacetime history of America. Bailing out the thrift industry—paying for the mistakes made by Congress, the White House, and thrift executives—is going to cost U.S. taxpayers upwards of $200 billion. That is more than the combined cost of rescuing Chrysler, the City of New York, Lockheed, and Penn Central. In real dollars adjusted for inflation, the price tag for cleaning up the S&L mess will be fully three times the cost of the Marshall Plan to revive the devastated economies of Western Europe after World War II.

But the real tragedy of the savings and loan crisis is not so much the enormous bill that taxpayers will have to cover as a result of official neglect and mismanagement. Rather, it is the extent to which the calamity has undermined the noble purpose of encouraging people to save money to make their own lives better.

Worst of all, it didn't have to happen. History had already provided the lessons that could have prevented the ruin.

I.
GOD
LOVES
SAVERS

S aving money, wrote Charles Dickens in 1864, is a practice that encourages its own success. "If you begin [saving] and go on with it for a little time, you come to have a sort of passion for it."[1]

But saving money is more than a commendable habit. It is a personal act of faith, a form of self-denial that expresses confidence in the future. A person who denies current comfort and pleasure for future happiness is demonstrating his belief in a destiny that can be controlled and improved. It is one thing to pray in church for God's favor. It is an altogether different proposition to spare today on food, clothing, and shelter in order to have a better life tomorrow.

The savings of immigrants seeking to improve their lives were responsible not only for the growth of the U.S. savings and loan industry but for much of the growth of the United States itself. Looking back, their willingness to save may seem to have been only prudent. But consider

what courage the act of saving required of those immigrants. The poor, shabby newcomer to nineteenth-
century America, perhaps a Jewish peddler from Eastern
Europe or a peasant farmer from Armenia, had to deprive
his family of often basic necessities in order to salt away a
few dollars in the care of a nameless banker operating
from a storefront along a crowded, noisy street in Manhattan or Boston or Philadelphia. That immigrant, usually
a victim of religious or political or economic repression,
justifiably had no faith in paper money or coins not in his
possession. Yet the immigrant saver still had sufficient
faith in the American dream, and in the durability of the
American political and financial systems to bet that those
few pennies and rare dollars would not only be secure,
but be available when he needed them for medicine or his
child's education or perhaps even the down payment on
a modest frame house.

That's what makes the wreckage of the U.S. savings
and loan business such a lamentable irony. For the fact is
that the origins and rich heritage of the thrift industry are
anchored in noble purpose—to provide common men and
women with a way of accumulating modest wealth to
improve their lives and the futures of their children. Indeed, they bear an indelible religious imprint, rooted in
the philanthropic funds accumulated and disbursed by
the church in the Middle Ages and the burial societies of
biblical times.

The origins of the modern savings and loan industry
in the United States are found in the "friendly" savings
societies that arose in England and Scotland in the early
nineteenth century. These societies were voluntary savings associations sponsored by small parish churches or
wealthy, socially conscious landed gentrymen. Their purpose was to help the poor cottagers of the time put away

small sums for annuities that would help them to avoid charity when they were too old or too sick to work.

The public policy behind the friendly societies wasn't entirely benevolent, of course. A more businesslike motivation was to reduce public welfare expenses. Between 1750 and 1800, though the population of England and Wales increased by only 12.5 percent, government expenditures of funds to help the poor jumped more than fivefold.[2] That increase in welfare costs prompted the British Parliament, in 1793, to pass the first act "for the encouragement of Friendly Societies" to stimulate savings among the "lower orders." As the preamble to that law stressed, increasing private savings would have several benefits, including "promoting the happiness of individuals and at the same time diminishing the public burdens."[3]

The precise model for today's thrift industry in the United States was developed seventeen years after the Friendly Societies Act was passed, in a modest parish church at Ruthwell Village in Dumfriesshire, Scotland. There, in the mild summer of 1810, the Reverend Henry Duncan established the Parish Bank Friendly Society of Ruthwell. Its purpose, Dr. Duncan said, was to be "an insurance office for disease and old age" of the parishioners.[4]

While the Ruthwell bank wasn't the first friendly society to be established following the 1793 act, Dr. Duncan's experiment was distinguished by three important differences that set it apart as the first modern mutual savings bank.

The first difference was philosophical. Existing friendly societies operated on the principal of charity; people banded together to help a neighbor in distress. By contrast, Dr. Duncan's Ruthwell bank was created to provide a way for one person to accumulate funds for his or her own benefit. The Ruthwell institution was not so much a charity as it was a repository for personal savings. The distinction is important. In simple charity, a needy person is given help for reasons of mercy. But individual pride and dignity often reject charity. Avoiding the charitable motivation behind other friendly societies, Dr. Duncan wanted to encourage independence, self-reliance, individual pride, and dignity.

The second difference was, to put it in modern terms, professionalism. Other friendly society banks were loosely organized and casually operated. The Ruthwell bank, in contrast, operated under strict rules, including minimum deposit requirements and early withdrawal penalties, all of which gave the institution soundness and durability.[5]

The third distinction of the Ruthwell bank was its safety. Fraud and mismanagement plagued many of the early friendly society banks. In fact, the problem of fraud was so severe that in 1819 Parliament revised the earlier legislation to provide government safekeeping of deposits, an early form of insurance guarantees. Dr. Duncan guarded against fraud with a simple device: He procured a lockbox that required three separate keys to open, and put three trustworthy parishioners in charge of the deposits.

The Ruthwell bank attracted considerable attention. In 1816, the staid and scholarly *Quarterly Review* reported the "astonishing" news that in the four brief years since its founding, the Friendly Society Bank at Ruthwell had accumulated deposits equivalent to some $10,000, up from a mere $1,600 at the end of its first year of existence.[6]

But the success of the Ruthwell experiment really wasn't so astonishing, considering the moral fervor with which the spiritual goodness of saving was advanced from the pulpits of Dr. Duncan and other sponsors of friendly societies. The Highland Society of Scotland noted in an 1815 tract: "We must remember that a poor man's savings are continually liable, while in his own custody, to be pilfered, not only by professional thieves but also (and it is an incomparably greater danger) by his family and by himself; that they are not unfrequently lost by being entrusted to improper hands; that in most instances they are worse than lost at the alehouse and gin-shop. . . ."[7]

But the security offered by the friendly societies was only relative. Fraud continued to be a problem, Dr. Duncan's three-lock deposit box notwithstanding. Said the Highland Society in that same essay on the proper operation of a savings organization: "Frequently [deposits] are embezzled by artful men who, by imposing on the inexperience of the members, get themselves elected into offices of trust."[8] In fact, most of the friendly savings societies that flourished throughout England and Scotland following Dr. Duncan's experiment at Ruthwell were eventually done in by the linear ancestors of the high-flying thrift executives whose banks have collapsed through fraud or mismanagement in recent years in Texas, California, Maryland, and Ohio. Things got so bad that in the mid-1850s, the British Parliament appointed a select committee to study the friendly savings societies and their vulnerability to fraud. The committee members were especially incensed by an embezzlement at the Rochdale Friendly Society bank, where a particularly clever dodger made off with 80,000 pounds sterling.

One answer to the problem of insider theft came in 1861, with the establishment of postal savings banks in Britain. These banks, which were sort of government-sponsored cousins of the friendly societies, reduced opportunities for fraud by imposing centralized government control. Through local post offices, the government accepted small deposits, usually limiting the amount of money that could be put away each year and paying a rate of interest lower than what could be earned at savings banks or friendly societies. The money deposited was used by the government to finance public improvements; in effect, it represented a low-interest loan from individual citizens to their government. But the purpose of the postal savings banks wasn't to provide funds for the government. Rather, the postal banks were intended to foster moral improvement throughout the Empire. One American observer commented about the British postal savings banks: "Good results almost always follow the opening of one of these savings-bank offices. Numbers of men and women, boys and girls, are gradually induced to become depositors . . . and habits of thrift and economy are formed."[9]

The system of saving through the postal banks proved enormously popular in Britain. By 1885, more than 3.3 million British depositors had entrusted almost 45 million pounds at local post offices.[10]

The British experience with postal savings banks was not ignored. By the end of the nineteenth century, postal savings banks had spread across the European continent and to North America.

Postal savings banks were established in the United States in 1910, after having been recommended by every U.S. Postmaster General since 1871. In fact, between 1873 and 1910 some eighty separate bills had been introduced in Congress proposing to establish a postal savings system.[11] But the U.S. postal savings bank never developed into the important financial institution that it became in

Europe. The principal reason was that a viable institution through which ordinary people could save had already been built in the United States—the mutual savings banks nourished by an energetic and thrifty immigrant population.

From its colonial birth to its post-Revolutionary adolescence, America was more than anything else a nation of small communities. Except for the adventurous pioneers who cut trails into the Western wilderness, most people lived their lives within a few score miles of where they were born.

The banking system that evolved in nineteenth-century America reflected to a large degree the community nature of the young nation's social and political systems. To be sure, there were public commercial banks similar to those that had long flourished in Europe. The first real national bank in the United States was the First Bank of North America, conceived by Revolutionary War financier Robert Morris of Philadelphia and chartered in 1781. This was followed by the short-lived First Bank of the United States, created by Alexander Hamilton in 1791. That institution collapsed in 1811, and was followed by the Second Bank of the United States, which was created in 1816 and lasted twenty years.

The year 1816 also saw the establishment of a more durable banking institution: the mutual savings bank, a bank owned not by stockholders but by its depositors. The first such bank in the United States was the Provident Institution for Savings of Boston, and it was quickly followed by similar mutual savings banks in Philadelphia and New York. The establishment of these banks mirrored a nation of small communities. People trusted their neighbors, and it was only natural that those people inclined to save prudently for the future would prefer to put their money in locally organized savings institutions that arose as groups of immigrants clustered in new towns or new neighborhoods. The growth of these mutual savings associations recalled Dr. Duncan's philosophy of people taking their destiny into their own hands; they were depositor-owned institutions whose profits belonged to the people who had entrusted their savings to them.

"The savings bank is a growth . . . of the common school, the common wealth and the common welfare," wrote a Boston historian in 1886, some seventy years after the founding of Boston's Provident Institution for Savings. "It is considered the duty of every citizen who has a standing, character and experience suitable to fit him for the place to be willing to serve as a trustee of the local savings bank in the place where he dwells."[12]

The key role played by the mutual savings banks in fueling the nation's growth was reflected in the limitations they observed on what could be done with depositors' funds. They were permitted under most charters to invest a portion in interest-bearing accounts at national banks. But most of the money had to go into bonds issued by cities and states for municipal growth and improvement. As a result, most of the myriad public works projects that transformed the nation in the heady period from roughly 1810 through 1890 were financed not by commercial or central banks but by small depositors investing in their own future through their local savings associations.

The savings accumulated by immigrants paid for waterways and roads in Ohio, sewage and sanitation systems in Pennsylvania, harbors and subways along the East Coast. It financed the building of the nation's railroads, new electric, telephone, and water utility networks, and the municipal debt that made possible the growth of great cities.

The importance of immigrants' savings to the nation's economic development cannot be overemphasized. Indeed, the explosive growth in personal wealth on deposit with the mutual savings banks in the United States paralleled the massive influx of immigrants into the Eastern Seaboard in the late nineteenth and early twentieth centuries. When the Civil War ended, there were 317 savings banks in the United States in which about one million people had deposited less than $250 million. By the end of the nineteenth century, there were a thousand banks holding almost $2.5 billion for more than six million individual depositors.[13]

In April 1920, Paul Warburg, former vice governor of the Federal Reserve Board, stressed the significance of immigrants' savings in a speech before the Inter-Racial Council of New York City. "The funds of the [immigrant] working class amount to billions," Warburg said. "And as increasing taxation decreases the importance of the one-time class of capitalists as the exclusive field to cultivate for . . . investment, so the savings of the masses will become an element of growing importance in . . . the future growth of our country."[14]

These immigrants were almost always poor people. They were day laborers and domestic servants, teamsters and hod carriers, ship's carpenters, tailors and cigar makers. Theirs was a dream of an America of golden streets and limitless opportunities. It was a dream sustained by scrimping on meager wages to put away money for a better future. And, as they saved, they were helping to finance the very economic expansion that eventually would make them prosperous. A turn-of-the-century journalist observed of the tellers' lines in lower Manhattan savings banks: "Whether you are watching the sad-faced Jew struggling to save the passage money which shall free his family from Russian persecution, or the Greek who has left his beloved Peloponnesus to push a peddler's cart in the city streets . . . you must be at least conscious that you are standing close to the process of a nation's growth."[15]

The point is that the immigrants who contributed to the growth of the U.S. thrift industry were unexceptional people. They were little different, removed only by time and technology, from the schoolteachers, computer programmers, medical technicians, secretaries, and retired civil servants who entrusted their financial future to the imperiled thrifts of the 1980s. The history of savings banks in the United States is, more than anything else, a story of ordinary people.

Unlike commercial banks, the savings bank would accept any small amount. In commercial banks, only safecrackers and burglars entered without a polite and deferential note of introduction. Not so in the savings banks. "Who are the savings bank depositors?" asked *The Century* magazine in 1901. "All classes—the millionaire and the beggar, the honest toiler and the scheming rogue: the sweller in Fifth Avenue and the sojourner in the penitentiary whose back still bears the marks of prison discipline. They are all there, touching elbows on the waiting line at the teller's window."[16]

At the same time the savings banks were amassing the dimes and dollars of immigrants, another foundation of the modern thrift industry was being crafted by a growing American middle class. These were the building associations formed to promote home ownership. Building associations, the roots of which can be traced to the English building clubs of the late 1700s, were owned by their members, just as the mutual savings banks were owned by their depositors. But there was one important difference: They were technically corporations, not banks, whose owners were required to make systematic contributions of capital, which was then loaned to individual members to construct homes on lots they already owned. For regularly employed workmen, these associations held great appeal. The first building society in the United States was formed in Philadelphia in 1840; by 1890 there were perhaps five thousand of them, with assets of about $300 million.[17]

The differences between the mutual savings banks and building and loan associations were essentially operational. At bottom, like the mutual savings banks and friendly societies from which they sprang, the building and loan associations were intended to help ordinary people determine their own individual destinies.

"The building and loan association gives a solution of the problem of working people's homes that is most essentially advancement by self-help," noted the journalist D. A. Tompkins in a 1903 magazine article. "It is a plan by which working people . . . solve the problems of betterment for themselves. There is nothing philanthropic about it. It is business, pure and simple. The man or woman who joins a building and loan association and builds a house sacrifices nothing of self-respect and nothing of dignity. Indeed, self-respect and dignity are increased."[18]

What's more, the building and loan associations served, or so it was believed, as a stabilizing economic influence during an era of violent labor unrest. In Pennsylvania, Tompkins observed, "the Philadelphia mechanics are usually members of building and loan associations and live in homes which they own through these institutions. On the other hand, the coal miners live usually in company houses and are inclined to strikes and squabbles."[19]

Before long, the building and loan associations began

to take on the coloration of savings banks. A member would join a building association and begin making deposits with the intention of borrowing for a home when the funds became available. But then he might change his mind. In the meantime, new members wanting loans as quickly as possible might have joined the building society. Increasingly, societies showed themselves willing to accommodate such desires; the earlier member would be allowed to withdraw his principal and some interest (less fines and service charges), while the newer members would be granted a loan immediately. This separation between savers and borrowers represented a significant step in the evolution of the thrift industry, and as the building associations grew, it became more common for them to accept savings deposits from people who did not intend to borrow for home ownership. In time, as the American middle class expanded and home ownership became possible for a broader range of people, the building and loan associations began to surpass the mutual savings banks in numbers of institutions, and depositors and amount of assets.

And so, as the United States entered the twentieth century, the thrift industry rested on three legs:

1. Depositor-owned mutual savings banks

2. Stock-chartered savings banks intended to profit investors rather than depositors

3. Building and loan associations, soon to become known as savings and loan associations

Of these, the safest by far were the mutual savings banks. The safety of mutual savings banks was a direct result of the prudence of their managers, which was in turn a reflection of the nature of their ownership. Since mutual banks were owned by depositors, not stockholders, there was little outside pressure on managers to produce inflated profits. The managers thus had little motivation to speculate with depositors' funds. No funds were put into risky stocks that required margin calls when the market collapsed. Money wasn't loaned on swamps in Florida. Instead, deposits were invested in guaranteed public bonds or gilt-edged utility debt—or simply kept in the safe. So it was that during the Depression year of 1930, the mutual savings banks had 8.7 cents in their vaults for every $1 on deposit.[20] That was sufficient to cover every call for cash by worried depositors. In contrast, the stock-chartered savings and loan associations held only 3.2 cents in cash for every $1 on deposit, which led to runs and ruin.

In 1928, almost 500 banks suspended operations in the United States; the next year, 651 closed their doors. In 1930, the Depression began rolling over banks with unprecedented force and 1,352 institutions failed. In 1931, another 2,294 banks became insolvent and closed.[21] As for savings and loan associations, 438 of them sank along with $67.3 million in depositors' funds in the three years before Franklin D. Roosevelt became President and the modern thrift industry was established.[22]

Yet between 1900 and 1933 only one small mutual savings bank failed, and none tumbled during the Depression. That's a distinction which suggests another irony in the destruction of the savings and loan industry:

The foundation on which the S&L industry was established, the mutual savings banks born of the friendly societies and nourished by millions of immigrants, managed to avoid the calamity that led to FDR's wholesale reform of the financial services industry. Nonetheless, they were swept up in the New Deal's regulatory embrace —an embrace that first protected the thrift industry, then ultimately led to its ruin.

2.
BUILDING THE SYSTEM

It is difficult for most people living today to understand what the U.S. banking system was like when Franklin Roosevelt took the oath of office as the nation's thirty-second President on Saturday, March 4, 1933. As a nation, our tribal memory of that era has been wiped almost clean by more than fifty years of largely uninterrupted growth and increasing affluence. It has been a half century marked by the development of an enormously complex system of financial services, by instant consumer credit with plastic cards and electronic transfers via computers, by a more mobile population, and by a host of other social, political, and economic influences that have propelled us to prosperity.

In March 1933, by contrast, the United States was embarking on its forty-first consecutive month of deflation. National income had plummeted by 52 percent since 1929, declining to $40 billion from $85 billion just three years earlier. At the same time, the national debt had increased by almost 21 percent. Bank loans were only 59 percent of what they had been in 1929. Frightened by the wave of bank failures, people were starting to hoard cash. Between January 1 and December 31, 1932, the supply of cash in circulation declined almost 25 percent, with some $1.36 billion draining out of the Federal Reserve System. People were growing desperate for a lack of money. In New York City, the Union Methodist Episcopal Church announced a moratorium on church offerings, while a merchants' association of Greenwich Village shopkeepers issued customers redeemable scrip to buy goods. In Reno, divorces were canceled because a county clerk's funds were tied up in a closed bank. The transit system in Salt Lake City began to accept silk hose and toothpaste in lieu of cash for trolley rides, while in Oklahoma City travelers paid for rooms at one hotel with pigs and chickens. The Lewiston, Maine, *Democrat-News* announced new sub-scription rates based on bushels of corn: one year for ten bushels, two years for eighteen, three years for twenty-six. The Louisville, Kentucky, *Courier-Journal and Times* paid its employees in scrip that could be used to purchase merchandise from advertisers, who could redeem the scrip for more advertising space.[1]

Of all the crises confronting the new President, none was more pressing than the collapse of the banking sys-tem. Banks were failing by the hundreds each month, leaving many depositors destitute. As a result, an anxious public started withdrawing money from the system at an accelerating pace. Net bank deposits began a decline in September 1931 that reached crisis proportions by Decem-ber 1932, with total deposits in state and national banks falling almost 16 percent, to under $25 billion from almost $30 billion only fifteen months earlier.[2] Runs on banks had prompted the governors of Illinois and New York to declare banking holidays on March 3, 1932, the day before Roosevelt's inauguration, that extended through Monday, March 6. In closing their doors, the money-center banks joined an ever-lengthening list of besieged institutions. Nationwide, fully thirty-four of the forty-eight states had either no banking facilities or only partial banking services the day Roosevelt took office. The historian Susan Estabrook Kennedy observed in her account of the banking crisis of 1933, "The United States had never stood so desperately in need of rescue as on that bleak March morning [when Roosevelt took the oath of office]."[3]

Unlike the more conservatively managed mutual savings banks, the stock-chartered savings and loan associations were every bit as vulnerable to the banking crisis as the commercial banks, perhaps more so. This was because they relied heavily on borrowing from commercial banks to meet their depositors' requirements for cash at a time when people were pulling out their money. When the banking crisis hit, it was estimated that savings and loan associations had run up a tab of almost $400 million in short-term borrowings from commercial banks. And as the S&Ls tilted and tumbled, losses to depositors grew. In 1930, 190 savings and loan associations failed, creating depositor losses of $24.5 million. In 1931, 126 more went under, with $22.3 million gone forever. The grim statistics continued: 1932 saw the failures of 122 savings and loans, leaving depositors out another $52.8 million. And in the darkest year of all, 1933, losses of almost $44 million were recorded by eighty-eight failed S&Ls. Altogether, during the 1930s, a total of 1,706 savings and loan associations went under, with direct savings losses totally an estimated $200.4 million.[4]

The mutual savings banks, of course, were more protected because they were less exposed to speculation. But even though their funds were directed to relatively safe investments rather than risky ventures involving real estate or stock manipulation, mutual savings banks in the Northeast still felt it necessary to begin enforcing rules to protect their cash reserves. As a matter of practice, most mutual savings banks had generally ignored the regulations that required depositors to give the bank thirty to ninety days' advance notice before making withdrawals. That laxity changed in 1933. On March 6, 1933, the mutual savings banks in New York City—where there were more of them than anywhere else—began to enforce the advance-notice rules. This extreme measure had been taken only twice before, in the panic of 1907 and during World War I.

As a result, the mutual savings banks remained secure. One bank historian observed: "While thousands of savings and loan associations and commercial banks were failing, these [mutual savings bank] institutions generated such confidence among savers that the result was a net savings inflow almost every year of the depression decade."[5]

But mutual savings banks represented only one small island of safety in a banking system increasingly awash in red ink. Overall, the problem was a classic Catch-22. In order for the banking system to recover its strength, public confidence in it had to be restored. But the public was likely to remain wary of the banking system until it regained its health.

How to break the vicious cycle? One idea that began to gain increasing support was some sort of government insurance to protect depositors' funds.

The idea of insuring small savers' deposits wasn't new. Indeed, as early as 1819, New York State enacted a bank guarantee law that was a primitive form of deposit insurance. By 1837, however, after a financial panic that led to scores of bank failures, the fund had been drained, and in 1842 the law was repealed.[6] Sentiment for deposit insurance revived after the Civil War, when deposit banking became more widespread. Between 1886 and 1933, fully 150 separate proposals were introduced in Congress to establish deposit guarantees.[7]

Deposit insurance had been tried by some states for more than two decades before the Great Depression, but until 1933, it had proved to be a dismal failure. The Midwest and Southwest, then as now problem areas for the banking industry, were the principal laboratory for the experiment. Beginning with Oklahoma in 1908, an unbroken chain of states from the Dakotas south through Texas on the Gulf Coast had established state savings deposit insurance funds. But however noble the idea may have been, it contained an inherent and ultimately fatal flaw: The funds were limited and the risk inadequately shared, with the stronger, well-managed banks supporting the excesses of weaker, more vulnerable institutions. If that sounds familiar, it is. Precisely the same problem exists today, only on a national scale.

For a while, the early state insurance funds appeared to work well. Assessments were made upon member banks to build and maintain a reserve fund, out of which depositors would be reimbursed for losses suffered in failed banks. Until 1920, there were few failures, and losses were paid easily and promptly. Then, in 1920, agricultural depression fell upon the Midwest like a smothering blanket. Farmers became unable to repay loans for seed corn. Workmen lost their jobs and began defaulting on home mortgages. Banks in the states with deposit insurance began to hemorrhage, then quickly sank into insolvency. "When agricultural depression came," noted *The New York Times*, "it was as though one fire insurance company had written all its business in Chicago, Baltimore or San Francisco."[8] In Nebraska, where insurance was compulsory, the fund paid out $17.7 million before it ran dry, unable to cover an additional $20 million in lost deposits. In Kansas, bank insurance was voluntary; there the fund paid off only $2.7 million before it was drained, leaving depositors an empty sack and $7.2 million in additional lost savings that would never be repaid. By 1929, all of the state deposit-insurance laws were either repealed or inactive.

Yet even with this history of failure, deposit guarantees continued to be regarded by many as essential to reform of the banking system. Certainly it was the most emotional issue involved in banking reform. Hundreds of thousands of Americans had at risk everything they had saved—an estimated $4 billion in all—when the nation's banks shut their doors for a four-day holiday declared on March 7, 1933, by the newly sworn President Roosevelt in order to buy time for a solution.[9] They wanted protection.

During the 1932 presidential campaign, Roosevelt had spoken out against insuring deposits, arguing that experience had shown that such guarantees simply didn't work. He believed federal insurance for deposits would only encourage greed, speculation, and irresponsibility on the part of bankers. Roosevelt was convinced that federal insurance of bank deposits would give savers and bankers alike a false sense of security. Risky loans would become commonplace as bankers relied more on insurance than on prudent lending practices to attract small depositors. This could only lead to higher insurance premiums for banks with more cautious lending practices, as speculative banks collapsed under a mounting weight of worthless loans.

Joining Roosevelt in his opposition were the big East Coast banks, which feared that such insurance would require them to pay the bill for supporting weaker banks in the South and Midwest, where wildcat management practices were more common. The big banks also believed that sufficient safeguards already existed; in the event of a bank failure, depositors could be repaid from bank capital, surplus, undivided profits, stock in reserve banks, and, finally, the failed bank's own reserves. Moreover, the big banks believed that since most plans put limits on the size of guaranteed deposits, they might actually prompt massive withdrawals by large commercial customers seeking to diversify their risk.

Where Roosevelt misjudged the issue was in regarding deposit guarantees as an esoteric topic with limited political appeal, one that could safely be ignored without jeopardizing his campaign. He may have been right about the political risk, but he was clearly mistaken about the popular appeal of deposit guarantees. For even though he would decisively defeat incumbent Republican President Herbert Hoover in the 1932 election, deposit guarantees would come to dominate the debate over banking reform after he took office.

The debate over deposit insurance began to boil over in the spring of 1932 when Representative Henry Steagall of Alabama, an intensely partisan Democrat who chaired the House Banking and Currency Committee, became convinced that the defeat of President Hoover was not the certainty it was widely thought to be. In particular, Steagall feared Hoover could make a winning issue of insuring bank deposits if the Democrats didn't act.

To be sure, Hoover and the Republicans were certainly vulnerable. The economic environment was more than just somber in the spring of 1932. Hoover was being blamed by the American people for having allowed the unemployment rate to almost triple since 1930—to almost thirteen million jobless workers, or 24.1 percent of the civilian labor force out of work in 1932. And public anxiety over spreading economic failure was increasing. On the surface, it appeared that the Democrats could hardly fail to recapture the White House after twelve years of exile.

Still, Steagall was nervous. He visited with Speaker of the House John Nance Garner of Texas one afternoon in the first week of April 1932 to express his political concerns.

"You know, this fellow Hoover is going to wake up one day and come in here with a message recommending guarantee of bank deposits," Steagall told Garner. "And sure as he does, Hoover'll be reelected." [10]

Garner agreed. The Texan, who was soon to become FDR's first choice for Vice President, had long supported a federal guarantee of bank deposits. Garner initially endorsed the idea in the 1908 congressional elections following the panic of 1907, when hundreds of banks collapsed in the Midwest and Southwest. By the 1930s, as banks began failing in growing numbers, Garner took the unusual step of providing his son, Tully, with a written guarantee pledging the Speaker's own modest personal fortune as security for funds that depositors had entrusted to the two banks owned by the Garner family in Texas.

"You're right as rain, Henry," Garner later recalled telling Steagall. "So get to work in a hurry. Report out a deposit insurance bill and we'll shove it through." [11]

Steagall followed orders. On April 14, 1932, he introduced a bill guaranteeing bank deposits up to $2,500. Five days later, the committee he controlled recommended that the bill be passed. Steagall then sought advice on timing from his Alabama colleague, acting Rules Committee chairman William B. Bankhead. Bankhead suggested waiting until May 25, six weeks before the Democrats would meet in Chicago to nominate a candidate for President—a time when the political climate would be most favorable. Steagall agreed, and on that late May morning, Representative Bankhead introduced the bill as a special order for consideration. With the support of the House's Democratic leadership, it was approved after only four hours of debate.

But then the bill withered without action by the Senate. As it happened, Roosevelt was not the only one opposed to guaranteeing depositors' funds; a more important enemy in the Senate was Senator Carter Glass of Virginia, former Secretary of the Treasury under President Woodrow Wilson and the self-described father of the 1913 legislation that created the Federal Reserve System. Glass's conservative background and political sentiments were with the money-center bankers who opposed insuring deposits. It was a curious coalition: the aristocratic but liberal Roosevelt from New York State, the equally patrician but archconservative senator from Virginia, and in the wings the American Bankers Association, controlled by the large East Coast banks.

What Roosevelt, Glass, and the bankers' association didn't count on was the wave of populist support that would break in favor of federal deposit guarantees, creating irresistible pressure on Congress. The pressure was especially severe in the Senate, where the Kingfish of Louisiana, Huey Long, led the fight for federal deposit guarantees with filibuster, threats, cajolery, biblical citations, and every other oratorical weapon in the populist arsenal. In the end, Long won. In fact, not only did Roosevelt back away from his opposition, but after the battle was lost he tried to make it look as if he had been on the other side all along. Several years later, reviewing the effectiveness of deposit guarantees and recommending their extension, Roosevelt said the "record amply justifies the confidence which we placed in deposit insurance as an effective means of protecting the ordinary bank depositor." His former Vice President, Garner, read the statement, winked, and said to a visitor: "I see Roosevelt is claiming credit for the guarantee of bank deposits."[12]

But Roosevelt certainly wasn't behind deposit guarantees when the Democrats met in Chicago at the end of June 1932 to nominate a presidential candidate.

The issue of guaranteeing deposits was raised on the convention's fourth day by William G. McAdoo, a U.S. senator from California and, like Glass, a former Treasury Secretary under Woodrow Wilson. McAdoo introduced to the convention a resolution saying the Democrats should "unequivocally" support guaranteeing the safety of small savers' deposits. "If the party refuses to go on record to make bank deposits safe, you'll lose more votes in November than you can count in a week," McAdoo told the convention, echoing the fears Steagall had raised to Speaker Garner almost two months earlier.[13]

The Roosevelt-dominated convention would not be stampeded. "A [deposit] guarantee plank in our platform would create anxiety, would cause disturbances in our ranks and would raise up opposition to our party in November which I regard as entirely unnecessary," Glass responded. "So why inject here a proposal which will cause to rise up against us the most powerful interests in the country?" He meant, of course, the big banks.

With the Roosevelt cadre in control of the convention, there was no question of the outcome. McAdoo's proposal was shouted down in a chorus of "No, no, no," failing to get enough votes even to force a roll call on the proposed resolution.[14]

Throughout the campaign and following his election, Roosevelt's opposition to deposit guarantees never wavered. Indeed, it became the first source of the friction between Roosevelt and Garner that finally led Roosevelt to dump Garner from the ticket in 1936. Even before the two took office in March 1933, their differences over deposit guarantees became public. The setting was a December 1932 dinner at the National Press Club in Washington.

Deposit insurance "won't work," Roosevelt said to Garner, who was sitting two seats away from him at the head table. "You had it in Texas and it was a failure, and so it was in Oklahoma and other states. The weak banks will pull down the strong. It's not a new idea and it won't work."

Garner had to lean around Press Club president Bascom N. Timmons, the Washington correspondent for the *Houston Chronicle*, to answer the President-elect.

"You have to have it, Cap'n, or get more clerks in the postal savings banks," Garner said. "The people who have taken their money out of the banks are not going to put it back without some guarantee. A national guarantee can be made to work. Depositors are not going to run on banks which have government insurance. It would be like making a run on the government itself, and the people know that the government coins money and issues currency."[15]

Roosevelt was unconvinced, but Garner didn't stop trying to change his mind. Three months later, the day before the March 4 inauguration, Garner visited Roosevelt as the President-elect rested in bed in his suite at the Mayflower Hotel in Washington. Garner brought with him Senator Gus Lonergan of Connecticut, another supporter of deposit guarantees. "I was on one side of the bed and Gus sat on the other side," Garner later recalled. "I told him I'd get Tom Love up here to tell him why it didn't work in Texas and as a state system elsewhere, but can be made to work as a national proposition." Love was a former Texas banking commissioner who had served in the Wilson administration as an Assistant Secretary of the Treasury. Along with Roosevelt, who was then Assistant Navy Secretary, Love was a member of Wilson's "little cabinet." He was someone whose advice Roosevelt could trust.

It wasn't enough. Roosevelt remained unconvinced, and didn't even bother to meet with Love. Yet Roosevelt, Glass, and the establishment banking community were grievously mistaken if they thought that the deposit insurance issue would die. On the contrary, it had an irresistible appeal to a broad segment of the public.

That should not have been surprising, given the fact the Americans were facing a financial crisis unparalleled in U.S. history, a crisis tailor-made for the populist demagoguery of Senator Huey Long of Louisiana, a late-arriving but forceful and persuasive supporter of deposit insurance.

Long's assault on the big banking interests and the conservative Democratic leadership in the Senate began in January 1933, when Glass delivered his proposals for banking reform to the Senate clerk. Glass, the Senate's self-ordained financial expert, recommended several significant alterations in the existing banking structure. Broadly speaking, Glass proposed separating commercial and investment banking to reduce opportunities for speculation; greater authority for the Federal Reserve over national banks; and allowing national banks to open branches in states that permitted branch banking by state-chartered institutions. The Glass bill also contained a limited form of deposit guarantees for national banks, proposing a federal appropriation of $125 million to finance a liquidating corporation that would pay off depositors and dissolve failed banks covered by the Federal Reserve System.

Long didn't spend much time on the Glass bill when it was first introduced on January 5. But when the measure was brought up as the main item of business on January 10, his Senate colleagues gradually realized that the Kingfish intended a filibuster. First, Long demanded that the previous day's journal be read in full, a formality never observed in the interests of saving time. Then he took the floor for more than four hours. With two Bibles as props—"Two Bibles is never too many," he said—he launched a scriptural attack on the Glass proposals. "Where is the preacher today that dares to get up in the pulpit and quote those words of the Lord: 'How hardly shall they that have the riches enter into the kingdom of God! For it is easier for a camel to go through a needle's eye than for a rich man to enter into the kingdom of God.' " [16]

Long told the Senate that he basically objected to the Glass bill because it did not embody his "Share the Wealth" program for bank decentralization. "We have elected a President who has deplored and denounced and renounced the concentration of the wealth of the country in the hands of a few people," he said. "I do not feel authorized, and am not authorized, to make any statement as to what the President-elect of the United States thinks about this matter except what he himself has said to the public. I am not going behind the scenes to quote any private conversations. . . . But . . . unless the President-elect has changed his mind and faced about and is going exactly in the opposite direction and is eating his own words, he would have to veto this . . . bill if it went to him after the 4th day of March." [17]

The next day, Long turned his attention to Glass's limited proposal for deposit guarantees. Long opposed both the proposed $125 million appropriation and the limitation of coverage to national banks; he wanted the protection extended to state banks as well, and argued that the banks should pay the insurance premiums. He attacked Glass directly. "We find here the distinguished senator from Virginia . . . proposing to take all the money that has been going into the United States Treasury from these banks and putting it into the pockets of the banking monopoly, and, in addition, giving them $125 million more. . . . It is a most monstrous proposition. There has never been heard of anything like this in my day or in my time. . . . If we want to protect bank deposits, here is a way by which to protect them without costing the Government anything; in fact, it will give the Government money at the same time: The net earnings that these banks make above 6 percent ought to be paid into the United States Treasury and used in the public interest for the protection of the depositors. . . . " [18]

Throughout the filibuster, Long kept returning to the issue of deposit guarantees and what he saw as the inequities in the Glass bill. While the deposit-guarantee provision was not the principal reason Long and other populists objected to the bill—the branch-banking proposal earned that honor—his continuing references to deposit guarantees provided hints that it would become the most controversial issue in banking reform.

"While there is suffering all over this country," Long said, "while we are begging for a few million dollars to construct various and sundry things needed for public improvement and to give people work, showing, evidently, that there is a need for funds which we cannot satisfy, we are asked to go into the Treasury today and to make the Government of the United States a partner in an agreement by which the United States is to put up most of the money [to pay off depositors in failed national banks]. This may be a New Deal," Long added in a sarcastic reference to Roosevelt's campaign slogan, "but it is from the bottom of the deck. They are not dealing cards off the top. What is proposed here contains every device of harm ever found in socialism and none of its good." [19]

Long's filibuster finally ended on January 25, two weeks after it began, following a January 19 attempt at cloture that was defeated by a single vote. The closeness of the vote suggested to Long that it was time to wrap things up. But he made a final, emotional appeal for defeat of the Glass bill. "We have dressed it up and crippled it up," he said. "We have taken off the right leg of the corpse and its right arm and chiseled into its lungs." It was time, Long told the Senate, to take the "carcass" to the burial grounds. [20]

Though the bill eventually was passed by a 54-to-9 majority, the President-elect was impressed by the extent of the opposition led by Long. Lacking a specific program of his own, Roosevelt passed the word to Vice President–elect Garner and other House leaders that he wanted the Glass bill to languish without action when it was received in the lower chamber. They acceded to his request, and banking reform remained suspended until Roosevelt's inauguration on March 4.

In his inaugural address, the new President advised the nation to take new courage. Addressing the banking crisis directly, he blamed the industry for the problems that were strangling the nation. "The money changers have fled from their high seats in the temple of our civilization," he said, declaring that with new leadership the nation's confidence would be restored with "social values more noble than mere monetary profit."

The next day, Sunday, March 5, Roosevelt announced that he was ordering a nationwide bank holiday that would extend through March 9. As legal authority for that order, Roosevelt relied on the 1917 "Trading with the Enemy" Act, which gave the President authority to "investigate, regulate, or prohibit, under such rules and regulations as he may prescribe . . . any transactions in foreign exchange and the export, hoarding, melting, or earmarking of gold or silver coin or bullion or currency." Some people questioned the legitimacy of both the wartime act and Roosevelt's use of it for domestic civil purposes. But no one—not even his critics—questioned the need for prompt, decisive action.

Beyond a pressing need to suspend banking for a few days to give the public, the banking industry, and Congress some breathing room to realize and appreciate that new forces were at work to solve the financial crisis, there was another, more immediate reason for the banking holiday: The simple fact was that neither Roosevelt nor his advisers had a ready solution to the crisis.

When Congress resumed deliberations on banking reform on Thursday, March 9, few members knew the details of FDR's hastily cobbled-together emergency banking bill. But they all knew they were there to act decisively. In his message to the House and Senate, Roosevelt essentially asked for executive control over the banking system and authority to open sound banks immediately and less solvent institutions at a more measured pace. He also wanted some existing laws amended in order to provide additional currency and coinage to relieve the liquidity pressures that were being felt by both banks and individuals.

For once, Congress did move with urgent speed. The emergency bill was introduced in the Senate at 1:40 p.m., approved by the Banking and Currency Committee by 4:10 p.m., and passed by the full Senate (by a vote of 73 to 7) at 7:23 p.m. The only interruption in the smooth parliamentary flow was the introduction by Huey Long of an amendment that would make state banks members of the Federal Reserve System in order that "little county seat banks" would also have the protection of emergency legislation. (The amendment was defeated on a voice vote.) In the House, representatives began their consideration of FDR's emergency bill at 2:55 p.m. They passed it on a voice vote just seventy minutes later. President Roosevelt signed the bill into law at 8:36 that evening, only eight hours after it first arrived on the Hill. Most of the representatives and senators who voted for it had never even seen the bill, much less read it.

The Emergency Banking Act was a tourniquet applied to a hemorrhaging wound. Title I retroactively legitimized the bank holiday declared by Roosevelt. Title II consisted of a plan to reopen national banks with impaired assets. Title III authorized national banks to sell preferred stock to the public in order to strengthen the capital structure of weak banks. Title IV broadened the ability of the Federal Reserve banks to advance cash to member banks. And Title V, the final section, appropriated $2 million to implement the legislation.

Nowhere was deposit insurance mentioned. That was a topic that would be dealt with in the administration's yet-to-be-drafted bill for overall banking reform.

Still, it was an issue that was starting to make the new President squirm. On April 26, *Business Week* reported:

> The bankers are trying to head off deposit insurance. They will not be able to get away with it. It is to be written into the banking bill beyond any question. This seemed almost sure a month ago, whether the President wanted it or not. In fact, at that time the President and [Treasury] Secretary Woodin were known to be flatly opposed to it. Senators and members of the House now say the President was misunderstood. He really opposed government guarantee of bank deposits, and so, they rush on, do we all. But he is not now opposed to insurance by the collection of a small percentage from the benefiting banks. . . . Down came the bankers with a vigorous, but quiet protest, and the Administration veered off again.[21]

When the Roosevelt brain trust unveiled its longer-range proposal for banking reform, what emerged was a marriage of the Senate's Glass bill and the House's Steagall measure. On May 10, 1933, companion measures were introduced in the two chambers. The basic difference between the two—what historian Kennedy called "a viper's nest of controversy"[22]—was the way each treated deposit guarantees. Steagall's bill called for the first $2,500 of all deposits to be guaranteed by a fund financed by insurance premiums paid by participating banks; this fund would be available to all banks, large and small, state as well as national. The Glass proposal, which was more acceptable to big banking interests, continued to be a government-financed sinking fund restricted to banks that were members of the Federal Reserve System, a restriction that would effectively prohibit deposit insurance for customers of state-chartered banks. As *Business Week* noted, this would have meant that virtually all state-chartered banks would be driven into the Federal Reserve

System, since "it is inconceivable that they would be able to attract deposits in any community where a member of the insurance fund was also operating."[23]

Long had already pounced on the Glass proposal as poisonous to the interests of small banks. "I realize that the death mask has already been put on the small financial institutions of this country," he said following the defeat of his proposal to put small state-chartered banks under the umbrella of the Emergency Banking Act. "You have condemned us to death in order that there might be a survival of the select.

"Mark my words: You have condemned 15,000 banks to close in order that you can keep 5,000 banks open.

"Mark my words: The 5,000 banks cannot stay open any more than the 15,000 banks can stay open."[24]

Support for deposit guarantees was also building outside the populist movement. Early in March 1933, *Business Week* noted, "A year ago, every banker was opposed to deposit guarantees. It has been interesting to see banker opinion slowly veer around until now a respectable minority are not a bit shocked by the idea, whether fully convinced or not."[25]

A month later, *Business Week* predicted that Roosevelt, Glass, and the American Bankers Association would have to submit to public pressure. "Bank deposit insurance will be written into the Glass banking bill," the magazine flatly declared on April 12. " . . . It isn't being included because the Senator has had any change of heart. He never has believed in bank deposit guarantees either through governmental underwriting or through mutual insurance. But he is yielding to the country's demand. . . . Washington does not remember any issue on which the sentiment of the country has been so undivided or so emphatically expressed as upon this."[26]

As the Glass-Steagall bill neared final debate, Long increased the pressure on the President. The Kingfish's biographer, Pulitzer Prize winner T. Harry Williams, wrote: "Huey . . . would accept the [Glass-Steagall] bill, but only if it contained a provision that he and other progressives had advocated at the last session [of Congress]: government insurance of deposits in all banks, national and state." [27]

The Senate Banking and Currency Committee reported the Glass bill to the full Senate on May 15, and debate concentrated for four days on the deposit insurance proposal. On May 19, Republican Senator Arthur Vandenberg of Michigan introduced an amendment providing for immediate insurance of bank deposits up to $2,500. "The savings of a nation," Vandenberg said some weeks before introducing the amendment, " . . . are utterly the most sacred trust with which we have to deal; and if there is one thing more than another that threatens the social system today, it is the failure of the American system to hold those savings inviolate." [28]

Thousands of telegrams supporting the amendment poured into Washington, Glass receiving more than a thousand himself. [29]

On June 17, Glass announced that the majority of his Senate subcommittee had had to discard its opposition to the insurance plan because "we realized, as sensible men, it was a problem from which we could not escape." [30] And so the Vandenberg amendment was approved in the Senate by a coalition of populists led by Long and Midwestern Republicans led by Vandenberg. It then went to a conference committee for inclusion in the Glass and Steagall bills and was passed by the House on May 23 and Senate on May 25.

Roosevelt was not impressed. He let it be known

through administration officials, principally Treasury Secretary William Woodin, that if the final banking reform bill included the Vandenberg amendment, he would veto it.

Long responded by turning up the heat. "Let us demand that Congress do its duty," he urged the Senate. "There are men enough in these two houses, if the bill meets with executive disapproval, to override the executive veto if we have a mind and heart here to do justice by the American people. I do not care what kind of *pronunciamento, ipse dixit* or anything else comes from the other end of Pennsylvania Avenue," he said to the laughter of his colleagues. "I want to protect the American people. I helped elect the gentleman who is occupying the White House, on the ground and on the promise and on the platform that he was going to help protect the American people. It is up to us here to put some action through this Congress and put this thing [deposit insurance] in the form of law and send it up to the other end of Pennsylvania Avenue. . . . "[31]

Then Long extended to Roosevelt an opportunity to accept defeat without publicly admitting that he'd been beaten. "I have yet to be convinced that the bill is going to be vetoed," Long said. "I discount seriously the rumors that are circulating around here to the effect that the bill may meet with the veto of the executive. I do not believe it will. I do not believe he has ever said so, and I do not believe he would do it. In fact, I know he would not do it if I have any mind at all as to what motives would actuate this man in correcting what seems to be a palpable injustice. . . . "[32]

From June 1 through June 7, Roosevelt held a series of almost nonstop conferences with Treasury Secretary Woodin, Glass, Steagall, and other officials involved in the insurance debate. One person he didn't consult was Long, whose attacks Roosevelt pointedly ignored.[33] On June 12, Roosevelt finally accepted the inevitable, acknowledging the strength of popular support behind the insurance guaranty issue. After all, the legislation approved by Congress would fulfill the Democratic platform of 1932 and could be altered in the future if necessary. And Roosevelt won at least a partial victory in that what finally emerged was something less than a full-fledged insurance system.

As finally agreed, the major insurance provisions in the bill were:

1. Deposits of up to $2,500 would be guaranteed immediately in all banks that were members of the Federal Reserve System, and to any nonmember state bank that could be certified as solvent by federal banking authorities.

2. The insurance fund would be financed by assessing participating banks a premium of 0.5 percent of their insured deposits.

3. To administer the fund, a Federal Deposit Insurance Corporation would be created, effective July 1, 1934.

Though mutual savings banks were permitted to join the FDIC, savings and loan associations weren't, a situation that placed them at a competitive disadvantage. So in 1934—and virtually without controversy—the Federal Savings and Loan Insurance Corporation was established to provide similar protection for deposits in thrift institutions.

But at least two major differences existed between the FDIC and the FSLIC.

The first was that the FSLIC was created as a subsidiary unit of the Federal Home Loan Bank Board (FHLBB), which had been established in the waning days of the Hoover administration to nurture home ownership. The FDIC, in contrast, was an independent agency with no other agenda but the protection of its member banks' deposits. This was not the case with FSLIC, for the FHLBB functioned not only as a regulatory agency but also as a spokesman for the industry.

The second difference established by legislation was that deposits protected by the FDIC were backed by the "full faith and credit" of the United States government. This meant that if the nation's banking industry suddenly collapsed, as it came perilously close to doing in 1933, the federal government would be legally obligated to assume responsibility for protected deposits.[34] But the private wealth stored in savings and loans institutions did not enjoy that same collective guarantee. Due to a quirk of congressional carelessness in 1934, the FSLIC was not backed by the full faith and credit of the United States government.

Depositors lulled by two generations of safety since 1934 may believe that the FSLIC has that backing, and the Federal Home Loan Bank Board often acts as if it does. But as a matter of law, savings and loan deposit insurance exists only to the extent that Congress can be persuaded to appropriate funds when the industry is in trouble. It is a distinction that later became critical when the FSLIC was unable to close insolvent S&Ls and pay off their depositors until Congress appropriated $10.8 billion of the requested $15 billion.

In addition to the deposit insurance features, the Glass-Steagall Act and the thrift legislation of 1934 contained several other important provisions designed to protect the thrift industry.

1. Only commercial banks, mutual savings banks, and savings and loans would be allowed to accept consumer savings deposits.

2. The thrift institutions—savings and loans and mutual savings banks—could not offer checking accounts, and their lending activities would be restricted to residential mortgage loans.

3. Strict limitations were placed on the interest rates both thrifts and banks could pay on deposits. However, thrifts were allowed to pay up to half a percent more in order to give them a competitive advantage in attracting deposits for residential mortgage loans.

4. And finally, commercial banks were prohibited from paying interest on checking accounts.

All of this worked extremely well as the nation climbed its way out of the Depression. The system designed in 1933 operated smoothly through and after World War II. Indeed, the regulatory framework established under Glass-Steagall contributed significantly to the orderly economic growth and stability of the postwar years. The new savings and loan industry, protected by a clear set of rules and deposit guarantees, became a haven for small savers' money. In the thirty years from 1935 through 1964, the number of insured savings and loan institutions nearly quadrupled, rising from 1,117 with assets of $711 million to 4,463 with assets of nearly $115 billion.

In addition to serving as the people's bank—by 1964, fully 36 percent of all personal savings in the United States was in savings and loans—the thrifts made home ownership possible on an unprecedented scale, revitalizing an

American dream that had been shattered by the Depression. The neighborhood savings and loan was not so much a commercial venture in the late '30s, '40s, and '50s as it was the focus of a proletarian socioeconomic movement. Applications for home mortgages were processed in small neighborhood offices or walk-up flats in cities. Thrift offices were open during the evenings and on weekends to accommodate working people. Most of the seed money for home ownership flowed through the thrifts as millions of veterans returned from World War II to Levittown tract houses with Betty Crocker kitchens and the latest in vinyl flooring. *Fortune* magazine noted in 1970 that the S&L industry did "more than any other kind of private enterprise to convert the U.S. from a nation of renters into one in which two out of three families own their own homes." The spirit of what the savings and loan industry gave to America was probably best captured in the 1946 Frank Capra film *It's a Wonderful Life*, in which Jimmy Stewart portrayed an idealistic S&L president who stops a run on his bank by reminding the scared depositors what the institution had done for the community, how it had given shelter to a financially pressed widow and a modest new home to a young couple beginning a life together.

For thirty years after the Depression, not much new happened in the way of regulation of the thrift industry. But then not much needed to happen. What thrifts could pay for deposits and how they could invest those deposits were both strictly regulated. As a result, the auditing of savings and loan associations' books became a matter of routine, requiring little skill and less analysis, and the examination process for thrifts began to atrophy into a set pattern that would remain unchanged even when the industry dynamics were altered by deregulation.

What Congress created in 1933 and 1934 was a framework for stability in the financial services industry. That it endured for almost fifty years through recovery from depression, global conflict, and steadily rising prosperity is remarkable, if not miraculous.

But the bank-reform legislation of the New Deal set a tripwire that would cause the S&L industry to stumble toward painful collapse in the 1980s. The regulatory restraints imposed on S&Ls by the New Deal had transformed them from principals responsible for other people's money into agents who merely processed that money; they accepted deposits that could earn only so much interest, and then lent that money into a narrow, restricted segment of the economy.

This worked well enough as long as interest rates remained stable. But the fact remained that the New Deal had turned the savings and loan industry into a creature of politics and law, rather than one of economic reason. Indeed, the basic economics of the industry no longer made much sense. What sane economist would propose creating a multibillion-dollar industry of private enterprises, federally insured against loss, whose business was to borrow short-term from small depositors (who could ask for their money back at any time) and then lend that same money to the same people for terms of up to thirty years?

The government tried to manufacture economic logic by fixing the interest rates that could be paid on S&L accounts, and discouraging savers from putting their money anywhere else by setting lower rates on bank savings accounts.

But the regulatory boundaries set in the New Deal didn't permit the thrift industry to keep pace with a changing America. And America was changing. Following World War II, suburbs sprouted from the industrial corridors of the East Coast to the Pacific beaches of Southern California. As people became more mobile, some once-familiar institutions began increasingly to be regarded as lingering relics of a more nostalgic past—the mom-and-pop grocery or butcher shop, the corner drugstore, the neighborhood service station. And with mobility also came the need for a broader system of consumer financial services—more flexible credit, charge cards, checking accounts, and branch banking. Yet as the nation's banking needs changed and grew more sophisticated, the thrift industry remained trapped in the regulatory mentality of the '30s.

3.
THE
FENCES
COME DOWN

T̶he forces that led to the downfall of the U.S. savings and loan industry were set in motion in the 1960s by a national government that tried to fight a costly war in Vietnam without sacrificing peacetime prosperity at home. Combined with the impact of the 1973 Arab oil embargo, which ended forever the era of cheap energy, the result was an extraordinary inflationary thrust that spiraled upward almost without pause for more than fifteen years. But while the cost of living rose a spectacular 162 percent between 1965 and 1980, the rate of interest paid on consumer deposits by thrift institutions remained locked in place by Depression-era regulations.

The interest-rate limits set by the Glass-Steagall Act in 1933 had a savage impact on both the thrift industry and the millions of trusting depositors who had committed their savings to it. Perhaps most significant, the combination of unchecked inflation and artificially restricted savings deposit yields led to a massive intergenerational transfer of wealth. Americans who had entrusted their savings to thrifts in the hope of securing a comfortable retirement—for the most part, older people who had believed in the system and faithfully put their money in passbook accounts—watched helplessly as double-digit inflation wiped out the interest they had earned and then began eating into their principal. At the same time, those deposits were being used to underwrite mortgages for younger home buyers who were reaping the benefits of borrowing at 8 percent a year or less to acquire property that was appreciating at 10 percent a year or more.

To appreciate the viciousness with which inflation eroded Americans' savings in the late '60s and early '70s, consider this example: A couple planning their retirement who in 1965 had deposited $10,000 in a savings and loan account that paid 5 percent interest compounded annually would have seen the purchasing power of their nest egg *decline* by almost 25 percent by 1980.

Of course, people with substantial sums available for savings, people who were willing to risk their money to uninsured accounts, could negotiate better interest rates. But those with little discretionary income for savings, which is to say most Americans, were faced with an unappealing choice. If they wished to save systematically and securely for retirement or their children's education, they could either put away money in their neighborhood thrift and receive an artificially low interest rate of 5 percent a year, or they could open a passbook savings account at a commercial bank and earn a maximum of 4.5 percent. The Glass-Steagall Act allowed no other savings options.

As a result, Americans quit saving as much as they used to. In 1967, the rate of savings in the United States was 7.5 percent of disposable income. Two years later, it had dropped to 5.5 percent. What was happening was a process bankers call "disintermediation"—instead of flowing through banks, money was beginning to flow around them, in search of a better return.

The institutions left highest and driest by this rechanneling were the S&Ls. In 1961, savings and loan associations had $85 on deposit for every $100 on time deposit with commercial banks. By 1970, that ratio had dropped to $69 at S&Ls for every $100 at commercial banks.

Economics may be an imprecise science, but money does follow some basic rules. Like nature, it abhors a vacuum; without an objective, it melts away. If water always seeks its own level by flowing downhill, money moves uphill toward the best possible return. Thus it was only natural that with the assistance of a creative financial services industry, people began to reassert control over what they would do with their discretionary income and how they would save.

The S&Ls may not have been prepared for change, but the people were. By the early 1970s, Americans needed checking accounts, credit cards, and a host of other financial services unfamiliar to the thrift industry. And in a few short years they would make a shambles of the regulatory framework established by Glass-Steagall. The people would force Congress to make changes that should have been obvious for almost a decade.

The first threat to the regulatory structure came in 1970, when the Consumer Savings Banks of Worcester, Massachusetts, proposed something called the negotiated order of withdrawal, or NOW, account. A NOW account was very simply an interest-paying savings account that functioned like a checking account.

On the face of it, such an account was illegal. The

Glass-Steagall Act prohibited banks and S&Ls from paying interest on demand deposit accounts—or, as they were popularly known, checking accounts. Interest could be paid only on deposits that could not be withdrawn without at least thirty days' advance notice—in other words, time deposits or savings accounts. (In practice, of course, most savings and commercial banks typically waived the advance-notice requirement for withdrawals.)

But American society had changed since 1933, and so had Americans' banking needs. In particular, as people became more mobile, the availability of their funds, whether through a checking account or through credit cards, became an increasingly important priority. Unfortunately, the savings institutions were woefully ill-prepared to meet that need.

The NOW account was a way of rectifying the situation. To begin with, what Consumer Savings proposed to offer was a savings account that would provide a depositor with a monthly statement rather than a passbook. More important, Consumer Savings also proposed to allow depositors to withdraw their money from this account with negotiable drafts that could be made payable to a third party—in effect, it proposed to let them write checks on an interest-bearing time deposit.

The idea was a clever one, but permission to implement it was denied by the Massachusetts Commissioner of Banking—on the grounds that it violated the thirty-day-advance-notice requirement stipulated by Glass-Steagall.

Undeterred, Consumer Savings took the matter to court. "It's the consumer's money," said Consumer Savings president Ronald Haselton, "and he should be able to get it whenever he pleases for whatever he wants."[1]

On May 2, 1972, after a two-year legal battle, the

Massachusetts supreme court ruled in the bank's favor, saying that the negotiated order of withdrawal was a "distinction without a difference" from customary withdrawal methods. In other words, since the banks had been allowing such savings withdrawals for years, there was no reason for them to stop now. And so, a few weeks later, on June 12, 1972, Consumer Savings went public with its NOW account. The bank required a minimum deposit of only $10 and paid 5.25 percent annual interest. It also assessed a charge of 15 cents for each check written. Three months later, savings banks in New Hampshire began offering similar accounts.

The innovation found a public not just ready but eager for change. By early 1973, some seventeen thousand New Englanders had opened NOW accounts with deposits totaling $30 million, and new depositors were signing up at the rate of more than a hundred a day.[2]

Deregulation of the thrift industry, whether wanted or not by Congress and the regulators, had begun.

Officials tried to slow the process, but they found themselves unable to do so. In Massachusetts, for example, an attempt to pass legislation banning NOW accounts failed in late 1972. The most Massachusetts regulators could do was to impose a brief moratorium on the opening of new savings-bank branches, the idea being to prevent the spread of what state banking commissioner Freyda P. Koplow called their "unfair advantage."[3]

Some people could see the danger in what was happening. Publisher Malcolm Forbes, Jr., noted in a January 15, 1973, editorial in his *Forbes* magazine: "Some savings banks are bound to discover to their sorrow that there is more to checking accounts than honoring checks."[4] An industry that had been creaking along with minimal supervision was beginning to deregulate itself. Up until then, no particular expertise had been needed to oversee the thrift industry. For years, it had been called, cynically, the "three-six-three" business: take in deposits at 3 percent, lend them out at 6 percent, and tee up at the golf course at 3:00 p.m. Although the numbers may have varied somewhat—interest rates did move up and down a bit—it was a fair description. Ever since Glass-Steagall, the thrift industry had been so limited in what it was allowed to do that supervision required no special skills or even intelligence.

But now the rules of the game were changing. To take in more money, you've got to pay out more in interest—meaning you've got to earn more. Yet, traditionally, the thrifts never had to worry about making money. Mutual savings banks existed for the benefit of depositors, not shareholders. And S&Ls operated under strictly regulated guidelines that determined their profit margins. They were thus poorly equipped, both philosophically and operationally, to alter their business so fundamentally. Nor were thrift-industry regulators prepared for the change either.

Moreover, thrifts offering NOW accounts faced a potential future liquidity problem. Commercial banks had long been subject to high reserve requirements for checking accounts; in the early 1970s, around 15 to 17 percent of demand deposit account balances had to be kept on hand. In contrast, because of the advance-notice requirement for savings withdrawals, thrifts were required to maintain a reserve of only 4 percent.

But such concerns didn't add up to much in the face of the growing public enthusiasm for NOW accounts. By 1976, NOW deposits in Massachusetts and New Hampshire totaled $943 million. As a result, Congress bowed to the inevitable and passed legislation officially authorizing federally chartered thrifts and banks in those two states to offer the accounts. (Playing catch-up would become a pattern for Congress when it came to dealing with the thrift industry throughout the '70s and '80s.) A year later, by which time more than two-thirds of all depository institutions in New England were offering NOW accounts, the figure had soared to $2.1 billion.

And the practice was spreading to state-chartered banks in other regions as well—first to New York, then to New Jersey and the Midwest. "NOW accounts have been a boon for the thrift institutions, the savings and loan associations and the savings banks," noted *U.S. News & World Report*. "For the first time, they have been able to offer their customers a service that competes with the checking accounts of commercial banks—and go them one up by paying interest."[5] By 1980, when Congress finally got around to approving NOW account authority for all federally chartered banks and thrift institutions, Americans had deposited almost $20 billion in interest-bearing checking accounts, more than 20 times over the 1976 level. During that same four-year period, deposits in ordinary passbook savings accounts nationwide declined from $454 billion to $381 billion, a drop of almost 16 percent.[6]

The system was starting to come apart. And the regulators seemed powerless to stop it.

If NOW accounts were the first loose thread in the regulatory structure surrounding the thrift industry, the fabric was torn asunder by money market funds.

By coincidence, the first money market fund also appeared in 1972, the same year that NOW accounts were born. It was offered by the Reserve Fund of New York City, an innovative new investment company. In essence, a money market fund was an insured savings pool not subject to the interest-rate caps imposed by Glass-Steagall. Glass-Steagall restricted only the interest that could be paid on individual savings deposits; commercial banks and other institutions were permitted to pay whatever rates of interest they liked on large, pooled deposits. Taking advantage of this loophole, money market fund managers bought high-interest, large-sum, short-term certificates of deposit, then sold off pieces in affordable chunks to consumers, offering them a higher return than they could have received at a savings bank. What's more, the fund managers allowed holders of money market accounts to write checks of withdrawal against their accounts—meaning that from the consumer's viewpoint, having a money market account wasn't much different from having a checking account that paid higher interest than they could earn on a savings or NOW account. Legally, of course, the money market account wasn't a checking account; it was a mutual fund that invested in government-guaranteed instruments.

At first, federal banking regulations required investors in money market accounts to lock in their funds for at least eight years in order to qualify for the higher rates. But in June 1978, Washington eased the rules, allowing banks and S&Ls to offer six-month money market accounts that paid interest at a rate tied to the annual Treasury-bill rate, which was then fluctuating between 10 and 12 percent.

With inflation continuing to gnaw huge chunks of value out of Americans' savings, the result was a mad flight of capital. Small savers rushed to the thrifts to move their cash from low-interest passbook accounts into high-interest money market accounts at an astounding pace. In just one month, April 1979, which was described by *Time* magazine as "the cruelest ever" for S&Ls, nearly $2 billion bled from thrifts to other investments. Later the drain would rise as high as $5 billion a month. Walter Wriston, chairman of New York's Citibank, observed: "Americans are not stupid. They have been seeking a better return on their money, and [now they are] getting it."[7]

It had taken the thrift industry more than 150 years to accumulate $250 billion in assets. Money market funds reached—and passed—that level by the end of 1979, just seven years after they were first introduced. At the beginning of 1979, Americans had just under $108 billion in six-month money market certificates. A year later, the total was nearly $291 billion. Six months after that, by June 30, 1980, $362 billion was parked in the new instruments. Over those same eighteen months, from January 1, 1979, to June 30, 1980, the level of ordinary passbook time deposits at banks and thrifts fell by 24 percent, from $907 billion to $690 billion.

The loss of time deposits, their traditional source of funds, wasn't the only problem the development and growth of money market investments posed for S&Ls. Far worse was the fact that by the late '70s, thrifts were having to pay 10 to 12 percent interest on short-term money market certificates in order to remain competitive with banks. Thrifts, said Saul Klaman, president of the National Association of Mutual Savings Banks, had "the worst of all possible worlds: high interest costs and disintermediation."[8]

What really hurt the thrifts was that they were still limited by law to investing those high-cost funds in residential mortgage loans—loans that earned them a lower rate of interest than the 10 to 12 percent they had to pay on money market accounts. Recognizing the problem, the Federal Home Loan Bank Board took several weak steps to correct the imbalance. The most significant of these was its December 1979 decision to allow federally chartered thrifts to begin offering variable-rate mortgages—mortgages whose interest rates were tied more directly to the real cost of funds. The bank board's recognition of the problem came a bit late; state-chartered thrifts in California had been allowed to offer variable-rate mortgages since 1974.

In any case, it wasn't enough. As a result of the squeeze, thrifts began swallowing red ink by the tankerload. By December 1980, as the newly elected Reagan administration was preparing to take office, industry analysts were estimating that almost half of the nation's four thousand or so S&Ls were losing money, and they were losing $4 billion a year.[9] According to a memo on the S&L industry that was circulated among members of the Reagan transition team, "the new Administration may well face a financial crisis not of its own making. . . . Confidence in the entire financial system could evaporate."[10]

The anonymous author of that memo was right. However ineffectual Reagan-appointed regulators and the Democratic-controlled Congress might later prove to be in confronting the crisis, its foundation was laid by Reagan's predecessors.

Indeed, what led to the immediate crisis confronting the S&L industry in 1980 was a miscalculation by the Carter administration on how to deal with the out-of-control inflationary spiral. By late 1979, the pressure of rising prices had become almost unbearable. In the four years of the Carter presidency, consumer prices had risen an average of more than 10 percent a year; by 1980, the consumer price index stood almost 45 percent above where it had been when Gerald Ford left the White House.

What one observer called "the death knell of the old era"[11] occurred on October 6, 1979, when Paul Volcker, the newly appointed chairman of the Federal Reserve, took action that indirectly spelled disaster for the thrift industry. In what came to be known as Volcker's "Saturday-Night Special," the Fed proclaimed that no longer would the federal government try to restrain rampant inflation by holding down interest rates. Instead, the effort would focus on controlling the money supply. Interest rates would be left to float where they might.

Volcker's Saturday-Night Special was the equivalent of trying to extinguish a kitchen blaze with gasoline. It touched off an inflationary and interest-rate firestorm that almost destroyed the thrift industry overnight. S&Ls were particularly vulnerable to rising interest rates, since their loan portfolios were almost exclusively tied up in long-term residential mortgages at fixed single-digit rates. Without the restraining hand of the Fed, interest rates started rising with increasing velocity. By early 1980, the prime rate that banks charged their most creditworthy corporate customers was approaching 20 percent. Meanwhile, the rate on short-term Treasury bills, which served as the rate for fixing interest rates on money market funds and short-term money market certificates, was passing 14 percent and still climbing.

The squeeze on the nation's S&Ls quickly became intolerable. As Citibank said in a remarkable headline in a January 1980 full-page advertisement promoting money market funds in *The New York Times:* "If You Keep Your Money in a Passbook Savings Account, You're a Loser."

Regardless of whether Congress and the regulators were ready, reform was clearly overdue. Indeed, some officials acknowledged that consumers had already made deregulation a *de facto* reality. Testifying before a Senate committee in June 1979, FHLBB member Anita Miller conceded: "Whatever we may believe about the role of [interest] rate control, it has become progressively less effective as savers have become more sophisticated with respect to alternative savings and investment [vehicles]. Rate control has itself provided an incentive for unregulated institutions to offer rates of interest higher than permitted by regulated depository institutions. The development of money market funds is an outstanding example of this."[12]

Once again, it was time for Congress to play catch-up. As it turned out, the House and Senate wound up taking two significant steps—the first in 1980, the second in 1982. If they had taken them together, and supplemented them with sufficient regulatory oversight, they might have accomplished something. But that's not what happened.

When Congress went to work in 1980 to do something about the liquidity crisis plaguing the nation's thrifts, it failed to grasp that the industry's problems demanded a solution more complicated than simply removing the lid on the interest rates S&Ls were allowed to pay on deposits. As Congress saw it, if the problem was that consumers were taking their money out of thrifts in order to get the better returns that were available elsewhere, then why not simply let the thrifts pay depositors higher rates? As a result, that's just what the Deregulation and Monetary Control Act of 1980 did. It deregulated only the liability, or deposit, side of the thrifts' balance sheet, largely removing the interest-rate limitations that had been imposed by Glass-Steagall nearly fifty years earlier. No attention was paid to the other side of the balance sheet —the assets, or loans, that provided thrifts with their revenues.

What this artlessly ignored was that the real problem facing the thrift industry was that most of its money was tied up in those long-term residential mortgage loans—loans that were paying a return of 8 or 9 percent at a time when depositors were demanding rates of 15 to 17 percent. You didn't need to be a genius to understand that if you were borrowing money at 16 percent and lending it out at 8 percent, you wouldn't remain in business for very long.

As a result of the 1980 deregulation bill, the thrifts found themselves in an inescapable bind. They really couldn't afford to pay the higher interest rates to depositors, but neither could they afford to let those depositors take their money elsewhere. Faced with a choice between two evils, they opted for what they regarded as the lesser of them: They decided that rather than risk a run on deposits, they would have to grit their teeth and pay higher rates.

Thus, as the Reagan administration took office and the new law went into effect, money began moving back into the S&Ls, helped along by a provision of the 1980 law that raised the limit on FDIC and FSLIC coverage from a maximum of $40,000 to $100,000 per account. Jonathan Lindley, executive vice president of the National Savings & Loan League, called the increase in deposit guarantees a "symbolic move. . . . Congress was saying, 'We'll make [the insurance limit] whatever we have to until you get the message [that deposits are safe].' "[13] But there was a subtle difference between the increased guarantees at commercial banks and thrifts. Because the FDIC was backed by the "full faith and credit" of the government, it could draw upon the Treasury's general revenues if it ran into trouble. The FSLIC, on the other hand, required congressional approval for additional funds if it ran dry. It was a distinction that would later prove to be of great importance.

At that point, however, the S&Ls weren't concerned with such niceties. The interest-rate squeeze was devastating them. In the first six months of 1981, they were paying an average of 10.31 percent for deposits—and that was before figuring in the cost of salaries and other operating expenses—while earning an average of only 9.72 percent on their mortgage portfolios. As a result, they lost a total of $1.5 billion in those six months—more than 5 percent of their total net worth. In the second half of that year, the return on mortgages rose to 10.53 percent, but the cost of funds rose even higher, to 11.53 percent. According to the FHLBB, nearly 85 percent of the nation's 3,786 government-insured S&Ls operated in the red between July and December 1981. For the year as a whole, industry losses totaled $4.6 billion, 17 percent of its entire net worth. As *Forbes* magazine observed, "You can't borrow at 12 percent to invest at 9 percent—unless you are prepared to let your company go down the drain. That, however, is exactly what's happening at many savings and loans." [14]

At his Senate confirmation hearings in April 1981, Richard Pratt, the Reagan appointee who headed the FHLBB from 1981 to 1983, put the problem in historical perspective, concisely listing the factors that he said were "threatening to undermine the integrity of the savings and loan industry":

> First, the rapid escalation in institutions' cost of funds fueled by inflation and dramatic variations in interest rates is causing serious shortfalls in earnings.
>
> Second, the combination of deregulation and the natural competitive process in the market is forcing savings and loan associations to acquire an increasing portion of their funds at costly open-market rates.
>
> Third, the growth of unregulated money market funds is

causing rapid disintermediation and threatening the liquidity of thrift institutions, which cannot compete for consumer savings on an equal basis. . . .

Finally, low-yielding mortgage portfolios are not turning over . . . returns as quickly as in the past, since inflation and high mortgage rates are encouraging borrowers to continue to hold their low-interest mortgages.

In short, savings and loan associations may very often be paying in excess of 15 percent for marginal funds, while their lending portfolios are yielding 9 percent or less. Even the most basic financial analysis of such a situation indicates a severe strain on liquidity, net worth and earnings.[15]

And things were getting worse. In the first six months of 1982, the S&L industry's net operating losses totaled $3.2 billion. "At that rate of decline," said Pratt, "the virtual elimination of the S&L industry . . . is more than a theoretical possibility."[16] Obviously, the 1980 legislation hadn't done its job.

That summer, aware that thrifts were in desperate need of new deposits, the FHLBB decided to allow S&Ls to accept more brokered deposits. Previously, they had been required to limit such "hot money" to no more than 5 percent of their total deposits. The reason the limit had been imposed in the first place was the fear that too high a level of brokered deposits could dramatically increase an S&L's cost of funds. What's more, brokered deposits were fickle. Unlike individual deposit accounts, brokered funds could be—and were—moved daily in search of better returns, their mobility enhanced by the use of computers. For the most part, individual savers had neither the ability nor the inclination to shift their money around that often.

With the lid now off, the more aggressive S&Ls began going after brokered deposits with a vengeance. Traditionally, thrift institutions had concentrated their operations in the regions where they happened to be located.

But in this brave new world, their need for funds knew no boundaries, and many S&Ls began advertising far and wide for hot money. If a thrift was willing to pay the higher rates, it could raise millions of dollars literally overnight from the fund brokers.

It didn't take regulators long to realize they might have acted imprudently in lifting the limits on brokered deposits. In the first year and a half after the lid came off, the amount of hot money on deposit at S&Ls doubled every six months, reaching $29 billion by the end of 1983.

In any case, that was hardly the only mistake the government made. Indeed, it paled in comparison to what Congress did in the fall of 1982 as it tried to come up with a cure for its 1980 cure. Once again, the legislators told the industry to feast on cake when what it needed was bread. If you need to earn more money on investments, Congress in effect said in the Garn–St Germain Depository Institutions Decontrol Act of 1982, then go out and invest in businesses that will earn you more money. What's more, it added, if S&Ls were having trouble maintaining the required 4 percent ratio of net worth to deposits, the answer was simple: lower the requirement to a minuscule 3 percent.

The Garn–St Germain bill was muscled into law mainly by two men, Rhode Island Representative Fernand St Germain, the chairman of the House Banking Committee, and House Majority Leader Jim Wright of Texas, both of whom had strong fund-raising ties to the thrift industry. What they accomplished was to get Congress to grant new and wide-ranging powers to S&Ls— powers whose implications few on Capitol Hill or elsewhere really understood.

To begin with, under the new law, thrifts were no longer restricted to just residential mortgage lending.

Now they could make loans for shopping centers and office buildings, raw undeveloped land and barbecue stands. Indeed, they could invest in virtually anything that struck their fancy, including junk bonds. And they could do all of this with less capital than ever before, and with no additional government supervision.

With Congress setting the tone, the regulators at the FHLBB joined in the frenzy, actively encouraging thrift owners to take advantage of the new relaxed regulations. In the FHLBB's Ninth District, which includes Texas, Louisiana, Mississippi, Arkansas, and New Mexico, the regulators created a traveling road show to explain the new opportunities to thrift owners. And in June 1983, only a month after he replaced Pratt as chairman of the FHLBB, Edwin Gray gave Texas thrift owners something of a pep talk. "Some savings and loan institutions . . . may not yet be fully aware of their options in applying [the new law] to their particular needs and circumstances," he said. "For instance . . . in order to utilize their commercial lending authority, they might choose to buy participations in commercial loan transactions without having to establish a commercial lending operation."

As it turned out, the loan participations Gray urged on the S&L owners would eventually prove to be the vehicle by which the cancer of mismanagement and fraud that plagued Texas thrifts was spread throughout the nation.

Beyond educating thrift owners in how to mismanage their way into insolvency, the regulators instituted an array of gimmicky accounting rules that completely ignored traditional notions of profitability, safety, and soundness.

The new accounting procedures, which had been approved by Congress, represented the most cynical kind of

misuse of official power. Known as "regulatory accounting principles," or RAP, they differed sharply from generally accepted accounting principles (GAAP). Perhaps
the most astonishing thing about RAP accounting was
that it simply denied the existence of losses suffered as a
result of interest-rate differentials. Under RAP accounting, a thrift that sold off its mortgage-loan portfolio at a
loss didn't have to record the loss in the period in which
it was incurred; rather, it could write it off over the lifetime of the sold-off mortgages. (GAAP would call for the
loss to be recognized at the time the portfolio was sold.)

For example, say that an S&L, desperate to increase
its portfolio yield in order to cover the high cost of deposits, sold a $50,000, 10 percent, twenty-year mortgage for
$40,000. (Such a mortgage would inevitably fetch less
than its face value because of its relatively low yield.)
Under RAP accounting, instead of recording the $10,000
loss in the year in which the mortgage was sold, the thrift
could amortize the loss over the next twenty years at $500
a year. Meanwhile, it could use the $40,000 it received for
the mortgage to make some new, more speculative investment—say, in commercial real estate or junk bonds—that
offered the kind of high return needed to pay for the high
cost of deposits. Of course, to make economic sense, the
new investment would have to do more than earn enough
to cover the cost of deposits; it would have to yield a
sufficiently high return also to cover that $10,000 time
bomb now ticking away at $500 a year.

The new accounting rules, however, seemed designed to obscure that fact. Say the new investment was a
$40,000 loan that paid 15 percent interest—or $6,000 a
year. Under normal accounting, the S&L would be obligated to record a $9,000 net loss on the transaction—the
$10,000 loss on the sale of the mortgage plus the loss of

the $5,000-a-year interest income that the mortgage had been producing, offset by the $6,000-a-year interest income that the new loan was bringing in. Under RAP accounting, by contrast, the same transaction would come out looking very different; instead of recognizing the full $10,000 loss on the sale of the old mortgage, the S&L would merely have to record one-twentieth of the loss, or $500. Thus, instead of netting out as a $9,000 loss, the deal would be viewed as having produced a $500 profit.

So which is it? Did the thrift make $500 or lose $9,000? Has its net worth been increased or decreased? Generally accepted accounting principles, as well as common sense, would say it was the latter. After all, all the paper-shuffling in the world can't turn a real loss into an imaginary profit—not over the long run.

By making the thrifts appear to be more solvent than they were, the new accounting rules not only hastened the day of reckoning that ultimately had to come, they also guaranteed that it would be worse. As *Forbes* noted, if the S&Ls had been treated like any other business, "they might never have gotten into the fix they are in now. They and the regulators would have been forced to face the music long ago instead of letting things slide until the situation was truly desperate." [17]

At the time, however, hardly anyone in the thrift industry or the government gave much thought to such warnings. Indeed, in April 1983, the FHLBB announced yet another relaxation of the rules—this one involving loan-to-value standards. Under the old rules, if you borrowed money from an S&L to buy, say, a house, the S&L was not allowed to lend you more than two-thirds of the appraised value of the house. On April 3, 1983, however, that limit was lifted. From now on, S&Ls could lend up to 100 percent of an asset's appraised value—meaning, for example, that a developer who wanted to buy a piece of raw land with an appraised value of $1 million could borrow the entire amount from an S&L and close the deal without putting up a penny of his own money. In short, it was an opportunity for speculators to make deals without any risk.

In addition, the new rules also allowed S&Ls to charge origination fees of up to 6 percent of the loan amount in deals involving real estate acquisition, development, and construction. This was another bonanza for speculators—one that encouraged wheeler-dealers not simply to borrow from thrifts, but to go out and buy their own S&Ls. Given the reduced net-worth requirements allowed by the Garn–St Germain Act, a speculator willing to put up just $3 million could open an S&L and attract $100 million worth of deposits. He could then lend out the entire $100 million to developers, charging them 6 percent in loan-origination fees—or $6 million. With that, he would not only have covered his original $3 million investment, he would have made an additional $3 million to boot.

What would happen if the $100 million loan went bad? Well, that would be the government's problem. After all, the deposits the speculator used to fund the loan would have been insured by the FSLIC.

What virtually guaranteed that this sort of reform would lead to disaster was that Congress and the Reagan administration neglected to accompany it with any sort of increase in government supervision. Indeed, oversight actually declined. In 1982, as the restraints came down, the FHLBB conducted 2,796 field examinations of thrift institutions. That was 12 percent fewer than the year before and almost 20 percent under the 1979 level.[18] Roy Green said in late 1987, as he surveyed the wreckage of the Texas thrift industry he had supervised as chairman of the FHLBB's Ninth District: "When Congress deregulated the thrift industry it forgot to deregulate the regulators."

Not everyone was blind to the implications of what was happening. The older, more conservative thrift owners understood all too well that the new accounting regulations and the other changes were bound to encourage massive speculation. As a result, many of them decided to get out of the business.

They didn't have to look hard for buyers. Indeed, the industry was ripe for a mugging. Virtually all the restraints had been lifted on what S&Ls could and couldn't do. Capital requirements for ownership had been eased. Risk had all but been eliminated by the increase in deposit guarantees.

As a result, opportunists flocked to buy whatever thrift charters were being offered for sale by more prudent sorts who were disgusted by what Congress and the regulators had wrought. In Texas, where most of the problems of fraud and mismanagement would occur, some fifty-five applications for S&L takeovers were filed in 1983 and 1984. "Texas real estate developers in particular have been drawn to the S&Ls and have begun to bid for thrifts in other states, too—sometimes to the consternation of the locals," the *Dallas Times Herald* reported in May 1985. "The newcomers have helped transform the profile of the state's savings and loan industry. Sleepy little thrifts have become aggressive financial institutions. S&Ls that once made home mortgages and little else now lend extensively for commercial real estate construction and land acquisition and sometimes act as developers themselves." [19]

In the beginning at least, these aggressive developers were greeted with open arms by federal regulators. "No one will admit it now, but at the time the Federal Home Loan Bank welcomed these guys into the industry," former Texas regulatory chief L. Linton Bowman told *U.S. News & World Report.* As Bowman described it, the bank board's response to this new breed of thrift owner was "Oh, you've got money? Come on in."[20]

4.
THE
COWBOYS

After Congress and the regulators took down the fences around the thrift industry, the new owners of savings and loans in Texas were like cowboys out on a drunken spree after a dusty trail drive. "Fast Eddie" McBirney, Don Dixon, Tom Gaubert, Jarrett Woods, Tyrell "Terry" Barker—they and a score of other real estate speculators forever changed the nature of the U.S. savings and loan industry. Of the twenty-four most deeply insolvent thrifts in Texas in 1987, twenty were owned by real estate developers who bought their way into the industry following deregulation in 1980.

As these cowboys took over S&Ls in 1981, '82, and '83, they found themselves in possession of a fresh license to do almost any kind of business they wished. Regulatory oversight had not been strengthened as broad new powers were granted to S&L owners; in fact, the examination process had actually been weakened. And so as the industry's new speculators spread across the Texas prairie, tens of billions of dollars in S&L deposits poured into ventures that had nothing to do with the thrift industry's traditional role, financing homes for people. One Texas thrift, Lamar Savings, announced plans to open a branch office on the moon. Another opened a chain of barbecue stands. A third backed a speculative residential development that would have required building a bridge over a ten-lane Interstate highway. McBirney, who referred to Sunbelt Savings' new, massive glass-and-pink-marble building in North Dallas as the thrift's "intergalactic headquarters," lent more than $3 million in insured funds to a terminally ill friend and business associate to buy a fleet of gaudily painted Rolls-Royces from Oregon cult guru Bhagwan Shree Rajneesh.

Novel phrases entered the language of the savings and loan industry: "daisy-chain land flips," "cash for trash," "trading a dead horse for a dead cow," "a rolling loan gathers no loss." They described transactions that reaped quick fortunes for insiders, but ultimately represented a burden of billions of dollars for taxpayers.

In addition to bizarre transactions that were unknown to a traditionally conservative and restricted industry, savings and loans poured funds into more conventional commercial real estate projects throughout the Southwest. Thrifts began to finance the acquisition of raw land and construction, offering development loans for new office buildings, apartments, and retail shopping centers. Towering construction cranes began to silhouette the skylines of Dallas, Austin, San Antonio, and Houston.

The industry was on a deregulation high. Between 1983 and 1986, S&L lending for land acquisition and development and other nonresidential real estate purposes nearly doubled, to $142.1 billion from $74.1 billion. In the Ninth FHLBB District, dominated by Texas, the growth of commercial real estate lending was even more dramatic. In Dallas, between the beginning of 1983 and the end of 1984, fully 29.3 million square feet of new office space came on the market—the equivalent of all of the office space in Miami at the end of 1988.[1] Many of the new buildings would never be occupied. By the end of 1987, there was more empty office space in the Dallas market area—almost 40 million square feet—than there was total office space in the entire central business district of Boston.[2]

While thrifts failed in other states, Texas was the flash point for fraud and mismanagement in the savings and loan industry. "Just because an institution is located someplace else . . . Virginia, Minnesota, Utah, Maryland . . . doesn't mean that a part of its asset problems are not in Texas," FHLBB chairman Danny Wall pointed out in 1988. "Chances are that if it is a troubled institution, some of its problems are in the state of Texas."[3] In Arkansas, for example, FirstSouth Savings and Loan Association of Pine Bluff failed because most of its $896 million in bad loans—64 percent of FirstSouth's entire loan portfolio was worthless—was owed by Texas developers, among them a group involving the then mayor of Dallas, A. Starke Taylor, Jr. Similarly, the main reason a small thrift in Mount Pleasant, Iowa, Capitol Savings & Loan, went under in February 1986, according to federal regulators, was a $20 million loss on loans to another Dallas developer and thrift owner, Democratic Party fund-raiser Tom Gaubert. In a May 11, 1987, article entitled "Deep in the Hole in Texas," *Fortune* magazine said "go-for-broke entrepreneurs" in Texas were largely responsible for turning a simple mess into a severe financial crisis. "By the time flat-footed regulators caught up with them, they had run amok," Fortune said. "At best, they shoveled government-insured deposits out of the vaults to finance doomed development projects. At worst, they simply stole."[4]

Why Texas? There are several explanations.

The first, and easiest, is what Texans themselves would have you believe. Texans will tell you that their S&L entrepreneurs were for the most part good ol' boys, imbued with a frontier spirit of pioneer adventurism, who saw an opportunity and took aggressive advantage of it. Okay, the reasoning goes, maybe some of them went too far; but hey, Bubba, there's nothing wrong with trying to turn a few million quick bucks, is there? That chauvinistic defense is at least partly valid. The fact remains, however, that Texas doesn't have a monopoly on resourceful business spirit. The same alibi could be made in New York, or California, or Florida, or any other state in a nation that was built upon entrepreneurial imagination and energy.

A more convincing reason is that Texas was a focus of the thrift whirlpool because rising oil prices in the late '70s and early '80s inspired a boomtown psychology that washed across the state, leaving in its wake a rosy glow of unbridled optimism. From Florida to Southern California, the Sunbelt was on a roll in the early 1980s. Chamber of Commerce types liked to say in those days that Texas was the golden buckle on the Sunbelt. The reason was oil, the vast pools of energy that lay beneath the Permian Basin in West Texas and the piney woods of East Texas. The Arab oil embargo of 1974 had combined with the inflationary spiral of the Carter years to boost oil prices to unprecedented levels. In July 1980 the average price of crude oil was just above $32 a barrel. A month later it was almost $1 higher, and the escalation was just beginning. By the spring of 1981 the price had risen to an all-time high of $35.53 a barrel.

Two years later, in the spring of 1983, oil prices had dipped back to around $30 a barrel,[5] but the oil-based Texas economy remained on a high that influenced all other industries in the state, especially real estate. Texas's population ballooned by more than 11 percent between 1980 and 1984, compared with an increase of less than 5 percent nationwide.[6] Vehicle rental companies reported a growing backlog of one-way reservations as thousands of families in the Midwest and Northeast packed their furniture in U-Haul trucks and trailers and made their way south to find jobs and a new future in the Lone Star State. It was a modern version of the post–Civil War era when ex-Confederates scratched "GTT" (Gone to Texas) on their doorframes before heading off to seek their fortune on the Western frontier.

By 1983, the Dallas and Houston newspapers were selling thousands of copies fattened with classified employment ads each Sunday in Detroit. The Texas jobless rate in 1982 was 6.9 percent, fully 29 percent below the national unemployment rate of 9.7 percent.[7] Employment in the Texas mining industry, the category for measuring jobs in the oil patch and related industries, rose to 302,270 by 1982, up almost 50 percent from 1979.

This meteoric growth generated a false sense of never-ending prosperity and led thrift owners to use their new lending powers to finance projects that would have been shelved in more prudent times. When the abrupt prosperity ended and oil prices started sliding—from $29 a barrel in the spring of 1983 to below $10 in early '86—the thrift industry in Texas responded by accelerating its already frenetic lending pace. Thrift owners were trying to make up for bad loans by increasing their volume, but that only made their problems even worse. By 1985, the industry was teetering precariously on the verge of disaster. Its vulnerability increased in 1986 when Congress revised tax laws to strip some real estate investments of the tax advantages they had enjoyed since 1982—and then made the change retroactive. The combination of falling oil prices and changes in the tax law turned the real estate boom into a bust almost overnight. Before long, Texas bankruptcy courts would be playing host to such well-known figures as the Hunt brothers, heart surgeon Denton Cooley of Houston, and former Texas governor and treasury secretary John Connally.

In all, when the regulators began trying to clean up the S&L mess in 1988, thrift losses in Texas alone—losses that taxpayers would eventually have to cover—totaled some $25 billion. Put in perspective, that was almost 20 percent of the entire federal budget deficit for 1988.

How much of that loss was due to mismanagement resulting from boomtown psychology, and how much was due to outright fraud? The answer to that question may never be known. The Federal Home Loan Bank Board told the Commerce, Consumer and Monetary Affairs subcommittee of the House Government Operations Committee in October 1987 that it estimated the total amount lost due to misconduct or fraud at $3.78 billion since 1984. But the subcommittee, chaired by Representative Doug Barnard of Georgia, said the FHLBB's estimate was unrealistically low—mainly because the regulators simply ignored some of the most publicized cases of potential fraud in Texas. The subcommittee noted in a report issued late in 1988: "Misconduct and criminality by financial institution insiders has been a major contributing factor to [S&L] insolvencies. . . . At least three-quarters of all S&L insolvencies appear to be linked in varying degrees to such misconduct. . . ."[8] In what amounted to an accusation of cover-up, the report noted pointedly that the data on fraud provided by the FHLBB "is so incomplete as to be almost worthless."[9] In particular, the report pointed out that the FHLBB had "excluded some of the more notorious Northern Texas institutions as to which there are major criminal investigations. It excluded [Tom Gaubert's] Independent American Savings Association . . . [Ed McBirney's] Sunbelt Savings of Texas and [Jarrett Woods's] Western Federal Savings Association—all of which, the subcommittee said, "were known for making reciprocal loan deals among themselves and for making loans to insiders" and all of which had had, as a result, most of their "major principals . . . removed and prohibited from entering the industry." To have examined possible misconduct at Texas S&Ls without including Sunbelt, Independent American, and Western, the subcommittee concluded, was "incredible."

"What is the Bank Board's motivation?" the subcommittee asked. "Information was provided . . . which indicated that, to reveal the full extent of FSLIC losses where misconduct played some role . . . could not help the industry and could possibly be 'inflammatory.' "[10]

And that leads to the third reason why savings and loan problems focused on Texas. This was the cozy relationships between Texas thrift owners, politicians, and industry regulators. The ties in Texas between regulators and the people they were supposed to be supervising went far beyond golf-course clubbishness. A typical example was that of Texas Savings and Loan Commissioner Linton Bowman, the highest official in charge of supervising state-chartered thrifts. Bowman was a partner in a real estate venture with Patrick King, a former colleague at the Texas Savings and Loan Commission who in 1987 became a target of an investigation and legal action by federal regulators in connection with the alleged "looting" of Don

Dixon's defunct Vernon Savings and Loan Association of Dallas, which went under in March 1987. (In 1989, King was indicted by a federal grand jury on charges of using S&L funds to make illegal campaign contributions.) When his relationship with King became widely known in 1987, Bowman resigned his position as head of the state S&L commission.

Nor was Bowman the only prominent political figure in Texas to have ties with high-flying thrifts. Indeed, when a Justice Department task force on thrift fraud descended on Dallas in 1987, the list of people whose records it subpoenaed amounted to a who's who in Texas politics, real estate, and banking in the early 1980s. Local politicos whose records were sought included former Governor Connally and Connally's business partner, former Lieutenant Governor Ben Barnes, as well as such less-known but nonetheless powerful local figures as former Dallas City Manager George Schrader, and Richard Strauss, son of former Democratic National Chairman Robert Strauss and the nephew of Dallas Mayor Annette Strauss.

Because of their ties with the industry, regulators simply weren't prepared to be vigilant in Texas. Two incidents illustrate just how ineffective regulators were in Texas. The first involved real estate developer Robert Hopkins, who acquired Big Country Savings Association of Stanford, Texas, in 1982. In four years, Hopkins transformed the slumbering $80 million thrift into a sprawling $800 million institution, which he renamed Commodore Savings Association, and moved to Dallas. When examiners arrived at Commodore in the spring of 1986, it was readily apparent that Hopkins should resign; the institution was more than $300 million insolvent when it was merged into another thrift under the FHLBB's Southwest

Plan in 1988. As for Hopkins, he was later convicted on 47 separate charges of illegally diverting thrift funds to political contributions to several important officials, including former Speaker Wright, and sentenced to 15 years in prison. The penalty seemed unusually severe for a relatively routine offense, but the judge said in the July 1989 sentencing that a strong message needed to be sent to people who would defraud thrifts.

The second illustration of the regulators' obvious impotence in supervising the thrifts came in early 1986, when the Federal Home Loan Bank Board issued its annual report on the health of the thrift industry. Among the specific institutions cited was Dixon's Vernon Savings and Loan Association. According to the FHLBB, Vernon had ended 1985 with a positive net worth of nearly $73 million, a reasonably healthy 6.04 percent of its almost $1.2 billion in assets. Fifteen months later, in March 1987, after a closer look at the books, the FHLBB declared Vernon insolvent with a negative net worth of $716.9 million. An incredible 96 percent of Vernon's loans, the bank board reported, were not being repaid. (Regulators get concerned when 4 percent of an institution's loan portfolio is not being repaid; when the 10 percent level is reached, the institution is regarded as terminal; anything over 15 percent means the thrift is brain-dead.)

Was it possible for Vernon to have gotten that sick in one short year, to have had its net worth decline by almost $790 million? Not really; the real estate market had dried up in Texas by 1986 and there were few if any new deals being done. The loans Vernon had in 1986 essentially were the same ones it had in 1985.

The fact was that supervision actually declined in Texas when the industry went on its growth bender. Why? The answer is to be found in the muscle the Texas thrift industry had with its regulators. Like all of the FHLBB's district banks, the Ninth District Federal Home Loan Bank, which is responsible for regulating and examining federally chartered S&Ls in Texas, Louisiana, Mississippi, New Mexico, and Arkansas, is owned by the same institutions that it supervises. And the Texas thrift industry dominates the district. As a result, some of the most powerful thrift owners in Texas have traditionally occupied top positions at the Ninth District bank. It is thus not surprising that when the thrift industry was white-hot in Texas, in September 1983, the Ninth District's board bowed to the wishes of its powerful Texas members and moved its headquarters from Little Rock to Dallas—despite the fact that only eleven of the district's forty-eight supervisory employees were willing to make the move. As a result of the move, and the consequent resignations, the board's remaining examiners found themselves overwhelmed by a fivefold increase in their workload. With the cowboys running wild, the timing of the headquarters move couldn't possibly have been worse.

Who were these cowboys? How did they operate? The stories of three of them—Fast Eddie McBirney, Don Dixon, and Tom Gaubert—provide illuminating insight into what exactly happened to the savings and loan industry in Texas.

A photograph of Chairman Edwin T. McBirney III published in a Sunbelt Savings Association annual report during the whirlwind days of the early 1980s shows a darkly handsome young man dressed in a conservative dark suit with the proper inch and a quarter of white cuff showing beneath the left sleeve of his jacket. McBirney's expression is one of intent determination. His right hand is in his pocket with studied casualness. He stands, legs apart, leaning slightly forward, his posture almost defiant, if not arrogant. The message McBirney seems to be sending recalls the portrait of Kaiser Wilhelm that was sent to the German embassy in Paris on the eve of World War I. In that painting, the Kaiser was dressed in the black cuirass of a Garde de Corps officer, his sword sheathed but the hilt thrust forward. "That is not a portrait," murmured General Gallifet of France. "It is a declaration of war." [11]

The bellicose impression McBirney conveyed in the photograph was accurate. McBirney acquired a reputation as a fiercely aggressive, nonstop dealmaker during the days when he built Sunbelt from a small-town thrift with only a few million dollars in assets into a giant wheeler-dealer known to friends and foes alike as "Gunbelt Savings." As McBirney's associates told reporter Byron Harris, Fast Eddie, as he became known, had two speeds: on and off. [12]

McBirney was twenty-nine when he appeared on the Texas thrift scene in January 1982. As the head of an investment group, he paid $6 million for control of Sunbelt Savings, an obscure savings and loan located in Stephenville, a rural community one hundred or so miles southwest of Dallas, on the fringe of the barren but oil-rich West Texas plains. McBirney quickly began merging Sunbelt with a string of other small community thrifts, and a few months later he moved the new, enlarged Sunbelt to Dallas.

By the middle of 1983, he had made a name for himself in the Dallas oil/real estate/banking establishment. Multimillion-dollar real estate deals were being cut by McBirney and other thrift owners over breakfasts at the Mansion on Turtle Creek, a five-star hotel favored by the glitterati, and over lunches at Jason's Steak House, a pricey North Dallas restaurant. McBirney's business often continued far into the night at the Rio Room, a trendy private club in Dallas's posh Park Cities where members paid up to $1,000 for the privilege of partying with the likes of Larry Hagman, Sammy Davis, Jr., and Adnan Khashoggi. It was a club where, as one observer noted, "the Rolex was the watch to wear, the Mercedes-Benz 380 SEC coupe the car to drive"—that is, if one didn't own a Rolls-Royce or Ferrari.

The reason McBirney so intrigued the Dallas business establishment was that no one knew much about him. In fact, McBirney, a Cincinnati native and son of a Philadelphia food- retailing executive, was far more qualified to run a savings and loan than some of the other new thrift owners with whom he did business, such as Terry Barker, who ran the Lubbock-based State Savings and Loan Association. Barker, a general contractor from California who bought control of State Savings in 1982, could read only at the third-grade level, according to a psychologist's report filed during the 1987 criminal trial in which he was convicted of fraud and sentenced to five years in prison.[13] Unlike Barker (who "wore dirty clothes and pounded nails" before buying the Texas thrift, according to one associate),[14] McBirney was well educated and reasonably well connected from his days as a student at Southern Methodist University, the breeding ground for Dallas's business elite. Moreover, McBirney had some experience in real estate.

McBirney's business career had begun in the early '70s while he was still at SMU, where he earned a healthy profit leasing small refrigerators to fellow students for $25 a semester. After graduating in 1974, McBirney bought an electronic-game distribution company, then in the late 1970s embarked upon a new career in real estate that would make him a millionaire several times over. He earned his first $1 million advising real estate investment trusts on how to work their way out of bad properties. But that first million was pocket change compared with what he would be able to squeeze out of owning a savings and loan.

Although he was relatively unknown to the Dallas power elite, McBirney's veneer of respectability and verifiable credentials gave credibility to some of the extraordinary transactions he was cutting with frequent companions such as Dixon of Vernon Savings, Gaubert of Independent American, and Western Savings and Loan Association's Woods over lunch at Jason's Steak House, where he would sketch out the broad outlines of an agreement on the tablecloth, which would then be turned over to Sunbelt lawyers with instructions to "paper the deal." [15]

What made these deals so extraordinary was that they were being cut by thrifts that only a few months before had been restricted to lending money to people who wanted to buy houses. With deregulation, that traditional business seemed to melt away in Texas. In June 1984, loans by Texas thrifts for one-to-four-family dwelling units accounted for nearly half their lending business. A year later, such residential mortgages represented only slightly more than a third of their outstanding loans. [16]

Under the newly liberalized rules of the S&L game, a thrift owner like McBirney could finance 100 percent of a commercial real estate deal, including both the interest payments and the loan-origination fees; require the borrower to use part of the funds to take an existing bad loan off his hands (the "cash for trash" transaction); then return to his office and pay himself a fat dividend from the profits on the 6 percent loan-origination fee. The borrower wouldn't be at risk, since he or she had put no cash into the deal. The only one with any exposure—from the old worthless loan or the new speculative one—was the federal insurance system. And with regulatory supervision at best inadequate and at worst nonexistent, thrift owners could trade bad loans among themselves, so that if the regulators happened to show up unexpectedly, the books would look clean. This practice was known as the "dead horse for a dead cow" trade in which a "rolling loan gathers no loss." Several thrift owners would get together and, with the help of friendly appraisers, form a "daisy chain" to "flip" a piece of property back and forth among themselves. Or they could pass the loan to an outsider—described by Terry Barker of State Savings as "the next greater fool"—artificially inflating the value of the land in the process. On each 100-percent-financed transaction, the thrift would make a profit from its front-end fees. On what Barker called the "Day of the Great Fool," the final outside borrower, dazzled by what appeared to be rapidly escalating value of the land, would be left holding the loan—and along with it, a property that was actually worth far less than its appraised value. *Caveat emptor.*

One of the most spectacular such transactions was a series of land flips that involved Sunbelt Service Corporation, an investment company formed by McBirney's Sunbelt Savings Association. Other links in the daisy chain were Barker's State Savings and Loan Association of Lubbock; Woods's Western Savings and Loan Association of Dallas; and Louis G. Reese, a Dallas real estate investor and speculator. The property involved was a 2,175-acre tract of raw pastureland and scrub hills covered by stunted mesquite trees with no developed improvements, in southwestern Tarrant County, about twenty miles from Fort Worth.

According to Tarrant County deed records, Reese

bought the property on October 28, 1983, borrowing the $17.25 million purchase price from First City Investments of Vancouver, British Columbia. Then, over the next two years, in a series of six separate transactions—some of them within hours of each other—the property escalated in value to almost $65 million, although nothing was done to improve the tract. On the same day Reese bought the land for $17.25 million, he sold it to his office partner, Jerry Parsons, for $24 million—a $6.75 million profit. Financing was provided by Barker's State Savings and Loan of Lubbock. Three days later, on October 31, 1983, Parsons sold the land to a joint venture he formed with Reese. On this transaction, the price did not increase; the Parsons-Reese joint venture simply assumed responsibility for the $24 million debt to State Savings and Loan. About four months later, in March 1984, Sunbelt Service financed sale of the tract for $44.7 million to another joint venture that included T. Cullen Davis, the Fort Worth oil millionaire who, before his bankruptcy, was known as the richest man ever to be tried for murder in the United States. (He was found not guilty.) In November 1984, Reese bought back most of the tract through a trust he had formed for his children; on this deal, the price declined to about $37.4 million, because part of the land had been previously sold to pay off First City Investments, the initial lender. Three weeks later, on December 20, 1985, Reese transferred the property from his children's trust to his own investment company, then finally sold the tract three days after that—for a whopping $64.4 million—to an investment group financed by Woods's Western Savings and Loan Association of Dallas. The *Dallas Times Herald*'s real estate writer, Ross Ramsey, put it in amusing perspective. Ramsey reported that Reese "bought land in south Fort Worth at the peak of the real estate boom. And bought it, and bought it, and bought it. . . ."[17]

On the Day of the Great Fool, the exposed link on the end of that daisy chain was a joint venture formed by outsiders. The joint venture filed for bankruptcy in October 1986, listing as its only asset the tract of land that it said was now valued at $85.5 million. The basis of that estimate was an appraisal done for Western Savings in 1985. When federal regulators finally got involved in August 1986, an independent appraiser said the tract of land was worth only $21 million, less than a third of its final sales price. Western Savings was closed by federal regulators in September 1986. As a middleman, Sunbelt Service stood to make almost $2.7 million in clear profit from fees for financing just one of the links in the daisy chain of flips.

That transaction wasn't even mentioned in the $630 million lawsuit filed against McBirney and his managers in 1986 by the federal government, which took over Sunbelt after the house of cards finally collapsed. According to that suit, McBirney and his associates were responsible for a number of illegal or unethical activities. Specifically, the suit charged that McBirney and his associates took kickbacks from borrowers, in one incident pocketing $805,000 that rightfully belonged to the bank and in a second grazing $3.4 million off the top of a $7 million loan. Another deal mentioned in the suit was a transaction involving loans on two office buildings in Atlanta. That deal looked so good, the suit said, that McBirney and his associates simply took it for themselves rather than directing it to the bank, thus cheating minority shareholders of their portion of $4 million in profits. In all, the suit charged, McBirney and other insider shareholders paid themselves nearly $13 million in dividends on Sunbelt common and preferred stock in 1985 and 1986, while the thrift's capital evaporated as the Texas economy—and along with it, the Texas real estate market—fell apart.

These dividends were in addition to McBirney's annual salary of more than $250,000 and the free use he enjoyed of company-paid limousines and four corporate aircraft.

Moreover, the government alleged that McBirney and his associates were guilty of abominable business judgment—for example, loaning $125 million to a fledgling Dallas real estate speculator, twenty-three-year-old Sam Ware, who ultimately defaulted on about $80 million of the debt. The government also claimed that a dummy corporation, CYA, Inc. ("aptly named," said the lawsuit, for "Cover Your Ass, Inc."), was created so Sunbelt could get rid of $8 million in bad loans to two of McBirney's associates through a "trash for cash" transaction.

McBirney's defenders—and there are quite a few of them in the real estate business in Texas—insist that Fast Eddie's business deals were not motivated by criminal intent. Rather, McBirney's advocates say, he was propelled by a gambler's faith that the Texas economy would not continue downhill and that his Sunbelt transactions would eventually reap huge legitimate profits.

Those betting instincts were part of the lavish lifestyle McBirney enjoyed while at Sunbelt's helm. A McBirney associate tells of how he visited Las Vegas with Fast Eddie in April 1985 along with several other Sunbelt executives, favored customers, and a few congenial women, some of them Sunbelt employees who were part of a cadre McBirney jetted to Nevada's pleasure palaces for gambling, sex, and parties.

Shortly after gathering at the Dunes Hotel, this associate recalls, the group moved to Caesars Palace, where McBirney had reserved a plush second-floor gourmet restaurant with its own private blackjack tables. After the first course was served, McBirney arose and walked over to a $5,000 blackjack table and put down $35,000 in chips to cover all seven hands. For the next fifteen minutes, according to the associate, "Eddie had the goddamnedest streak of bad luck I've ever seen. He lost every hand dealt to him. Figure it takes about a minute and a half to play a hand of blackjack. He was losing money at a rate of almost one and a half million dollars an hour." Between the soup and the salad courses, McBirney reportedly dropped almost $250,000.[18]

Sunbelt's Las Vegas excursions for favored customers were part of a high-flying pattern that became the talk of the industry in Texas. On one Las Vegas trip, described by Byron Harris in *Texas Monthly* as "the most outrageous jaunt of all,"[19] the entertainment was provided by four women who performed a striptease at a cocktail party in McBirney's suite. When their clothes were gone, Harris reported, the women "proceeded to perform sexual acts on some of the businessmen." Harris called the affair "the most memorable extravaganza in a long string of Sunbelt excesses."

By 1984, when Sunbelt was at the height of its apparent prosperity, the excesses had become orchestrated events. McBirney threw a Halloween party that year for hundreds of guests who feasted on exotic wild game—including lion and antelope—while being entertained by a magician who performed feats of levitation behind a swirling curtain of fog produced by smoke machines. A pair of obese disco singers, billed as "Two Tons of Fun," provided the music. For that bash, McBirney dressed up as royalty, complete with robe, scepter, and crown. The Halloween festivity was followed two months later by a Christmas party that was less elaborate but still memorable. For it, McBirney rented a large film studio on the outskirts of Dallas. Entertainment for the hundreds of Sunbelt customers and other guests was supplied by Ben

Vereen, who performed on a soundstage that had been transformed into a winter wonderland.

The lavish partying continued without interruption in 1985 even as Sunbelt was sinking into insolvency and the Texas economy went down the tubes. McBirney's Halloween party that year had an African safari theme. A tropical jungle was created in a huge warehouse. A live elephant added to the ambience—until a magician made the beast disappear, to the amazement of the crowd. The menu included water buffalo ribs. Banker McBirney was costumed as Bwana McBirney, the Great White Hunter, replete with pith helmet and binoculars. Six weeks later the now-famous Sunbelt Christmas party had a Russian winter motif. A North Dallas furniture warehouse was converted to resemble the snow-blown Russian steppes. Waiters dressed as serfs. Manhattan Transfer provided the entertainment.

According to a civil lawsuit filed by Sunbelt's managers after McBirney was finally forced out by federal regulators in 1986, the savings and loan spent more than $1 million on parties in 1984 and 1985. Part of that sum, $32,000, was reportedly paid to a company called Rapture, Inc., for helping to organize the parties. The owner of Rapture, Inc., was Jamie McBirney, Fast Eddie's wife. The lawsuit also alleged that McBirney, acting without authority from his board of directors, approved a $200,000 loan to Rapture, Inc. The loan was in apparent violation of the law, since the amount exceeded the $100,000 limit on loans that could be granted without board approval. Nor were lavish parties McBirney's only excesses. According to the filing, McBirney improperly spent Sunbelt funds on $278,000 worth of gifts from Neiman Marcus and other trendy stores, on limousines, and on lunches at Jason's.

The aggressive, defiant McBirney pictured in Sunbelt's annual report was still in evidence after the roof fell in on Sunbelt. Seemingly unrepentant, he responded to the lawsuits with a countersuit and accusations that all of his problems were caused by the regulators. In his only public comment on the charges, McBirney insisted that the mission of federal regulators, when they finally arrived at Sunbelt in the spring of 1986, was "to write down Sunbelt as quickly as possible so that it would stop growing."[20] That defense was somewhat like a drunken driver blaming the insurance company for negligence after he wraps his car around a tree. The only concession McBirney made was to acknowledge that Sunbelt might have been overly aggressive during the boom years of the early '80s. "Everybody gets caught up in the fever when the economy is exploding," McBirney explained.[21]

According to McBirney, the parties and other expenditures for gifts and entertainment were all part of an energetic marketing campaign. "We felt that a banking business had to establish personal relationships; we felt that parties were the most effective approach," he said. As for the Las Vegas excursions, McBirney insisted that he had never engaged a prostitute for himself or for anyone else. But he would not comment on what other Sunbelt officials might have done. "What they all do for a weekend in Las Vegas, I can't control," McBirney said. "Men will be men."[22]

If lavish parties for hundreds of customers and friends were the thrust of Sunbelt's marketing efforts, Don Dixon of Vernon Savings focused on a smaller group: powerful politicians. It was a strategy that would pay off—for a while.

Among the influential public figures cultivated in the

early 1980s by Dixon was then House Majority Leader Jim Wright of Fort Worth, later to become Speaker of the House of Representatives, a post he ultimately resigned in 1989 amid charges that he violated House ethics rules no less than sixty-nine times. Another was Representative Tony Coelho of California, the House Majority Whip and principal Democratic fund-raiser for House congressional candidates. (Like Wright, Coelho also wound up resigning from the House in 1989 because of alleged ethics violations involving favors received from a thrift owner.) Dixon's guest list for parties aboard Vernon Savings' Potomac River yacht, the *High Spirits,* included Democratic congressmen J. J. Pickle and Jim Chapman of Texas, along with Coelho and influential thrift industry lobbyists. According to the ship's log, Coelho used the *High Spirits* for eight fund-raising affairs during the summer of 1986 at a cost to Vernon of $25,184. Not that Dixon was partisan. He also placed his fleet of six aircraft at the disposal of such influential Republicans as former President Gerald Ford and Senator Pete Wilson of California and Senator Paul Laxalt of Nevada.

Like McBirney, Dixon knew how to enjoy the newfound wealth that came from owning a savings and loan. If anything, he was even more lavish than McBirney, according to lawsuits filed by federal regulators. Not only did he live rent-free for eighteen months at a $2 million mansion purchased by Vernon Savings in Del Mar, California, according to the FSLIC, he also billed Vernon for more than $500,000 in personal living expenses, including $36,780 for flowers, $37,339 for telephone calls, $13,446 for catering services, and $44,095 for "out of pocket" incidentals. When Dixon and his wife, Dana, filed for personal bankruptcy in California in April 1987, an action that prevented the FSLIC from seizing their personal assets, the Dixons' possessions included an art collection valued at almost $1 million; twenty-four cases of wine valued at $1,300 each; six Fabbri shotguns and other expensive firearms valued at almost $170,000; a Victorian-era Steinway piano worth at least $15,000; hundreds of thousands of dollars' worth of jewelry; and several luxury cars, including a Rolls-Royce and a Ferrari. The list of possessions filed with the bankruptcy court was as long as it was opulent. Between 1983 and 1986, Dixon allegedly withdrew more than $8 million from Vernon in salary, bonuses, and dividends, not counting the bills paid by Vernon for living and entertainment expenses. In all, according to the FSLIC lawsuit, Dixon and six other former executives looted Vernon of $40 million in inflated compensation and dividends while they squandered some $350 million of the institution's assets.

Vernon's insured funds supported Dixon in ways that are only a dream for most Americans. The Dixons took their friends on European vacations at Vernon's expense. A diary of one two-week trip in 1983 to Paris and southern France described the holiday as a "flying house party . . . of pure unadulterated pleasure." The diary, entitled "Gastronomique-Fantastique," was kept by Dana Dixon, who recorded every meal at the seven three-star Michelin restaurants at which they dined in France on fare ranging from roebuck (in Alsace) to truffle soup (in Lyons). The bill, which came to $22,000, was paid by Vernon Savings and Loan. But the high point of the Dixons' European tours was an audience with Pope John Paul II in 1985. It had been arranged by the Catholic bishop of San Diego in return for a charitable donation Dixon had made to a church university. Dixon gave the Pope a painting valued at $40,000. "I was very well aware of everything that I said and that I was in the presence of someone very special," Dixon commented afterward.[23]

Dixon's opulent life-style as a thrift owner was a

world apart from his roots in rural Texas. Dixon was born in Vernon, Texas, a farming and ranching community about two hundred miles northwest of Dallas, near the Red River, which separates Oklahoma and Texas. In 1938, when Dixon was born, it was hard country. Yet not everyone who lived in Vernon was a dirt-poor oil roughneck or hardscrabble farmer. Dixon's father, W. D. "Dick" Dixon, was known as a hustler, the description meant as a compliment rather than a criticism. The elder Dixon was a journalist, who began his career in 1924 as a twenty-year-old reporter for the *Vernon Record*. By the time Donald was born, Dick Dixon was general manager and a partner of the company that owned the newspaper and a local radio station.[24]

After Dick Dixon died of a heart attack in 1952, his widow, Frances, took over the upbringing of their only child. According to the journalist Bill Adler, "about the only disparaging comment that might be made about her is that she spoiled her son rotten," with lengthy California vacations, the latest in fashionable clothing, and a new pea-green Thunderbird—"the first in Wilbarger County" —as a high school graduation gift.[25]

In 1956, Dixon entered Rice University in Houston to study architecture. During his freshman year there, he changed his mind and decided upon a career in business. As a result, Dixon transferred to the University of Southern California and then to UCLA, where he received a bachelor's degree in business in 1960. Returning to Dallas, to be near his hometown roots, Dixon embarked upon a career in real estate. After a series of partnerships in various real estate deals, Dixon entered the home-building business, and in the late 1970s formed his own company, Dondi Group, Inc. By 1981, Dondi Group was the second-largest home builder and the largest condominium developer in the Dallas market, its structures winning awards from architectural groups for their distinctive designs that favored red tile roofing.

Along the way, Dixon realized something fundamental about the home-building business: Lenders played the tune, borrowers did the dance. For example, some lenders often required part ownership in return for financing real estate projects. With deregulation, savings and loans started making the same demands. So Dixon decided that owning his own S&L in addition to building homes made more sense than just digging holes and putting up houses.

The path that led him to Vernon Savings and Loan began in 1976, when Dixon was introduced to Louisiana businessman Herman Beebe, Sr., by a mutual acquaintance, former Texas lieutenant governor Ben Barnes, who had abandoned politics after his name was linked to the Sharpstown bank scandal in Texas in the early '70s. At first, the relationship between Beebe and Dixon was strictly business. In 1976, when Dixon was a partner in a home-building company called Raldon Homes, he started borrowing money from financial institutions that Beebe controlled in Houston and Louisiana. But a genuine friendship soon developed between Dixon and Beebe. The two were kindred spirits, Dixon finding traits in the older Beebe that he admired and wished to emulate. Principal among these apparently was Beebe's ability to enjoy the material fruits of his various enterprises. Dixon often visited Beebe at the older man's compound of modern Southern-style mansions at the end of a private road near Shreveport. The two men also traveled together frequently on Beebe's private plane, sipping bourbon and playing gin. Dixon reportedly became so close to Beebe that he began calling him "Pawpaw."[26]

The only problem with emulating the gray-haired, grandfatherly Louisiana businessman was that Beebe was a crook. His own son once said: "Dad would make a deal with the devil if it looked good."[27] Through a holding company called AMI, Inc., Beebe controlled a bewildering maze of companies involved in nursing homes, insurance, and motels. He also had extensive though shadowy interests in banks and savings and loans. According to a series of confidential reports by investigators from the U.S. Comptroller of the Currency, Beebe controlled or exerted a major influence over forty separate banks and S&Ls in Louisiana, Texas, Alabama, Arkansas, Colorado, and Oklahoma.[28] He was directly involved in the failure of two banks and three savings and loans, according to federal investigators. As a result, Beebe was indicted twice for financial misdeeds and convicted once; he entered the federal correctional institute at Fort Worth in the fall of 1988 to serve a term of one year for conspiracy and wire fraud in connection with a $1 million loan from the Small Business Administration.

The friendship Dixon enjoyed with Beebe led in the spring of 1981 to Dixon's acquisition of Vernon Savings. Like many of the cowboys, Dixon realized early that the new power of S&Ls to attract millions in new deposits through unregulated interest rates offered a dazzling opportunity for bold entrepreneurs who could find profitable ways to use that cash. And, coincidentally, the community savings and loan in his own hometown just happened to be on the market. Vernon Savings and Loan Association, formed in 1960, was one of the strongest thrifts in all of Texas, with only about $90,000 in bad loans out of $82 million in assets, a delinquency rate of 0.1 percent. Vernon's owner, R. B. Tanner, had been a bank examiner during the Depression, and he "ran his thrift with a rigid discipline born of that experience."[29] But now he was sixty-five, and he wanted to retire. Dixon, a natural salesman who could peddle warts at a beauty contest, visited Tanner and earnestly assured the flinty old banker that he wanted to return to his roots and be a contributing member of the community he loved. Dixon, Tanner said, "painted us a real pretty picture"—so pretty that Tanner agreed to sell Dixon his majority interest in Vernon Savings for a reported $6 million, of which $1.75 million was in a note that would ultimately prove to be worthless.[30] Dixon's principal source of financing was provided by Beebe.

As soon as he purchased Vernon Savings, Dixon opened a branch in Dallas and, for all practical purposes, moved its operations to the city. He descended on Dallas with a flashiness that drew gasps from the more staid real estate and banking establishment. Now that he was a lender, Dixon abandoned the conservative pinstripes he wore as a borrowing home builder, favoring open-collared shirts, ropes of medallion-laden gold chains around his neck, and a mustache that produced a vague resemblance to singer Kenny Rogers. His business cards were bogus $3 bills, which bore his likeness, his signature, and the phrase "Chairman of the Bored" on one side, and on the other side the mock-Latin slogan "Red Tillibus Roofum," which referred to his award-winning building designs. The bills were inscribed: "In Don We Trust."

Through a series of complicated stock transactions, Vernon Savings was wrapped into Dixon's Dondi Group as a subsidiary. Although technically Dixon was never an officer of Vernon, he functioned as its chief lending officer. The prudent banking practices of former owner Tanner were quickly abandoned. Under Dixon's guidance, the savings and loan began to accumulate artwork that was valued at about $5.5 million on Vernon's books when the S&L was taken over by federal regulators in 1987. Much of the artwork was gone by then, though; Dixon had appropriated some of it for his Del Mar mansion and generously given other pieces away to favored customers of the institution. Dixon also gave managers flashy new Mercedes-Benzes as company cars and started fattening the payroll. Among the new employees were his wife, Dana, her sister, and his stepdaughter, who took charge of decorating Vernon's expanding network of branches.

In the first eighteen months of Dixon's stewardship, as expensive brokered deposits were sucked in from across the nation and then redistributed to impetuous entrepreneurs speculating in real estate development, Vernon ballooned to an institution with more than $440 million in loan assets, more than five times its size when control changed hands in 1981. Vernon became known as a lender of last resort—the bank a borrower would visit if he or she couldn't get a loan anywhere else. The price was high; Vernon charged up to 6 percentage points as front-end fees on loans. But it wasn't hard to pay, since Vernon would advance borrowers 100 percent of the principal and interest on the loan as well as the front-end fee. As Vernon's de facto chief lending officer, Dixon encouraged his subordinates to speculate. "If a developer came in with a proposal that didn't make sense, they would work on the deal to try to make it work," said Rick Ramsey, who worked with Dixon for several years in the late 1970s and then joined Vernon after Dixon bought control.[31] Because profits were based on front-end fees rather than on any reasonable expectations of repayment of loans, Vernon loan officers were given short-term, paid-in-advance bonus incentives to lend as much as possible. According to federal regulators, more than $22 million was paid in

bonuses during the four years Dixon owned Vernon—
$4.5 million of it to Dixon himself.

Given such incentives, the loan officers accelerated
their lending on extraordinarily speculative ventures. By
the end of 1985, Vernon Savings showed almost $1 billion
in loan assets on the books. But many of the assets were
of dubious value. Example: Dixon had extravagantly over-
estimated the market for condominiums, as a result of
which Dondi Residential Properties, Inc., one of Dixon's
many subsidiaries tied in with Vernon, had about seven
hundred unsold condos on the market. Internal estimates
indicated that Vernon could lose as much as $11 million
on the DRPIs (for Dondi Residential Properties, Inc.), or
"Drippies," as they were known. The problem of the
Drippies was not solved, federal regulators said, but
Dixon did conceive a scheme for getting rid of them
through an elaborate series of almost fifty paper transactions in which the condos were to be packaged with other
real estate loan deals—the "cash for trash" technique. If
federal regulators hadn't arrived before the deals were
consummated, the result would have been a paper profit
of $25 million instead of the $11 million loss.

As early as 1983, it was apparent that Vernon was
headed for trouble. In October of that year, federal examiners made a cursory visit to Vernon and reported "significant regulatory violations, unsafe and unsound practices,
lending deficiencies, inadequate books and records and
control problems." By August 1985, bank examiners reported that Vernon Savings was "out of control." With
1986 came tumbling oil prices and an abrupt end to the
wealth-without-end optimism about the Texas economy.
By this time, thrift examiners had targeted Vernon as the
most problem-ridden institution in the state. On July 15,
1986, the FHLBB issued a cease and desist order against

certain practices uncovered at Vernon by state S&L examiners. These practices included falsifying reports to federal examiners to avoid reporting delinquent loans, ignoring earlier demands to curtail acceptance of brokered deposits and high-risk loans, and the now-familiar swapping of bad loans among thrift owners to stay a jump ahead of the bank examiners. Dixon's attorney later admitted that there was an informal confederation of thrift owners that moved bad loans from one institution to another, but he insisted it was because of arbitrary and selective regulatory enforcement. "Hell, yes, there was a network," Dallas attorney William Ravkind told the *Dallas Morning News.* "But it was a network of [savings and loan] associations with serious problems who had to come together after federal regulators changed the rules and made their lives more difficult. Between the bad economy and the re-regulation of the industry [in 1986], thrifts were left with no choice but to move their bad loans around. They didn't do it to hide from the regulators. They did it *because* of the regulators." [32]

But by the late summer of 1986, Dixon's days as a thrift owner were numbered. In October of that year, Vernon's minority directors told bank regulators they had been "lied to and deceived" by Dixon and his senior officers. Still, Dixon tried to hang on. And as the regulators sought to oust him from control of the thrift, he wheeled out his big gun—the politicians he had favored over the years with the free use of airplanes and his yacht for fund-raising parties. Specifically, he called Jim Wright.

Wright later told journalist Bill Adler that all he did in response was make a telephone call on behalf of a Texas constituent—a call to FHLBB chairman Edwin Gray. As Wright told it, he said: "Ed, I don't know anything about this guy. I don't know anything about his situation. But

I'm telling you what he said to me. And Ed said, 'There's no way. They can't close him down.' And I said, 'He thinks they will. Would you mind looking into it?' "[33]

But the preponderance of evidence presented to Gray suggested more than just simple mismanagement at Vernon Savings. The perks Dixon bestowed upon himself were too lavish—the California mansion, the generous living expenses and opulent parties, the six aircraft, the European "gastronomique-fantastique," the Ferraris and Mercedes-Benzes and Rolls-Royces, all bankrolled by Vernon. Regulators continued to press for Dixon's removal. In February 1987, Wright intervened again, meeting with William Black, chief counsel for the Federal Home Loan Bank Board, and the two top officials of the Dallas FHLB, chairman Roy Green and chief enforcement officer Lou Roy. According to sources present at the meeting, Black attempted to contradict Wright's version of Dixon's problems, which the Speaker attributed to legitimate business judgments that merely miscalculated the Texas economy. The meeting reportedly ended when Wright lost his temper and began shouting at Black and cursing.

Apparently realizing that he couldn't salvage Dixon through the regulators at the FHLBB, Wright changed his strategy. He moved to prevent Congress from providing the funds that would be required to close down insolvent thrifts. The Federal Home Loan Bank Board had been seeking $15 billion in appropriations to restore the FSLIC's ability to pay off depositors and liquidate such insolvent thrifts as Vernon, which had been taken over by regulators on March 20, 1987, with a negative net worth of $350 million. Wright said he would not support any bailout measure that exceeded $5 billion, an amount too small to cover even a fraction of S&L losses by 1987. As one analyst put it, "You could start with $5 billion in downtown

Dallas and not even make it to D/FW [the Dallas–Fort Worth airport]."[34]

On April 28, 1987, after the FSLIC filed a lawsuit seeking $540 million in damages from Dixon and six other former Vernon officers—at the time, the largest such claim the agency had ever filed—Wright backed down and said he would support the $15 billion bailout plan. *The New York Times* called Wright's change of heart an "embarrassing reversal."[35] Congress eventually compromised on the two figures and in October authorized the FSLIC to issue $10.8 billion in long-term bonds to rescue the thrift industry. Even at the time, everyone acknowledged that the amount was woefully insufficient to deal with just Texas thrift losses, much less the national problem.

But it was enough for the FSLIC to be able to shut down Vernon, and on November 19, 1987, the regulators closed the thrift's doors and committed $1.3 billion—records continued to fall to Vernon, for the bailout at the time was the largest ever—to liquidating its assets. Vernon's few good loans were transferred to a new institution, Montfort Savings.

Vernon Savings, the small-town thrift that Don Dixon wanted to use to give something back to the community of his birth, as he told R. B. Tanner when negotiating its purchase not quite seven years before, had ceased to exist. What's more, its former Dixon-appointed president, John V. Hill, had pleaded guilty to charges of violating federal banking and bribery laws by arranging sexual favors for the thrift's officers and directors and by making illegal political contributions with thrift money. (According to the indictment, Hill had flown two women from Dallas to San Diego at Vernon's expense in June 1985, then hired as many as ten other prostitutes in Southern

California, so "sexual favors would be available to Vernon officers and directors in connection with their service to Vernon and Vernon's owner, Don R. Dixon.")

Dixon's own legal problems were so complex that they seemed likely to be tied up in court for years. Not only did he face the criminal fraud investigation, the FSLIC lawsuit, and his personal bankruptcy, he began 1989 as a defendant in some forty other lawsuits filed by creditors and borrowers. Though his attorney claimed Dixon was broke—most of his personal possessions, including the artwork and the expensive firearms, were sold at auction by the bankruptcy court in June 1988—like McBirney, Dixon remained defiant, blaming the regulators for all of his problems.

"I'm not a guy who flew into town to rape the savings and loan business," Dixon told the *Dallas Times Herald* in September 1987. "The regulators in Washington decided that entrepreneurs are bad and said: 'We'll sink the ships to kill the captains.' " [36]

Despite the results, Dixon insisted that his strategy had been reasonable. Instead of lending thirty-year money on home mortgages, Dixon said he intended to concentrate on short-term loans for land development, construction, and commercial projects. Since most of the loans would be repaid within three years, Dixon said, interest rates could be adjusted to reflect changing market conditions. As Dixon told it, the regulators approved of the strategy. "We were accepted with open arms, encouraged, patted on the back." [37]

Dixon was less convincing when it came to justifying his lavish life-style, the fleet of six aircraft, and the five full-time pilots. At a 1988 bankruptcy hearing in California, Dixon was the only person in the courtroom to keep a straight face when he suggested that his company-financed Ferrari was a conservative vehicle because it had four doors and served as "the family Ferrari." The airplanes, he explained later, were a result of Vernon's rapid move into the national lending arena. "The only way I could find to get decision-makers to pay attention to opportunities and problems from Florida to California was to send them in and out of there on a daily basis with a private airplane," Dixon said.[38] Perhaps, but no other financial institution in the state of Texas—including such failing giants as RepublicBank Corporation and InterFirst Corporation, each of them fifteen times larger than Vernon and with long-standing reputations as national and international banks—maintained six aircraft. As for the Del Mar mansion, Dixon explained: "The beach house was acquired . . . as a project to refurbish, redecorate and sell for a profit. What the FSLIC doesn't say is that even when you add to the purchase price the cost of redecorating and refurbishing, company entertainment and my living expenses, the house was sold at a handsome profit."[39] That may sound reasonable, but it really doesn't wash. According to the FSLIC, Vernon took a "substantial loss" on the property, which was sold to Bruce West, a Dixon business partner, for no money down. Vernon financed 100 percent of the deal.[40]

Still, Dixon made no apologies. When the industry got in trouble, he said, the regulators needed scapegoats to conceal the FHLBB's culpability in helping create the crisis. That was why he and Vernon Savings had been singled out. The regulators, Don Dixon said, "have killed me."[41]

When Jim Wright went to Don Dixon's aid, he claimed "not to know anything about this guy." Wright didn't try that same apologia in 1987 when he applied his political muscle on behalf of Thomas M. Gaubert, the expansive, cigar-chewing Papa Hemingway look-alike who owned Independent American Savings in Irving, Texas, a suburban community between Dallas and Fort Worth. The simple fact is that it would have been laughable for Wright to suggest that he didn't know Tom Gaubert.

Gaubert (the name is pronounced Guh-bert) had long been a Democratic Party fund-raiser, and the walls of his office were adorned with pictures of him with prominent Democrats, including such luminaries as former House Speaker Tip O'Neill, former President Jimmy Carter, former Vice President Walter Mondale—and, of course, Wright. In late 1985, Gaubert directed a fund-raiser in Fort Worth for Wright and other congressional candidates that set a new record for a single congressional campaign event, raising a remarkable $1.6 million in one evening. As a result, in early 1986, Gaubert was named national finance chairman of the influential Democratic Congressional Campaign Committee. In that post, he worked even more closely with Wright and House Majority Whip Tony Coelho, the principal fund-raiser for House Democrats. Thus it was only natural that Gaubert would turn to Wright when his problems with regulators began.

Gaubert, a Minnesota native born in 1940, built his first house in Dallas in 1958 with funds borrowed from a local lumberyard. That first deal earned him a profit of about $150. He then worked for a concrete company in highway construction, and after serving in the U.S. Army returned in the late 1960s to Dallas, where he started building homes on a larger scale, concentrating on middle- and lower-income residences and apartment complexes. He also became, in his own words, a "junk dealer," specializing in difficult real estate rehabilitation projects. In the process, he acquired a reputation as a smart deal-maker with a good mind for assembling the complicated financial packaging needed to put unprofitable real estate projects back in the black.

As Congress began dismantling the regulatory structure surrounding the S&L industry in the early '80s, Gaubert wasted no time in taking advantage of what he recognized as a remarkable new opportunity. "When you are interested in politics, you pay attention to what is going on in government," Gaubert told the *Dallas Morning News* in a 1987 interview.[42] "I thought how wonderful it would be to have a savings and loan association that would really, truly care about and cater to the individual home builder."[43]

And so, in January 1983, Gaubert came calling when the ailing $40 million Citizens Savings & Loan Association of Grand Prairie, a Dallas suburb, went on the market after the death of its majority owner. Gaubert paid $1.05 million for 51 percent of the thrift, renamed it Independent American Savings and Loan Association, and moved its headquarters to a new building a few miles north in the futuristic Irving, Texas, community of Las Colinas, only a mile or so from Texas Stadium, where the Dallas Cowboys play football.

Gaubert then embarked upon a growth bender that paralleled what was happening at other Texas thrifts. He began by buying up branches of other small S&Ls and merging their operations into Independent American. At the same time, he encouraged out-of-market brokers to funnel scores of millions of dollars into high-interest accounts. Such brokered deposits swelled from $221.6 million in 1983 to more than $1.57 billion by 1985. Almost as fast as the money came in the front door, it was ladled out the back—to high-risk real estate acquisition and development projects. Accounting and control procedures were incredibly lax. One former executive quoted by *Business Week* magazine recalled walking through Independent American's offices collecting loose checks from desktops; by the time he had completed his stroll, he had some $20 million in his hand.[44]

Gaubert's difficulties with regulators began almost as soon as he acquired Independent in 1983, when he proposed to take over an inventory of unfinished apartments and condominiums financed by Empire Savings and Loan Association of Mesquite, Texas, just east of Dallas. Gaubert's plan was to package the project and sell it to investors seeking tax shelters. That proposal—and Gaubert—attracted the attention of regulators, who denied approval of the project because Empire was at the time the subject of an extensive federal investigation for fraud and conspiracy among its owners and officers, who were believed to be flipping land and raking off millions in illegal profits.[45] A few months later when Empire collapsed, Gaubert himself became the target of an investigation into his dealings with an Iowa thrift. Regulators looking into a series of transactions involving a tract of land south of Dallas suspected that Gaubert had pocketed $1 million from flipping the property. Gaubert denied the charge—though he made an out-of-court settlement of a civil claim arising from the transactions—contending that he never received the $1 million, which he described as a standard loan-commitment fee.

But even though Gaubert ultimately was not found to be liable for any civil or criminal wrongdoing in the case, he had drawn the attention of regulators. So when in 1984 he proposed to buy twenty branches of United Savings Bank of Houston, the FHLBB was wary. The bank board reluctantly agreed to permit Independent American to acquire the branches. But the thrift also had to agree to absorb another Texas S&L, the failing Investex Savings Association of Tyler in East Texas. The regulators said the transaction would save the FSLIC $50 million, which is what it would have cost the government to close down Investex and pay off its depositors. And that wasn't the only price the regulators exacted: Gaubert had to agree to distance himself from Independent American until regulators finished their investigation of the Iowa transactions, and he had to guarantee personally his S&L's net worth, even though he was barred from participating in its management. Against the advice of his attorney, Gaubert signed the agreement with regulators on December 28, 1984.

Then came a sequence of events that resembled a television sitcom, complete with stand-in characters and complicated transactions popping in one door and out another. First, it turned out that Independent American lacked sufficient net worth to absorb both the United branches and Investex. As a result, regulators agreed to permit Independent American to raise capital by selling land—specifically, a 4,200-acre tract around the man-made Joe Pool Lake in southwestern Dallas County that had been acquired in a $26 million deal financed by Fast Eddie McBirney's Sunbelt Savings Association. Gaubert agreed to sell the parcel for $53 million to a development company headed by a former Sunbelt officer. The lender was Gaubert's Independent American. It was an inventive way of raising capital without having to persuade an outside investor of the bank's stability and worth.

Then Gaubert, the majority owner of Independent, put himself at arm's length from the thrift by having his brother, Jack, elected chairman. (Nonetheless, Tom Gaubert continued to draw his $240,000-a-year salary, and he kept his part-time chef on the payroll.) Gaubert also kept pressing regulators for the "fair and impartial" investigation they had promised him when he agreed to remove himself from Independent American's day-to-day management. On the tenth day of each month, Gaubert told the *Dallas Morning News*, he would visit the FHLB Dallas headquarters to deliver an affidavit of his nonparticipation to chief enforcement officer Lou Roy. "I would sit in the lobby, sometimes all day, until he would see me," Gaubert said. "When I handed it to him I would ask him, 'Where is my fair and impartial investigation?' "[46]

Gaubert's political pull finally paid off in August 1985 when a meeting was scheduled—it is unclear whether Wright actually arranged the session, although he has acknowledged talking with regulators on Gaubert's behalf —with FHLBB officials at the bank board's Dallas headquarters, which happened to be right across the street from Independent American's principal offices. Among those present, in addition to Gaubert and Roy, was the tough-minded enforcement chief from FHLBB headquarters in Washington, Rosemary Stewart. According to participants, Stewart called Gaubert a crook and declared that she was determined to have him thrown out of the industry. "I know you are a crook. I don't have it yet, but I am going to get you," one witness quoted Stewart as saying.[47] Gaubert left the room in tears.

After the meeting, Roy and Gaubert encountered each other in the men's room and, according to Gaubert, Roy said, "Tom, I can't go up against her. She is head of the enforcement division. She enforces me, too." As a result, Gaubert said he would step down officially from Independent American, but only if regulators would tear up his personal guarantee of the thrift's net worth. The regulators agreed. Gaubert very simply outnegotiated the regulators when he won that agreement; otherwise, he would have been personally responsible for the millions of dollars necessary to maintain the institution's net worth. It was a precedent, too, although no one realized it at the time.

Meanwhile, Independent American's financial condition continued to deteriorate as the slump in the Texas economy worsened. The S&L ended 1985 with $1.92 billion in assets and a stated net worth of $62.2 million, according to FHLBB data. A year later, its asset base had slipped to $1.30 billion, while its net worth had eroded to a negative $468.4 million.

In March 1986, Roy asked Gaubert to join him in Washington for an emergency meeting. Independent American's insolvency was getting out of hand. Roy asked Gaubert if he would agree to remove his brother, Jack, and the other handpicked directors. In return, Roy promised Gaubert that the regulators would recruit a top management team to turn the thrift around. Gaubert agreed, and by the next day the resignations of Jack Gaubert and other top officials were in hand.

Roy then placed Independent American in the care of Thomas E. Hendricks, a tough-minded senior executive with the FHLB Dallas. Hendricks, said Roy, "was obnoxious, belligerent and smart as hell. I felt if anybody was smart enough and tough enough [to put Independent American back on track], it would be Hendricks." [48]

Hendricks hired a consulting firm that specialized in problem loans, J. E. Roberts & Co., to take a look at Independent's loan portfolio. According to a confidential report cited by *Business Week* magazine, the Roberts group discovered "a large number of complex, unorthodox and 'screwy' deals," including a "network" of S&L owners and developers that conspired to inflate earnings. [49] Many of the deals, the Roberts report said, were structured "to create fictitious profits or to accomplish some other 'network' purpose."

Gaubert's response to the allegations was that "we never participated in anything like that at Independent American." Gaubert's contention notwithstanding, Hendricks responded to the Roberts company report by carving away at the thrift's loan portfolio with a meat cleaver rather than scalpel. Hundreds of millions in loans were written off as worthless. As a result, in the third quarter of 1986, the thrift reported a $314 million loss. At the same time, Independent American's new managers filed a lawsuit against Tom and Jack Gaubert and other senior officials, charging that they had looted the S&L by selling shares of Independent American stock at exaggerated, unrealistically high prices to an employee stock option plan.

Believing he had been betrayed, and furious with Hendricks, Gaubert filed a countersuit alleging that the thrift's new managers had engaged in a scheme to "artificially write down as many . . . assets as possible." Gaubert was convinced that it was part of a regulatory plot to discredit him. He visited with Jim Wright, seeking to get the "fair and impartial" investigation he had been promised. "I . . . spent hours with Wright, telling him the whole thing," Gaubert told the *Morning News*. "A lesser man than Jim Wright would have distanced himself from me."[50]

Of course, Wright couldn't distance himself from a man who had raised some $9 million in a single year for House Democrats. Wright telephoned FHLBB chairman Gray and arranged for Gaubert to have yet another hearing from federal regulators. "It is very difficult when you have a man complaining who is very close to the next Speaker of the House," Gray told *Newsweek* magazine.[51]

So, in October 1986, after a three-hour session between Gray and Gaubert, the FHLBB appointed an independent counsel, Nashville attorney Aubrey B. Harwell, Jr., to look into the Independent American mess. Harwell's investigation concluded that there were no white-hat good guys. "I faulted everybody," Harwell said. Harwell reported that there was no basis to Gaubert's contention that the FSLIC had caused Independent American's financial problems. However, Harwell also concluded that the regulators had treated Gaubert unfairly in some procedural matters, particularly in forcing him out of the business at a time when it was growing rapidly as a result of the Investex and United Savings acquisitions, and by requiring that he sign a personal guarantee of the institution's net worth. Harwell tempered that criticism of the regulators with the observation that "it is not clear that this arguably unfair or improper conduct resulted in any harm to Gaubert."[52]

Armed with an independent investigator's report suggesting improper conduct by the regulators, Gaubert tried to stage a coup. On the morning of January 20, 1987, pro-Gaubert shareholders led by Jack Gaubert dismissed Hendricks and reassumed control of Independent American. The restoration to power lasted less than a day. A few hours later, Texas Savings and Loan Commissioner Bowman placed the thrift under state control and asked for the keys. Independent American was no longer independent. On April 20, 1987, Independent American officially went into federal receivership, and it was officially dissolved on August 19, 1988, when it was merged with seven other savings and loans—including McBirney's Sunbelt and Jarrett Woods's Western Federal Savings Association—in a $5.5 billion rescue that gave the federal government ownership of what one industry analyst called "a bigger carcass, but still a carcass."[53]

During the brief year he ran Independent American without regulatory problems or intervention, Gaubert kept outside his office a polished scale model of the *Titanic*, six feet long and gleaming. It had been taken as collateral on an unpaid loan. It was, in more ways than one, an appropriate symbol.

This sort of thing had happened before, although on a much lesser scale. A decade earlier, on June 28, 1976, federal regulators closed the doors of the Citizens State Bank of Carrizo Springs, a relatively small bank in South Texas. A subsequent investigation by a subcommittee of the House Banking Committee revealed that the bank had been sunk by an intricate network of insider loans and self-dealing. Between 1972 and 1976, several investor groups had taken control of as many as twenty small Texas banks. Through a series of interconnected loans—"a rolling loan gathers no loss"—the groups shared large sums of money that sometimes were not repaid, leaving some of the banks insolvent or severely disabled.

Many of the same figures uncovered in that investigation surfaced again in the 1980s as the new entrepreneurs gained control of Texas thrifts. Texas's former lieutenant governor Ben Barnes, the man who introduced Herman Beebe to Vernon Savings' Don Dixon, figured prominently in the investigation. So did Beebe himself. Another name that surfaced in the 1976 probe was George J. Aubin, a Houston financial consultant who subsequently was banned from the banking business in Texas. One Aubin protégé was J. B. Haralson, who in 1983 purchased Ben Milam Savings of Cameron and Mercury Savings of Wichita Falls, both of which ultimately had to be taken over by the government—at a cost to the taxpayers of $73 million. Another Aubin associate was Jarrett Woods of Western Savings and Loan Association.

Yet in a 1976 statement following the Carrizo Springs bank failure investigation, Democratic Representative Henry Gonzalez of Texas, who would later become chairman of the House Banking Committee and a key player in the cleanup of the S&L wreckage, had singled out federal regulators as "the one bright spot" in the mess. Declared Gonzalez: "The Federal Home Loan Bank Board is aware of the situation and is plainly working hard to turn it around." Of course, he added, "we probably must consider strengthening [the FHLBB's] enforcement powers" to make sure this sort of thing didn't happen again.[54]

Gonzalez's concerns were echoed by Representative Fernand St Germain, chairman of the investigating subcommittee. In his 1976 statement on the investigation, St Germain declared that the "buying and selling of banks . . . the 'Texas Rent-A-Bank' scheme, must be dealt with effectively and dealt with immediately."[55]

If congressional leaders had been so concerned, why, then, was the thrift debacle allowed to happen? The regulators say they were hamstrung by Texas regulatory rules that were so weak as to be wholly ineffective. Once an application for a thrift charter had been approved by federal authorities, state regulators said, there was nothing they could do to block the transfer of the charter to anyone—even someone who had been convicted of a crime in connection with financial institutions. "Let's say I had to deal with a lot of people I didn't necessarily want to deal with," said former Texas Savings and Loan Commissioner Bowman.[56]

Yet even that explanation begs the question: Why weren't the federal regulators more aware and aggressive?

5.
THE
GAMBLERS

T he techniques used by the cowboys to ravage the deregulated thrift industry captured public attention at least partly because of their lurid appeal—the outrageous fraud, the extravagant expenditures, the sex junkets to Las Vegas, the questionable trades that netted insiders millions of dollars. Moreover, the results of what might be called the Texas method were usually painfully visible —in the form of row upon row of empty buildings that had been financed by imprudent thrifts. If nothing else, the Texas method was easy to illustrate on television.

But the Texas method was small potatoes compared to what might be called the California method—a far slicker game that reduced the thrift business to nothing more than a legal crapshoot. Because it was—and is— legal, and because it continues to be played, the California method of gambling with depositors' insured funds poses an open-ended risk that could ultimately result in a tax- payer liability that far exceeds the $157 billion or so already estimated by Congress. As bad as it was, the Texas debacle is pretty much over; the bill for it has already been plotted. The taxpayer tab for California-style abuses is still piling up.

The California and Texas methods were as different as the reputations of the two states. Like the rawhide frontier the phrase evokes, the Texas method was crude and unrefined. To be sure, the Texas method wasn't confined to the Lone Star State. It took down thrifts in other states, too—Iowa, Maryland, Florida, Colorado, Louisiana, and Oklahoma, to name just a few. But it was practiced most widely in Texas. In many respects, it was nothing more elaborate than a modern version of the old shell game played by slick hustlers in the cowtown saloons of the Old West. It didn't require much financial sophistication to flip land until an unwary outsider could be lured into a daisy chain, or to get cash in exchange for trash, or to swap a dead horse for a dead cow.

The California method was something else again. If the Texas method was primitive, hiding the pea under the shell, the California method was sleekly modern, a kind of computerized roulette that involved sophisticated wagering with depositors' insured funds on a grand scale. It was made possible by the willingness of California legislators, in the heady days after passage of the Garn–St Germain Act, to give state-chartered thrifts virtually unlimited license to throw their assets into just about any type of investment they wished. The immediate result was predictable, as Rosemary Stewart, director of the FHLBB's Office of Enforcement, observed: "California . . . with its unlimited power of state-chartered thrifts to do whatever they wanted, attracted people who were interested in doing high-risk things."[1]

Like the Texas method, the California style represented a response to the new realities of the thrift business. Among other things, these new realities included:

—A frenzied building market.

—A flood of cash in the form of brokered deposits drawn in by the offer of unusually high yields.

—Borrower willingness to pay big up-front loan-origination fees.

—New lending powers and accounting gimmicks.

—Federal S&L deposit insurance that virtually removed risk from the thrift owner's business equation.

—An ineffective, understaffed regulatory agency and a shortsighted Congress.

Given all this, it's no wonder that more than 150 investor groups rushed in to apply for California thrift charters when Washington and Sacramento threw open the casino doors in 1982. And it's no wonder that the activities of most of them followed a standard pattern.

To begin with, practitioners of the California method invariably took advantage of the easing of restrictions on brokered deposits and the elimination of S&L interest caps by offering unusually high-yielding accounts to lure in billions of dollars in "hot money." In the early '80s, California S&Ls were paying 11 to 14 percent interest on brokered accounts, an unusually generous offering, considering that their mortgage portfolios were yielding only 9 to 10 percent at the time.

Of course, the unfavorable spread didn't really matter, since the new accounting regulations—the so-called regulatory accounting principles (RAP)—encouraged S&Ls to sell off their mortgage portfolios and use the proceeds to book higher-yielding, if much riskier, new loans. Whether or not those new loans could or would ever be repaid was beside the point. What mattered was that RAP accounting allowed you to amortize the loss you invariably took on the sale of your old mortgage portfolio over the lifetime of the sold-off mortgages, while at the same time permitting you to record as current-year income the usually exorbitant origination fees you got from the new loan. The result was that even though the real consequence of such a transaction might be to lock in a long-term loss several times larger than your thrift's capital base, you could actually show a paper profit on the deal —a paper profit that you could make quite real by paying yourself a hefty cash dividend.

The net effect of this sort of thing was to put a thrift in the position of a penniless gambler deeply in debt to the mob, with the deadline for payment rapidly approaching. Under such circumstances, the best possible course is not only to keep gambling, but to make the riskiest possible bets. After all, if you're already dead, you might as well bet the pot. You can be killed only once. And who knows? You might hit the long shot, be able to repay the loan shark and save your life.

In technical jargon, the availability of easy brokered money and the incentives provided by the new accounting rules accelerated the yield-time curve for thrift investments. As a result, once their vaults were bulging with brokered deposits and cash from the sale of mortgage loans, the Californians often didn't bother lending out the money for speculative commercial real-estate projects or flipping land in the manner of the Texas cowboys. That required time and effort, and the Californians didn't want to wait. Instead, the more sophisticated thrift owners on the West Coast began to play a high-stakes game of chance that was all perfectly legal. They began betting their insured deposits on interest-rate swings. Thanks to the loosening of restraints by the Garn–St Germain Act in

1982, thrift funds that traditionally had been used to finance homes for people now began flowing into junk bonds and mortgage-backed securities.

It took almost three years after the rules were relaxed in 1982 for regulators to see that junk bonds represented a cannon loose on the thrift industry's decks. In this area as in so many others, the regulators would be playing catch-up with an industry running wild.

Indeed, the chronology of regulatory attention to junk bonds is another depressing example how the system was victimized by congressional ineptitude and regulatory ineffectiveness. It wasn't until 1985 that the regulators first began to consider taking action to limit S&L investments in junk. In April of that year, the Federal Home Loan Bank Board staff told Senator William Proxmire of Wisconsin, a member of the Senate Banking Committee, that the agency was "in the process of proposing fairly stringent diversification requirements" for thrifts that invested in junk bonds.[2] No action was forthcoming, however.

Five months later, on September 20, 1985, an associate general counsel of the FHLBB told a House banking subcommittee that the "board is gravely concerned that excessive investment by savings institutions in below-investment-grade bonds issued to finance [corporate] takeovers would in effect provide a federal subsidy" to corporate raiders.[3] Still, nothing concrete was done to limit thrifts' investment in junk.

Fully one year later, on September 8, 1986, FHLBB general counsel Harry Quillian admitted to the *Wall Street Journal* that "our attention got distracted" from junk bonds.[4] As it happened, Quillian added, a bank board study had reached the "tentative conclusion . . . that junk bond investment isn't bad in itself"—though "on general principles there ought to be some limitation on it."[5]

In fact, the FHLBB staff had concluded from a study of loan defaults that junk bonds were actually safer than residential mortgage loans. Of course, significant investments in junk bonds had only been pursued for about four years, which didn't amount to much of a track record for safety and soundness. Moreover, comparing the safety of junk bonds to the safety of residential mortgage loans was a classic case of comparing apples and oranges; the two are simply not analogous.

In any case, early in 1989, the FHLBB at last became sufficiently concerned about the thrift industry's junk bond holdings to take some action. Unfortunately, the action was almost wholly meaningless. What the bank board did was to prohibit insolvent S&Ls from keeping junk bonds in their portfolios without FHLBB approval. It did nothing to prevent still solvent thrifts from continuing to roll the dice.[6]

Compared to their appetite for junk bonds, the eagerness of California S&Ls to invest in mortgage-backed securities may seem a bit more appropriate, given the thrifts' traditional role as a financing agent for residential housing. In fact, the thrift owners' motivation for buying what were known as collateralized mortgage obligations, or CMOs, had much more to do with speculation—with betting on interest-rate swings—than with any desire to help Americans realize the dream of home ownership.

CMOs first appeared on the scene in 1983. In essence, they were nothing more than a bond backed by a pool of home mortgages, most of them insured by one of the three federally sponsored mortgage agencies: the Government National Mortgage Association (popularly known as Ginnie Mae), the Federal National Mortgage Association

(Fannie Mae), and the Federal Home Loan Mortgage Corporation (Freddie Mac).

Thrifts were the principal purchasers of CMOs, though initially they did little more than dip a toe into the pool to test the water. In the first twenty-four months, only $18 billion worth of CMOs were sold nationwide.[7] But then the trend accelerated. By the middle of 1988, federally insured thrifts held more than $230 billion in mortgage-backed securities—almost three times the amount held by commercial banks.[8]

The use of mortgage-backed securities to bet on interest-rate swings caught on early in California, and by the end of 1985 six of the ten largest CMO portfolios were held by California S&Ls. The leader was American Savings & Loan Association of Stockton, California, with $6.36 billion in mortgage-backed securities.

Under the California method, if a thrift believed that interest rates were heading down, it would buy long-term CMOs and lock in then-current yields. If it turned out to be right, the short-term interest it would have to pay out on deposits would soon be lower than the long-term interest it would be earning on the bonds. Similarly, a thrift betting the other side of the gamble—that rates would rise —would sell long-term bonds and invest in shorter-term instruments.

The basic problem with the California method—a situation ignored and unforeseen by Congress and the regulators—was that in such a gamble there had to be a loser for every winner. And so overwhelmingly did S&Ls dominate the market for mortgage-backed securities that it became virtually a zero-sum game for the industry. For just about every thrift that bet interest rates would go up and sold its portfolio of interest-sensitive securities, there was a thrift that bought those same securities in a gamble that rates would go down. This helps to explain why, by 1988, roughly a third of the nation's thrifts were profitable, a third were unprofitable, and a third were just breaking even. In a zero-sum game of chance with a large universe of bettors, it could work out no other way.

To make matters worse, as part of the deregulation frenzy, capital requirements had been lowered to the point where thrift owners had hardly any of their own money at stake. With the government requiring S&Ls to maintain a capital reserve of just 3 percent, a speculation-minded thrift owner with, say, $3 million could attract $100 million in federally insured short-term brokered deposits by offering to pay, say, 10 percent interest. If he thought that rates were going down, he could then bet the $100 million pot by purchasing mortgage-backed securities paying 12 percent. If interest rates fell by 1 percentage point, the $100 million pot of mortgage-backed securities could then be sold for $107 million, or a profit of $7 million—more than twice the thrift owner's original equity investment. Of course, if interest rates went up 1 percentage point, the $100 million in mortgage-backed securities would now be worth only $93 million. But most of the loss would be the FSLIC's, which had insured the deposits. And anyway, the losers didn't have to sell the devalued portfolios because the new accounting principles didn't require that the losses be recognized. So the losers just kept on taking in new deposits and playing the game like a compulsive gambler on a binge, while the winners kept cashing in their chips and taking out the profits.

The potential for profits was even more spectacular when the pot was bet on junk bonds. By putting the $100 million of deposits into higher-yield, higher-risk junk securities paying 16 or 17 percent, the thrift owner's entire $3 million investment could be repaid in the first six months and doubled every year thereafter. Never mind the high risk of investing in junk bonds. All the thrift owner had at stake was 3 percent of the $100 million. The bulk of the risk was borne by the FSLIC if the bonds became worthless.

So the real and potential losers weren't the thrifts that failed to make winning bets on whether interest rates would go up or down, or the thrifts that put up the money for junk securities. The ultimate loser was the deposit insurance fund and, by extension, the American taxpayers. Some cynical thrift owners recognized that fact openly. "Heads I win, tails FSLIC loses" was a common saying in the thrift industry in the early '80s, as S&Ls sold off conventional home mortgages and amassed vast portfolios of junk bonds and mortgage-backed securities. By the end of 1988, the U.S. thrift industry had accumulated almost $135 billion in corporate paper[9]—usually a euphemism for junk bonds when thrifts were involved—and more than $214 billion in highly liquid, federally guaranteed mortgage-backed securities.[10]

These statistics suggest the most ominous difference between the California and Texas methods. However appalling the results may have been of Texas-style fraud and mismanagement in the thrift industry, at least the losses left by the Texas method have been recognized and calculated. In a very real sense, the California debacle is still unfolding, its ultimate cost still beyond reckoning. All it will take is a new round of sharp interest-rate swings and the now-moribund S&Ls that played the California game will generate additional billions in losses—billions that will have to be covered by the FSLIC (and hence the taxpayer) and that have not been counted in the $157-billion estimate of what the S&L bailout will ultimately cost taxpayers.

How did things come to this pass? It is difficult to

avoid placing much of the blame at the feet of Congress and the regulators—in particular, for allowing the S&Ls to replace traditional accounting rules with the perversely illogical regulatory accounting principles that made it possible for thrifts to record paper profits even as they incurred huge real losses. Jonathan Gray, a respected thrift-industy analyst for the Wall Street firm of Sanford Bernstein & Co., noted in a 1988 study he did for the Federal Deposit Insurance Corporation: "Current accounting rules permit distortions of the true economic conditions of thrift institutions, and divert management from operating strategies that will enhance the long-term economic value of their firms."[11]

As an example of how the ersatz accounting rules distort reality, Gray cited the case of California-based Financial Corporation of America, which in 1987 was able to report $1.3 billion in profits from sales of mortgage-backed securities by its operating unit, American Savings & Loan. From the beginning, American Savings & Loan had been the largest single player in mortgage-backed securities, holding nearly $15 billion—or 48 percent of all its assets—in CMOs. Gray pointed out that despite the reported gain of $1.3 billion, FCA actually lost $1.6 billion on its CMO portfolio that year.

"If it is possible to show a profit when you have a loss," Gray noted, "the illusory profit can be paid out as a dividend and the cash flow obtained from deposit growth. Unless current accounting rules are drastically revamped, the safety of insured deposits can never be secured."[12]

That's the danger: The safety of insured deposits can never be secured as long as deceptive accounting rules permit thrifts to trade in speculative securities and defer their losses, while immediately taking out any profits that accrue. The RAP method of accounting for losses helped the Texas-method cowboys only partially, permitting them to get rid of their unprofitable residential mortgage loans and then use the proceeds for speculative real estate investments. But for the gamblers playing the California game, the new accounting rules opened the doors to a permanent floating crap game of trading in junk bonds and mortgage-backed securities, with the federal deposit insurance system the only certain loser.

Take Financial Corporation of America, the example noted by analyst Gray. As the concealment of $1.6 billion in real losses on its financial statements suggests, FCA had absolutely no reason to worry in 1983 about the fact that it was paying out an average of 2 percentage points more on deposits than it was booking in loan interest income. Thanks to Congress and the regulators, FCA could ignore the traditional lending concept that required interest received from loans to exceed interest paid for deposits. By selling its mortgage portfolio, trading in securities, and charging exorbitant loan-origination fees that it could book as current income, FCA could show profits so long as it played interest-rate roulette by sucking in deposits and placing new bets at an appropriately furious pace. Later in the game, it occurred to FCA that all the fuss and bother of lending to homebuyers—or even profit-crazed developers—could be avoided if its customer deposits were used to purchase junk bonds. Where would the funds come from? Why, just offer high rates of interest for brokered deposits. Shovel the money in the front door from deposit brokers and out the back to Drexel Burnham Lambert and other junk bond underwriters.

Moreover, the game-show fun could be intensified by using Wall Street option contracts to bet on the future direction of interest-rate swings. Of course, if you bet wrong, you could get into big trouble very quickly. And that's just what happened to FCA, which skyrocketed from $8 billion in assets to almost $34 billion in just five years. In the early '80s, with the approval of federal regulators, FCA's hyperaggressive chairman, Charles Knapp, borrowed more than $5 billion in short-term deposits and invested it all in long-term mortgage-backed securities, betting that interest rates would fall. When they didn't, FCA hid behind the blue lights and mirrors of RAP accounting to report record profits while deferring enormous losses.

In 1984, however, the Securities and Exchange Commission made Knapp restate FCA's earnings to show the losses. That sparked a run on deposits. It also prompted thrift regulators finally to act, forcing Knapp's resignation. He was replaced by another longtime FCA executive, William J. Popejoy, who immediately proceeded to follow the same strategy Knapp had employed—he borrowed short and invested long, gambling once again on a decline in interest rates. "It's a case of the greater fool theory," was how one Wall Street investment banker characterized FCA's investment strategy.[13]

As it turned out, the 2.5-to-3-percent spread Popejoy had anticipated from falling rates didn't materialize. Instead, rates started rising. By the end of 1986, FCA's net worth had shrunk to just $294 million and the firm was staring into the abyss. At that point, an additional 1-point increase in interest rates would reduce the value of its CMO portfolio by about 6 percent, or some $300 million. In other words, a 1-point rise in long-term interest rates would wipe out FCA's net worth.

That's just what happened. Between the end of 1986 and the end of 1987, longer-term interest rates (based on the thirty-year Freddie Mac rate) rose from 9.46 to 10.35

percent. As a result, by the end of 1987, FCA's net worth was thrown almost $800 million in the red. Popejoy's bet had gone bad, just as Knapp's had before him. In all, the company recorded a whopping net loss of $486 million in 1987, almost all of it—$425 million—the result of the shrinking value of its portfolio of mortgage-backed securities.[14] On Wall Street, wags began referring to FCA as "Financial Corpse of America."

The inevitable happened in 1988, when FCA washed up on the beach and publicly pleaded for a $1.5 billion government bailout. After negotiations with several potential investors, including Ford Motor Co. and a group headed by former Treasury Secretary William Simon, FCA's only operating subsidiary, American Savings, was rescued by Texas billionaire Robert M. Bass in a sweetheart deal that will ultimately wind up costing the government as much as $1.7 billion.

FCA was just one of the bastard children of the California method. Not all of them wound up in ruins. Indeed, perhaps the most striking example of how the game was played on the West Coast was a thrift that also bet the pot, but came out a winner—the spectacularly successful Columbia Savings & Loan Association of Beverly Hills.

THE MAN
WITH THE
LUCKY COIN

B—————————————

y the summer of 1982, the Columbia Savings &
Loan Association of Beverly Hills, California, was dead,
awaiting only the coroner's official verdict of insolvency.

Like most of the nation's thrift institutions, Columbia
had been caught in the fatal embrace of partial deregulation that seemed almost intended to destroy the industry.
Now that the caps on what they could pay for deposits
had been lifted, S&Ls had to offer depositors high yields
in order to be competitive. Yet thrifts were still locked into
long-term, low-interest residential mortgage portfolios.
As recently as 1980, the industry was still ahead of the
game, paying depositors an average interest rate of 8.94
percent, while earning an average return on mortgage
loans of 9.34 percent.[1] That amounted to a net interest
margin of almost half a percentage point, down from a
spread of almost one and a half points in 1979 but still
favorable. Then in 1981 the impact of 1980's partial deregulation struck with brutal force. The cost of funds indus-

trywide jumped nearly two full points to 10.92 percent, while the return on mortgage loans rose only half a point to 9.91 percent.[2] And in the first six months of 1982, the gap widened even further.

The industry was quickly sliding into insolvency. Nationwide, the thrift industry's net worth dropped an alarming 21 percent between 1980 and 1982, to $26.2 billion from $33.3 billion only two years before.[3] Even more alarming, that $26.2 billion represented only 3.7 percent of the industry's total assets, less than 1 percentage point above the 3.0 percent level that triggered regulatory concern for the safety and solvency of an individual thrift institution.

Columbia Savings & Loan was just one more steerage passenger on that sinking ship in 1982. Columbia had been teetering on the brink of insolvency ever since 1977, when thirty-six-year-old Thomas Spiegel had been brought in by his father, Abraham, to run the family-controlled institution, which the elder Spiegel had bought in 1974. In 1980, it had lost $626,000 on a capital base of just under $12.5 million.[4] The loss deepened in 1981, growing to $3 million as Columbia ended the year with a reduced capital base of $9.6 million supporting assets of $372.5 million. In fact, Columbia's financial condition would have been even worse if it hadn't been lucky in speculating in mortgage-backed securities. In 1981, Columbia managed to record a gain of almost $1 million from trading mortgage-backed securities.[5] This was a respectable profit from a limited business activity. But it was not enough to offset Columbia's losses.

By the spring of 1982, great uncertainty prevailed throughout the nation's financial services industry about which direction interest rates would take, both short-term and long-term. Since December 1980, when it hit an all-time high of 21.5 percent, the benchmark prime lending rate had been bouncing like a cork atop a tidal wave. In 1981 there were thirty-nine separate changes in the prime, which began the year at 20.5 percent and drifted gradually downward to close in the 15.5-to-16-percent range at year's end. Despite that downward drift, though, in the spring of 1982 it still appeared as though there would be no end to the inflation-driven spiral.

Indecision over the direction of interest rates was especially perplexing for thrift owners such as the Spiegel family. Like most S&Ls, Columbia was caught between a rock and a hard place. The rock was an asset portfolio heavily weighted toward low-yielding residential mortgage loans. In 1981, that portfolio produced a total of $7.4 million in interest income. The hard place was a deposit base that cost the thrift more than $7.8 million in interest expenses in 1981—or almost $500,000 more than what its loan portfolio was generating. And the outlook was grim. Over the course of 1981, the proportion of Columbia deposits in short-term accounts paying 12 to 17 percent interest jumped from 26 percent to 73 percent of all deposits.[6] When you're paying out 16 cents for a dollar that earns you 8 cents, you don't make up the difference in volume.

As a result, Columbia's young president and chief executive officer, Tom Spiegel, made a remarkable decision at the thrift's quarterly board meeting in the spring of 1982. We're through, gentlemen, Spiegel reportedly told his somber directors, and the only thing we can do is bet the pot. We can either bet that rates are going up or that rates are going down. What do you think? Are rates going up? Or are they going down?

In the end, Spiegel and his directors decided to bet the pot that interest rates would fall. According to one story that circulated throughout the industry—a story that Columbia officials deny but decline to discuss—Spiegel made the choice by flipping a coin. Whatever the basis of the decision, Columbia raised the rate it offered on deposits in order to attract funds and then threw $260.6 million into mortgage-backed securities yielding 14.02 percent.[7] By locking in that rate, Columbia would be dead if interest rates started rising again. But if interest rates tumbled, Columbia would be jerked from the Red Sea and thrown into the Black.

Unlike FCA a few years later, Spiegel and Columbia won their bet. Interest rates started falling, with the prime rate descending from its 1982 high of 16.5 percent to 10.5 percent one year later. As a result, Columbia enjoyed a growth surge that was phenomenal even by the garish standards that were starting to characterize the thrift industry. Within eighteen months, Columbia would command $5 billion in assets—more than ten times its size only two years earlier—and Tom Spiegel would be corporate America's highest-paid executive. In 1985, his grateful board paid him almost $9 million in total compensation. In addition to a base salary of $960,000, Spiegel was voted a $3 million bonus and a $5 million contribution to his individual retirement account. *Forbes* magazine noted that a $5 million IRA slug wasn't a bad start toward early retirement for someone Spiegel's age. "You can't start working on retirement too early," the magazine said. "Spiegel is already forty years old."[8] Forbes also noted that Spiegel's compensation figure didn't include the options his appreciative board had granted him to buy 307,500 shares of common stock at an average price of $20.37 each; in 1985 Columbia's shares were selling around $32 each, meaning the options were worth $3.6 million.

For his part, Spiegel was not at all embarrassed by his good fortune. "My compensation was based on a formula set by the board," he said. "When the formula was set in early 1985, no one foresaw that Columbia would make $200 million pretax before employee bonuses."[9] But the generosity of Columbia's board to its president was questioned by federal regulators, who began a three-year inquiry that prompted Columbia to cut Spiegel's annual salary back to $3.8 million in 1986. It was a sharp reduction, to be sure, but it still left Spiegel making more than the CEOs of California's three largest publicly owned companies—Arco, Occidental Petroleum, and Chevron— put together.[10]

However excessive Spiegel's salary may have seemed to federal regulators, the fact remained that his gamble that interest would fall unquestionably saved Columbia from insolvency in 1982. What Columbia's success concealed, of course, was the fact that its profits inevitably represented another thrift's losses under the zero-sum gambling game of the California method. In any case, Columbia's 1982 turnaround was the beginning of a remarkable period of growth in which the thrift's profits would rise to almost $200 million a year by 1986, and its return on equity average 60 percent over the next five years.

All of this prosperity may have begun with a lucky or astute guess, but it was sustained by Spiegel's and Columbia's close ties—made possible by deregulation—to Michael Milken, the Drexel Burnham Lambert wunderkind who virtually singlehandedly created the junk bond market. Tom Spiegel's relationship with Drexel dated back to the early '70s, when he worked at the firm's New York retail sales office. According to at least one account, Spiegel's forte was more partying than sales. In her chronicle of Drexel's junk bond business, *The Predator's Ball*, author Connie Bruck quotes one Drexel executive as recalling that Tom Spiegel "would be out till four a.m., never got in to work until ten-thirty or eleven—then he was hung over."[11]

Spiegel didn't stay with Drexel for long. By 1974, he had moved from the securities business to real estate, marketing condominiums in Iran for the Starrett Corporation. That same year his father, Abraham, a Czechoslovakian refugee who emigrated to the U.S. after World War II, acquired a controlling interest in the forerunner to Columbia Savings & Loan. The elder Spiegel had entered the home-building business shortly after arriving in California in 1948. By capitalizing on the postwar housing boom, he amassed a modest fortune in a relatively short time. He first got into the savings and loan business in 1958, when he acquired a small Los Angeles–area thrift that he sold a few years later to a subsidiary of U.S. Life Insurance Co. In 1965, Abraham Spiegel tried the business again, buying another small thrift in Long Beach. That thrift, too, was soon sold. The Spiegel family's permanent entry into the business came in 1974 with the acquisition of Eastland Savings & Loan Association, a small Beverly Hills–based thrift with $43 million in assets. Abraham Spiegel paid $2 million in new capital for a controlling interest in Eastland, installed himself as chairman, and changed the association's name to Columbia. In 1977, he installed his son Tom in the executive suite as president and chief executive officer.

Columbia rocked unsteadily along for three years under Tom Spiegel's leadership. Then, in 1980, Spiegel attended a dinner party where he met Mike Milken. Spiegel's and Columbia's fortunes—and, to a lesser degree, Milken's as well—were dramatically altered by that meeting. For his part, Spiegel quickly became a disciple of Milken, who convinced him that a fortune was waiting for any S&L executive bold enough to use his thrift's funds to invest aggressively in junk securities. When the 1982 deregulation legislation made it possible for S&Ls to do just that, Spiegel wasted no time in acting on his new faith, the gospel according to Milken. Milken's sermon to Spiegel was compelling: Why lock money into thirty-year residential mortgages at 8 or 9 or 10 percent (or even 12, with interest rates rising) when you can buy Drexel's trash bonds and earn 16 or 17 or 18 percent or more? It was a persuasive argument, and by 1984, *Forbes* magazine was reporting, "Spiegel is a big source of commissions for Drexel Burnham."[12] But there was more to it than just commissions. Milken had become Spiegel's financial guru.

"Mike has really been the major influence in expanding my business perspective," Spiegel told *Business Week* magazine in 1987.[13] Indeed, according to Connie Bruck, Spiegel was Milken's "star" protégé, and the junk bond wizard was "clearly" speaking of Columbia when he said: "Many of the savings and loans, who have used different investment techniques, and different ways to build their capital structures, will be the survivors and the savings and loans of the future. . . ."[14]

None of this would have been possible had Congress not passed the deregulation acts of 1980 and 1982. Taking the lid off interest rates and raising the deposit insurance limit in 1980 allowed Columbia to gorge itself on brokered deposits. The 1982 Garn–St Germain Act authorized federally chartered thrifts to invest in corporate debt securities and commercial lending, which gave the Spiegels and other thrift owners more latitude in matching maturities of assets and liabilities, a critical problem for thrifts that borrowed short-term and loaned long-term. To be sure, federally chartered thrifts were barred from investing more than 10 percent of their assets in junk securities. But for S&Ls like Columbia that operated under California state charters, there were virtually no restraints. California law allowed state-chartered thrifts to create subsidiaries that could be assigned up to 100 percent of the parent company's assets, which could then be invested in any type of instrument the owners wished, including junk bonds. For Milken and other underwriters of the junk bonds that were being used to finance a new wave of corporate buyouts, the relaxation of rules on what thrifts could do opened access to a treasure trove of more than $1 trillion in S&L funds, most of it federally insured. It's no wonder that Milken and Spiegel connected; each had a lot to offer the other.

And so Columbia Savings went on a deposit-gathering and junk-bond-buying binge. Over the next several years, its deposit base ballooned from $220.5 million at the end of 1981 to $1.88 billion just eighteen months later. By the end of 1986, deposits had more than doubled again, to $5.19 billion.[15] Columbia achieved this growth by selling several billion dollar's worth of high-interest intermediate- and long-term certificates of deposit through a nationwide network of retail brokers. Because the CDs could not be withdrawn without a penalty, Columbia was assured of a stable deposit base.

Columbia's investments in corporate securities—make that read junk bonds—was on an equally breathtaking scale. Columbia's first bet on junk bonds in 1982 may appear modest in retrospect, a mere $135.9 million. But that represented more than 10 percent of the thrift's total assets at the time—and nearly 600 percent of its entire $23.8 million capital base. In subsequent years, Spiegel began to throw more into the junk bond pot—$844.3 million in 1983, $1.92 billion by the end of 1984, $2.49 billion in 1985, $3.27 billion in 1986, and by the end of 1987 a total of $3.91 billion, or more than a third of the thrift's assets, which by then totaled $11.23 billion.

What began as a two-file-cabinet operation in 1982 eventually would require its own research staff to keep up with Columbia's growing portfolio of junk bonds. By its own admission, that portfolio consisted largely of bottom-of-the-barrel junk. According to Columbia Savings' 1987 annual report to the Securities and Exchange Commission, fully half of its almost $4 billion corporate bond portfolio was rated less than BBB by Standard & Poor's or Baa by Moody's. These are the minimum ratings required for a bond to qualify as "investment grade" and thus be eligible for inclusion in the portfolios of pension funds and other legally regulated investing groups. Included in Columbia's trash portfolio were bonds issued by corporate raider Saul Steinberg's Reliance Group, $109.9 million in bonds issued by Frank Lorenzo's takeover-hungry Texas Air Corporation, $89.3 million in trash debt issued by Wickes Cos. to finance a leveraged buyout, and $88 million borrowed by a Canadian investment group that put up virtually no cash to buy out the billion-dollar Zale retail jewelry chain.[16]

In short, Columbia was one of Drexel's best customers for junk bonds. For Milken, Columbia Savings & Loan was almost a private treasury, effectively functioning as his merchant banking unit. Indeed, because of the strengthening relationship between Drexel/Milken and Columbia/Spiegel, Drexel obtained a 5 percent ownership position in the thrift. And as Bruck reported, Columbia maintained a branch on the second floor of Drexel's Los Angeles office building—a branch that wasn't open to the public. Its sole purpose apparently was to service business with Milken.[17] In return for acting as merchant banker for Drexel-underwritten bonds, Spiegel and Columbia got the high-yield assets they needed in order to continue showing a profit from a base of high-cost deposit liabilities. Never mind the risk, or that the corporate securities were called "junk" for the simple reason that financial experts considered them hazardous investment vehicles.

As it happened, Columbia's gamble on junk bonds paid off. The thrift saw profits rise from $14 million in 1982 to $40 million in 1983, $43 million in 1984, and $122 million in 1985, and in 1986 there was a meteoric leap to a record $194 million. In the first half of 1987, profits began to fall off, which bothered Spiegel. He told *Business Week* that he was "concerned that the profitability in that [junk bond] business will decline as more players enter the market."[18] Then came "Black Monday," the stock market collapse of October 19, 1987. The Wall Street crash had a psychological impact on bond trading as well as the stock market, and Columbia's investment portfolio was shaken. For all of 1987, Columbia's net income dropped a steep 39 percent, to $119 million. In 1988, Columbia's profits were squeezed further by rising interest rates, and—as Spiegel had feared—increasing competition in the junk bond market.

Then, too, there was the bothersome matter of the federal probes into alleged insider trading by Drexel and Milken. Spiegel and Columbia were not targets in the investigations, but along with other major clients, the thrift reportedly received subpoenas for information on its relationship with Drexel and Milken. Troublesome rumors persisted that Milken, Columbia, and other insiders had traded and profited handsomely in 1983 on advance information that Caesars World, the publicly owned Nevada gambling operation, intended to exchange some debt for equity. Since the effect of the trade would be to reduce debt, anyone who bought Caesars World bonds before the exchange offer was announced would be in a position to reap large returns. According to depositions obtained by Connie Bruck, Columbia Savings "may have done well, along with Milken, on the Caesars World exchange" by acquiring several million dollars in bonds before the offer was announced.[19] Milken insisted in the depositions that he had not spoken with Spiegel or other Columbia officials about the Caesars World deal. Still, as Bruck noted: "This was the kind of rumor that had swirled around Milken and his inner circle for years: that first he had created these players such as Spiegel . . . made them his captives with their pools of capital at his disposal, and then rewarded them further (sometimes personally, other bond buyers speculated) with . . . inside information."[20]

After the SEC concluded its investigation of several Milken-led transactions, Drexel admitted to some criminal violations and in 1988 agreed to pay a $650 million fine. Abandoned by Drexel, Milken resigned from the firm and bitterly proclaimed his innocence, vowing to fight charges that he committed illegal acts while earning a reported salary in 1988 of $552 million by making junk bonds the linchpin of Drexel's business operations. For their part, Columbia Savings and Spiegel were not charged with any improper activities.

Nonetheless, the unorthodox "California method" business practices of Columbia and Spiegel had caught the attention of federal regulators. For one thing, Spiegel's lavish $9 million compensation package in 1985 looked too much like the questionable riches the Texas cowboys were taking out of thrift vaults. For another, there were questions about what appeared to be overly generous benefits bestowed on corporate executives, even though Columbia never challenged the excesses of the Texas cowboys. Spiegel and his executives enjoyed the use of two corporate jets and a company gymnasium staffed by four fitness instructors, including a full-time karate coach who often traveled with Spiegel.[21]

Another characteristic Spiegel shared with the Texas cowboys was his penchant for cultivating powerful political figures such as House Democratic Whip Tony Coelho. Indeed, it was as a result of a proposed ethics investigation into a favor Spiegel did for Coelho, involving the congressman's 1986 purchase of $100,000 worth of junk bonds issued by Beatrice Cos., that led the California representative to resign from the House in May 1989. At the time Coehlo bought the bonds, with money borrowed from Spiegel and Columbia Savings, Congress was considering legislation that would limit the amount of junk securities thrifts could own. In the end, the House leadership, of which Coelho was the third-ranking member, kept the junk-bond bill from ever making it to the floor.

Columbia's questionable behavior—the thrift's political maneuvering, the apparently lavish perks enjoyed by its executives, Spiegel's outsized salary, the heavy investment in junk bonds—never sat well with Wall Street investors. Columbia's stock began to be traded publicly in 1984, when the thrift entered the over-the-counter market; it was listed on the New York Stock Exchange at the end of 1985. But despite the institution's remarkable success since Spiegel's lucky coin toss, Columbia's common stock was the Rodney Dangerfield of Big Board trading: it got no respect. "Some stocks Wall Street just can't bring itself to love," *Business Week* noted in June 1987. "Take Columbia Savings and Loan Assn. It would seem to have all the right statistics: record profits in 1986, a 60 percent average return on equity in the past five years, assets that grew to $10 billion from $1 billion in the same period, and twice as much capital as regulators require. But look at the stock. While most stocks sell now at 21 times earnings, Columbia hovers around 2—rock bottom, even for a thrift. . . . Analysts worry about the [junk] bonds' riskiness and also about Columbia's heavy reliance on securities gains."[22]

Then came the October 19 market collapse, which put a $30 million dent in Columbia's $350 million stock portfolio, and rising interest rates, which began to put a crimp in Columbia's favorable interest spread on junk bonds. The combination of these two indirectly related developments led Spiegel and Columbia to review the wisdom of their heavy involvement in junk bonds. And Spiegel concluded that it was time to do things differently. In November 1988, *Forbes* reported: "Tom Spiegel wants Columbia to become more of a 'merchant banker'—get Columbia involved early enough in financings for leveraged buyouts and the like so that it can influence the structure of the deal before committing to buy. It will, in short, compete more directly against the Merrill Lynches, the Morgan Stanleys, the Salomons. . . . Spiegel is also trying to step up Columbia's real estate development activities . . . and hopes to sell 10 to 15 high-priced homes in southern California that were built by a subsidiary."[23] That last item— providing more residential mortgages—was significant. Columbia's executive vice president, Lawrence Fish, told *Forbes* that the thrift intended to increase its residential mortgage lending and thus return the thrift to its original role. "We need to build a more steady foundation of more predictable core earnings," Fish said.[24]

What goes around comes around. It was time for Columbia Savings & Loan to follow a more prudent course. But other thrifts continued to gamble. Although Columbia's portfolio was still heavy with $3.2 billion in junk bonds as the industry's bailout began in 1988, it had been surpassed in the junk bond business by Franklin Savings

Association of Ottawa, Kansas, which held $4.42 billion worth of the securities. By December 31, 1988, Columbia's investment securities portfolio had risen to $3.86 billion, 33 percent higher than 12 months earlier, but it now stood fourth in the industry in junk bond holdings. Just as Spiegel had anticipated, other S&Ls had gotten heavily into the game. Hunter Savings Association of Cincinnati, for example, had 15.7 percent of its assets in junk bonds at the end of 1988, while such California thrifts as Far West Savings & Loan Association of Newport Beach, United California Savings Bank of Anaheim, Imperial Savings Association of San Diego, and Lincoln Savings & Loan of Irvine each had more than 10 percent of their assets tied up in junk.[25]

That's why the importance of the California method to the thrift crisis cannot be overstated, for the game of chance involving interest-rate swings and junk bond investments continues. When regulators finally became aroused to realization that the industry was in trouble, all of their attention was focused on the cowboys and the Texas method that was taking down thrifts throughout the Southwest. The regulators were wholly unequipped—in both staffing levels and supervisory expertise—to understand what was going on in California. And while regulatory expertise has improved since 1986, when the crisis became evident, it still is not sufficient fully to assess the risks created by the California method. After all, most regulators had been trained only to examine simple residential mortgage portfolios and to determine whether a thrift was paying the correct percentage interest on a passbook account. Asking the average thrift regulator to conduct an audit of a thrift with billions of dollars in brokered hot money, junk bonds, and interest-sensitive securities was like asking a school nurse to perform brain surgery.

7.
THE
REGULATORS

By 1985, it was apparent to the staff of the Federal Home Loan Bank Board that the U.S. savings and loan industry was sliding into an abyss of insolvency at an accelerating rate. And as the pace of thrift failures quickened, graveyard humor began to penetrate the FHLBB's Washington headquarters.

At the bank board's 1985 Christmas party staff members wore T-shirts with the slogan "FSLICAID" imprinted on the front, a reference to the mounting bankruptcy of the thrift insurance fund. On the backs of the shirts, printed in reverse, was the statement "We do it with mirrors!" A year later the humor got rougher. The 1986 Christmas party featured a ventriloquist whose act suggested that Bank Board chairman Ed Gray was a dummy who merely parroted words spoken by William O'Connell, the chief lobbyist for the powerful U.S. League of Savings Institutions.[1]

Those two jokes were quite revealing, recognizing as

they did the two main weaknesses that prevented the principal regulator of the thrift industry from exercising the muscle required to keep the cowboys corralled and the gamblers away from the roulette table. The first weakness was a critical lack of trained examiners and supervisors—"We do it with mirrors"—which was a direct result of Reagan-era deregulation. According to the Reagan administration, deregulation meant not just fewer regulations, but fewer regulators as well. The second weakness was more fundamental. It was essentially a structural problem that stemmed from the way the Federal Home Loan Bank Board, its captive insurance agency, and its pliant leadership had been conceived by the New Deal and had developed over the fifty or so intervening years.

A comparison with the commercial banking industry is useful. The federal regulatory framework established by Glass-Steagall in 1933 for commercial banks had several levels—the Federal Reserve System, the Federal Deposit Insurance Corporation, and the Office of the Comptroller of the Currency. These were all independent agencies, each fulfilling an examination and oversight role and each exercising a broad degree of autonomous authority.

Not so with the thrift industry. The Federal Home Loan Bank Board was not only an extension of the White House, it was also the sole federal agency overseeing savings and loan institutions. Even more incestuous, the eleven district Federal Home Loan Banks were actually owned by the S&Ls they supervised. As was the case in the commercial banking industry, the Federal Home Loan Bank Board's supervisory role was augmented by local S&L commissions in each of the states. But the dual regulatory system didn't help. In fact, instead of working together, the federal and state agencies more often competed over prerogatives.

As noted earlier, for half a century the industry had operated within strict guidelines for accepting deposits and making loans, guidelines that allowed little latitude for the member institutions and whose enforcement required virtually no expertise on the part of regulators. It didn't take much education or training to determine whether an S&L was paying interest within the legal limits, or investing in anything more elaborate than residential mortgage loans.

It's thus not surprising that over the years the chairman of the Federal Home Loan Bank Board, who also acted as the chief executive officer of the industry's deposit insurance agency, the Federal Savings and Loan Insurance Corporation, as well as the executive in charge of supervisors and examiners for both the FHLBB and the FSLIC, had become little more than a figurehead. The FHLBB chairman served the dual but essentially incompatible roles of chief regulator on the one hand and principal industry spokesman and public relations agent on the other. The chairman and the two other members of the bank board were political appointees who were usually selected with the comfort of the thrift industry uppermost in the White House's mind. Indeed, until deregulation, being appointed chairman of the Federal Home Loan Bank Board was like being named ambassador to a minor nation. It was a prestigious appointment, but one without power, influence, or meaning. The skills required were diplomacy, tact, and the willingness to spend plenty of time massaging a constituency that was a powerful source of political clout and campaign money. If the appointed chairman had some knowledge of banking and economics and could make change for a dollar without counting out loud, that was a plus. But expertise wasn't a critical asset. The most important characteristic required was a good sense of public relations.

All of which seemed to make Ed Gray an ideal candidate for the chairmanship of the Federal Home Loan Bank Board in 1983. Gray, who went on to become the president of a $1-billion-plus Florida thrift, was a forty-two-year-old former public relations executive when he was named head of the FHLBB on May 1, 1983. A former radio and wire service reporter, Gray was amiable, smooth, and articulate, and he actually had at least a passing knowledge of the thrift industry, gained while working for six years in public relations at San Diego Federal Savings and Loan Association. Moreover, Gray was politically acceptable to the free-market ideologues of the Reagan White House. A conservative Republican, he had served Reagan as a press aide, first when Reagan was governor of California and then later during the 1980 presidential campaign. Following the campaign, Gray joined the White House staff as a deputy assistant to the President for policy development, and played a role in both writing and winning passage of the Garn–St Germain deregulation bill. Gray was also friendly with Nancy Reagan, an association that helped him gain White House appointments (though it would later work to his disadvantage when he crossed swords with Treasury Secretary Donald Regan, no friend of the First Lady). In short, Ed Gray seemed to be just right for the chairmanship of the Federal Home Loan Bank Board.

The only problem was that deregulation had quietly but dramatically altered the requirements for the job. As a result of deregulation, a war had started in the thrift industry. The minor nation to which the FHLBB chairman was emissary was no longer insignificant. It was the scene of an ever-widening battleground between a small band of regulators with few weapons and no leadership, and a group of well-armed thrift owners who, like guerrilla chieftains, were exploiting the weaknesses of a system that time had left behind. What the FHLBB needed was a Pattonesque general—a tough son of a bitch with an instinct for the jugular and the ferocity of a barroom brawler —not a socially polished banana-pudding diplomat. Gray, the quintessential nice guy, very simply was in over his head.

But if anyone thought he would just fold up and go away, they were wrong. Once he discovered the danger of insolvency threatening the insurance fund shortly after he took office in 1983, Gray was transformed. Almost overnight, he became a re-regulator in a political environment that demanded deregulation. Like a reformed alcoholic who must preach the virtues of sobriety to reinforce his own conversion to righteousness, Gray turned into an evangelist for stricter controls. Beginning with testimony before a House banking subcommittee on October 7, 1983, Gray began talking about the critical need to impose regulations on an industry that was running out of control. He repeated that message countless times over the next four years, in speeches before industry groups, testimony on Capitol Hill, and press interviews. As early as March 1984, Gray was telling the industry that it was "out of control," and that if it went under "you will have only yourselves to blame."[2] The implicit message Gray conveyed—the one neither the industry nor the administration wanted to hear—was that you can't deregulate without controls. In short, Gray became a nag who quickly became wearisome to the disciples of deregulation in the Reagan administration and to the industry lobbyists who were determined to preserve the newfound freedoms provided by Garn–St Germain.

It's hardly surprising that Gray was unable to stop the steamroller on its downhill rush toward chaos. He had neither the tools nor the personnel nor the political toughness necessary to carry out a battle on several fronts against a host of enemies. Those enemies, some natural, some made by Gray and circumstances, included powerful members of Congress, especially House Majority leader (and soon-to-be Speaker) Jim Wright and House Banking Committee chairman Fernand St Germain of Rhode Island; industry lobbyists, particularly officials of the U.S. League of Savings Institutions; state regulatory officials who were jealous of their turf, principally in Texas where most of the problems with fraud and mismanagement occurred; and opponents within the administration, mainly Treasury Secretary Regan.

"It would have been so easy for me to have been a good old boy and gone along," Gray mused in the spring of 1989 almost two years after leaving office. "I was always known before I became a regulator as a nice guy. Mr. Nice Guy. You'd never know that now. Everybody liked me. I didn't have to be a policeman and give out tickets, send people to jail. . . . [But] I considered myself as protecting the FSLIC. People used to call me Mr. Ed. You know, Mr. Ed, the talking horse? They said there was only on thing I could talk about. The FSLIC."[3]

Gray took office seven months after passage of the Garn–St Germain deregulation act. As he tells it, it was three months later, at an August 1983 briefing on the condition of the FSLIC, that he first became aware of mounting problems in the thrift industry. The signal, according to Gray, was the rapidly escalating level of brokered deposits—"hot money"—that was flooding into federally insured S&L accounts. The flood had been unleashed by Gray's predecessor as FHLBB chairman, Richard Pratt, who in 1982 removed the 5 percent cap on brokered funds. Pratt, a former professor of finance at the University of Utah and a protégé of Republican Senator Jake

Garn of Utah, "brought to the table some basically deregulatory ideas," Gray said. "You know, let the market do
its thing. . . . The problem was, especially in retrospect,
that people confused deregulation and free-market con-
cepts. Thrift institutions, you see, aren't free-market players. They had always been regulated."

With the limit on brokered deposits removed, financial services institutions could package small investors'
funds in $100,000 increments, thus qualifying for federal
insurance, then shop them to the S&L paying the highest
interest rate. "All you had to have was a retail base like
Merrill Lynch," Gray said. "Don Regan developed that
[base] when he was at Merrill Lynch [as chairman and
chief executive officer, before joining the Reagan admin-
istration]. There was absolutely no risk [to the brokers].
They got a nice commission. All they had to do was package it up to insurability and ship it to the guy who paid
the highest rate. And Merrill Lynch was funneling money
to the S&Ls as fast as they could get it." Most of that
brokered money went to the Sunbelt—in particular, to the
newly aggressive S&Ls of Texas and California.

Gray regarded the trend with alarm. "It was scary,
what was happening. And it was happening quickly . . .
the reserves of the FSLIC were deteriorating at an alarming rate. The rate of FSLIC reserves to deposits was drop-
ping even faster, which meant that we had less cushion
for the losses from these increased deposits, which were
going into bad assets. Going really quickly." At the time,
the FSLIC was taking in $700 million a year from insur-
ance premiums and interest. But new brokered deposits
were entering the system at the rate of billions of dollars
a year, and the $700 million, as Gray put it, "was a drop
in the bucket compared to what we could be losing."

He began sounding the alarm early and kept at it. His

first public warning came in his October 1983 testimony to a subcommittee of the House Banking Committee. "In light of the rapid growth in money brokering," Gray told the hearing, "I would urge that the Congress revisit the whole matter of what federal deposit insurance is and what it ought to be used for in the future. The issues [for the FSLIC] are of such magnitude, I believe they ought to be addressed and resolved in the legislative process."[4]

A month later, in a speech to industry leaders in Albuquerque, Gray criticized what he called "open trafficking in brokered funds by those who have little or no concern for the safety and soundness . . . of the deposit insurance funds. . . . We must question philosophically to what extent the resources of the federal deposit insurance system should be put unnecessarily at risk as the result of money brokering activities."[5]

That wasn't what either the industry or free-market enthusiasts in the administration wanted to hear. In particular, Gray's concern about the rapid growth of brokered deposits aroused the ire of Treasury Secretary Regan. Secretary Regan, Gray said, "had ideas that were very different from mine. He wanted to decontrol rates as quickly as possible." When he was running Merrill Lynch, Regan hadn't had the advantages of a deregulated thrift industry. As Gray put it, "They had to go out and get money with no deposit insurance. They had to do it on their own." Now that the walls had come down, Regan was not about to let anyone rebuild them. "I said we're going too fast. We're going to hurt the S&Ls. It didn't make any difference. Don Regan was going balls out to get rates decontrolled."[6]

A month after the August 1983 briefing that made him aware of the problem, Gray met with FDIC chairman William Isaac, who agreed that brokered deposits were getting out of hand. Together, Gray and Isaac proposed a joint regulation that would prohibit any money broker from placing more than $100,000 in a depository account at any insured bank or thrift. They announced their plan on October 25, 1983, and formally proposed the new regulation on January 16, 1984. "It was like ice water being thrown in the faces of all those who were sailing along happily in the new deregulatory spirit," Gray recalled.[7]

Pressure to abandon the proposed regulation was immediate and forceful. "Donald Regan dispatched the full resources of the Treasury to prevent me . . . from proposing the brokered funds resolution," Gray noted in a January 1989 letter to the *Washington Post*. "The pressure on me by Treasury Deputy Secretary Tim McNamar during the weeks preceding January 16, 1984, the day the Bank Board proposed the brokered funds regulation, was particularly intense." According to Gray, on January 15 he spent seven hours on the telephone with McNamar, who had been assigned the task of twisting arms because Regan had had to disqualify himself from involvement in any matter relating to Merrill Lynch. McNamar "appealed to my patriotism," Gray later told *Barron's* magazine.[8] "He said that in interfering with the free flow of money I was being disloyal to [President] Reagan." McNamar, in a statement released by Regan's office, said his diary and communications logs for January 15, 1984, show no telephone contact with Gray. But while he didn't remember talking with Gray on that day, McNamar told *Barron's* that "we did not think it was a good idea to cut off liquidity at a time when the thrifts were in bad shape."[9]

Gray said urgent demands to abandon the regulation came from all sides—from the administration, from "fierce lobbying" by the U.S. League of Savings Institutions, from members of Congress who were beneficiaries of campaign contributions from the thrift industry. In all, said Rosemary Stewart, director of the Office of Enforcement under Gray, the lobbying effort to kill the brokered deposit regulation "was indicative of how much the industry did not want to be part of re-regulation, which is what that [the proposed regulation] was trying to do." [10]

As it turned out, all of Gray's efforts to put a leash on brokered deposits were as pointless as they were agonizing. In an immediate court test once the new joint FHLBB-FDIC regulation took effect in March 1985, a federal judge ruled that the regulation was arbitrary and unreasonable. The re-regulators had lost their first major fight. It would not be their last defeat. They were—and would continue to be—outmanned, outgunned, and outsmarted at almost every turn.

Ed Gray's biggest problem wasn't political infighting with Treasury Secretary Regan. The major difficulty he and his fellow regulators faced was a critical lack of skilled examiners and supervisors. At no time in 1984 and 1985 did the number of FHLBB professional examiners and supervisors vary much from the 750 level that had been reached when Ronald Reagan took office. Indeed, in the early years of deregulation thrift examinations actually declined, which was wholly consistent with the Reagan adminstration's emphasis on cutting back on regulators as well as regulations. Only in 1986, after Gray transferred the field examination force from Washington headquarters to the district banks in order to avoid White House restraints, did the size of the field examination force increase, doubling to 1,531 by the end of the year. [11] But by that time it was too late; the damage had been done.

According to Gray, staff problems were critical. "Look what I faced—a 25 percent turnover in the field [examination force] every year; in the Ninth District, the figure was 29 percent. Half of the examiners had been on the job for less than two years. Their average salary was $25,000, and the highest entry-level salary we could pay was $14,000. It was laughable."[12]

The inadequacy of the bank board's examination and supervision force was a direct result of how the thrift industry regulatory structure had developed over the years. FHLBB examiners had been trained only to verify that thrifts were paying interest on deposits within prescribed limits and that residential mortgage loans were being made within set guidelines. The examiners and supervisors were not equipped to understand the complex financial transactions that began taking place in the newly deregulated thrift industry—the equity investments in retail businesses, the loans to real estate developers to buy and improve raw land, the trading of loan participation agreements, the plunge into junk bonds, interest futures, and so on. The thrift business was no longer simple; deregulation had made it an immensely complicated chess game.

Joe Selby was a senior career supervisor with more than thirty-two years of experience in the Comptroller of the Currency's office—for seven months in the early '80s he was acting Comptroller of the Currency—when he was brought to the Dallas Federal Home Loan Bank in 1986 as director of supervision. His assignment was to help clean up the mess that deregulation had created in Texas. He wasn't prepared for what he found.

"On May 1, 1986, when I came [to Dallas], there were any number of thrifts that had not been examined for two to three years during this period of deregulation and high growth," Selby said. "And basically, the examination system that was in place was an ineffective one. Examiners in the bank board system were—and still are, to a large part—not decision-makers. Examiners in the bank board system are fact-finders. When I got to the Dallas bank their reports made no recommendations to management, made no decisions. Those reports were a compilation of facts that were given to the supervisors. The process of supervision was long, tedious, and basically ineffective, too." [13]

When he first got to Dallas, Selby immediately increased the budget for examination and supervision in the Ninth District to $30 million from about $11 million. He didn't accomplish that without resistance.

"The quirk is that the Federal Home Loan Banks are run by a board of directors, of which a majority are the industry members," Selby continued. "And about the time I got to Dallas those same directors started squawking about the fact that they were having to cut back at their institutions, on their budgets and spending, and therefore the Dallas bank should do the same. And so, immediately, they began talking about a zero-based budget, a zero budget for 1987."

But money was the least of Selby's worries. The lack of training was a far more pressing problem. Compared to their counterparts who watched over the commercial banking industry, the thrift examiners "were not up to date in the sophisticated changes in products and services that financial institutions were engaged in. The Federal Reserve, the Comptroller, the FDIC examiners—all were much better trained." [14]

As an example, Selby cited a regulation approved by the FHLBB in December 1985 requiring examiners to analyze loans from several perspectives. The regulation was called "loan classification." As Selby put it: "Now, the Comptroller's Office and the commercial-bank regulators had loan classifications for a hundred years. But the bank board didn't adopt it until 1985, because all of a sudden thrifts could make commercial loans. And here these [FHLBB] examiners had one training program on loan classifications and they didn't understand it. The only thing they understood was that a mortgage loan had to be supported by an appraisal. That was their only guideline. Then, all of a sudden, they had to look at loans in terms of cash flow, payment ability and the financial worth of the borrower, and so on. . . . A lot of [the examiners] just weren't competent to understand it."

According to Selby, the flaws in the personnel structure of the Federal Home Loan Bank system were a direct result of politics. "Because the bank board is such a political animal there is very little continuity," he said. "The head of it, rather than being a career supervisor, has traditionally been a political appointee, as has the head of the FSLIC. Therefore, every three or four years, when the chairman changes the head of supervision changes, too."[15]

One indication of the low esteem in which thrift regulators were held was their low pay and poor benefits. In 1985, the FHLBB was paying "exceptionally qualified and experienced" senior financial anaylsts a maximum annual salary of $37,599. In contrast, the FDIC, the Fed, and the Comptroller of the Currency paid their senior analysts up to $48,876 a year, a differential of almost 30 percent. And while the FDIC could offer its field people regional pay differentials of up to 10 percent of base compensation, thrift regulators were granted no such differential. To add insult to injury, FHLBB employees had to pay 40 cents a month for each $1,000 of basic life insurance coverage, while employees of the Federal Reserve Board paid only 14 cents for the same protection. The bank board was also at a disadvantage in other areas, including bonus plans for senior executives and subsidized employee savings programs such as 401-K plans.[16] The disparities were magnified even more when FHLBB compensation and benefit plans were matched against those offered by private industry.

According to Gray, the result was enormous difficulty in recruiting and keeping employees. According to the bank board, one prospective employee, an MBA candidate at the Wharton School of Business, was "incredulous" when offered a starting salary of $21,804; the graduate student said he wouldn't consider a job for less than $42,000. Another candidate for employment turned down the FHLBB in favor of the FDIC because the thrift agency could not pay his relocation expenses. Senior secretarial vacancies at the bank board remained open for six months or more because the agency simply couldn't compete with salaries and benefits offered by private industry. Between June 1984 and June 1985, the FHLBB lost sixteen attorneys from its general counsel's office to private industry. In all, the FHLBB's employee turnover rate in 1984 was 23.6 percent—almost twice the turnover rate for all federal government employees. Attrition was especially severe in the bank board's major policy offices. In 1985 alone, the general counsel's office lost 52 percent of its employees, the Office of Examinations and Supervision 39 percent, and the Federal Savings and Loan Insurance Corporation 33 percent.[17]

The bank board's personnel problems were due in part to the agency's position on the federal organizational chart. Because it is an executive rather than independent agency, the FHLBB is subject to restraints on hiring, compensation, and benefits imposed by the Office of Personnel Management and the Office of Management and

Budget, both of which report directly to the White House. This dependence on executive pleasure is not shared by the independent banking regulatory agencies—the FDIC, Federal Reserve, and Comptroller's Office—or, indeed, even by the eleven district Federal Home Loan Banks. Since the district banks are owned, legally at least, by the member institutions they supervise, they can set their own budgets and establish their own levels of staffing, compensation, and benefits. Indeed, as a result, the Washington FHLBB staff often loses people to the district banks. Between 1984 and 1986, twenty of the Washington office's most experienced financial, professional, and legal managers, including six attorneys from the general counsel's office, were lured away by recruiters from the district banks.[18]

Just as he incurred the displeasure of Treasury Secretary Regan and the thrift industry's lobbyists when he sought to put a lid on brokered deposits, Gray ran into an ideological roadblock when he tried to solve the agency's staffing problems. When he tried to get approval to hire more people and to pay more money to the people he already had, he got what he called "preachment lectures" from Carol Crawford, the OMB associate director in charge of the FHLBB budget. According to Gray, Crawford told him in 1985 and again in 1986 that he "was no longer on the Reagan team, that I had betrayed the Reagan revolution—and especially the policy of deregulation."[19]

But it wasn't simply ideology that prevented Ed Gray from doing what he took to be his job. There was also the matter of the thrift industry's "dual charter" system, which allocated powers over S&Ls between the states and the federal government. When Gray was unable to increase compensation, benefits, and staffing levels for the

FHLBB's examination and supervisory force, he solved the problem by transferring many of those functions to the eleven district banks, which operated with more autonomy than the central bank board. A solution to the problems arising from the dual-charter system would prove to be more elusive.

Under the regulatory system established during the New Deal, a thrift institution could be chartered to do business by either the federal government or by the state in which it intended to operate. One idea behind this dual-charter separation of powers was to duplicate the commercial banking system, which also allowed banks to choose either state or federal governance. There were advantages and disadvantages to each, but the difference essentially was one of regulatory control: State-chartered thrifts were supervised by state commissions and operated within limits set by the various state legislatures, while federal thrifts operated within guidelines set broadly by Congress and administered by the Federal Home Loan Bank Board. The Federal Savings and Loan Insurance Corporation, under the Bank Board, oversaw any thrift with federal deposit guarantees.

Legally, only thrifts with federal charters were required to pay FSLIC premiums and enjoy the protection of deposit guarantees. But as a practical matter, virtually all state-chartered thrifts chose to seek the protection of FSLIC. After all, a state-chartered thrift without federal deposit guarantees would be all but crippled in the competition for depositors' funds. In Texas, for example, only one of 254 state-chartered thrifts in 1982 operated outside the shelter of the FSLIC. Nationwide, about one-third of all S&Ls operated under federal charters in the early 1980s, while the remainder were state-chartered. The effect of this was that two-thirds of the industry enjoyed the protection of the FSLIC but operated under guidelines set by the states rather than the Congress. It was not a healthy mix.

The deregulatory fervor that gripped Washington in the Reagan years washed across state legislatures, too. Particularly in Texas and California, local lawmakers outdid Garn–St Germain by passing legislation that permitted state-chartered thrifts to do virtually anything they wished. In California, for example, the Nolan Act of 1982 allowed a state-chartered thrift to create a subsidiary service corporation with literally unlimited powers to do business, and then permitted the thrift to assign 100 percent of its assets to the subsidiary. Gray called this "the California honey-pot . . . the most irresponsible legislation" in thrift history.[20] Not to be outdone, Texas followed in 1983 with a similar relaxation of rules for its state-chartered institutions. The Garn–St Germain Act, said FHLBB enforcement chief Rosemary Stewart, "triggered a lot of states to liberalize. . . . It had much more of an effect than just the words in the law."[21]

According to Gray, whatever the original purpose of the dual-charter system, its main raison d'être was to provide a source of political contributions for candidates for state office. "Without the dual thrift system," Gray said, "there would be no need for political contributions from the thrift industry to state legislators and governors and other state officers. . . . The so-called dual thrift system is really . . . nothing more than a scam, a rationale artificially generated to create the need for thrift industry contributions to state officials. There is no sound reason for having a dual thrift system which is insured by the federal government."[22]

It's hardly surprising, then, that Gray aroused the

vipers in the pit when in 1985 he proposed both regulations and legislation that would limit state-chartered thrifts. Among the proposals: restricting the growth of state-chartered thrifts to their ability to generate earnings; restraining direct investments, which turned the thrifts into business owners rather than lenders; and charging extra insurance premiums to state-chartered thrifts engaged in business activities not permitted to S&Ls operating under federal charter.

These proposals, Gray said, "caused every state regulator, and governors and legislatures, to put pressure on the Reagan Administration and members of Congress to lobby the Bank Board to gut or rescind the regulations." According to Gray, political pressure from state officials led more than half the members of the House of Representatives to sign a resolution calling for derailment of the direct-investment regulation. But what finished Gray off was his attempt to limit the power states enjoyed over S&Ls. It was this effort, Gray said, that caused Don Regan "to tell the White House staff that he wanted me out, and he wanted me out soon." [23]

In theory, at least, the dual-charter system should have provided sufficient safeguards to prevent thrift abuses. Federal regulators from the bank board would oversee the one-third of the thrifts that were Washington-chartered, state supervisors would keep an eye on the other two-thirds, and the FSLIC would be a backstop for both. But in actual practice the system broke down.

To begin with, it appeared that the state regulators were even more incompetent and understaffed than the federal examination and supervision force. In Texas, for example, state law in 1983 gave the Texas Savings and Loan Commission virtually no authority. Indeed, until

1984, the Texas S&L Commission didn't even have the power to deny an application for thrift ownership if the applicant met the requirements for capital adequacy and other administrative preconditions. According to former Texas S&L commissioner Linton Bowman, who occupied the state's top thrift post from 1982 through 1987, the weaknesses of the state regulatory framework were what permitted a Herman Beebe to slip into the system through partial ownership of Don Dixon's Vernon Savings and Loan Association. Beebe, it will be recalled, was the later-convicted criminal who was implicated by federal regulators as early as 1976 in playing a role in the downfall of at least five banks or savings and loans through questionably legal transactions and insider dealings.

Bowman learned shortly after Dixon bought control of Vernon that Beebe was one of Dixon's backers. He said, "I told Dixon that I didn't think he could survive in the business connected in any way at all with Herman Beebe, and if there was a way he [Dixon] could get loose . . . it would be the only solution to saving his capital." As a state regulator, however, there was nothing Bowman could do himself to force Beebe away from Dixon. "He [Dixon] went through a lot of gyrations to convince me that he had in fact separated himself from Beebe," Bowman said. "But I don't think anybody ever separates from Herman. I think you gets with Herman and you stays with Herman."[24]

With hindsight, Bowman says both state and federal regulators were "naive" in encouraging real estate developers such as Dixon to become thrift owners. "What happpened was that we saw an opportunity to get these guys [into the industry], not so much for the men themselves but for their cash, to shore up the industry," Bowman said. And because the basic business of thrifts had been residential lending, "we felt like the logical marriage was someone whose business was real estate. It seemed to make sense to Washington and Austin. What we didn't recognize was that the builder who makes a lot of money makes it because he gets around the city council, because he gets around the planning and zoning commission. And the developers [who bought thrifts] saw us as just one more of those regulatory bodies they needed to get around. They saw that they could make more money if they could circumvent the regulations than if they played by them. It is the nature of the developer to circumvent regulations. He was already of a mind-set to do that. We were the ones who were naive."

The FHLBB's chief enforcement officer, Rosemary Stewart, concedes that developers were welcomed into the business. But she insists that was because the regulators really had no other choice. "These people had capital, or at least access to capital, and that's what the industry desperately needed," Stewart says. "Besides, there were not a lot of other business groups looking at investing in the industry in 1982. It's not like we turned down a Wall Street banker to get the real estate developer. The real estate developer was really the only person I can recall who was here applying [for thrift ownerships], wanting institutions, promising he would put in capital. And we said yes."[25]

But the weakness in the thrift regulatory systems of states like Texas went far beyond their inability to close the doors on people who had no business owning or operating a savings and loan. In the most important respects, the shortcomings of the state regulatory framework resembled those of the federal system. Indeed, if anything, they were worse.

To begin with, the snug relationships between the

regulators and the industry that existed in Washington were duplicated on the state level. For example, in 1981, when he was deputy S&L commissioner in Texas, Bowman entered into a small real estate deal with one of his employees, Patrick King, who was then director of supervision for the Texas Savings and Loan Department. It was a minor transaction, involving ownership of only two duplexes—four housing units—in northwest Austin. And, Bowman said, he made sure that the Texas State Finance Commission, the oversight agency for the Savings and Loan Department, knew about it. "Every year I'd say, 'If you guys got a problem with this let me know.' " And every year, even after King left the state agency in 1987 to go to work for Dixon at Vernon Savings, the Finance Commission said it saw nothing wrong with the deal. The matter became public knowledge in 1987, and was one factor that led to Bowman's decision to resign. "If I could have sold those damned duplexes I'd have been long gone from that deal," Bowman said, noting that the units were still unsold on the dreary Austin housing market in early 1989.[26] The attitude of the State Finance Commission says something about how Texas officials viewed—or didn't view—potential conflicts of interest.

The relative weakness of the supervisory force in Texas was another parallel with the situation in Washington. If the FHLBB examination and supervisory force was thin, the state thrift examination staff in Texas was positively skeletal. Bowman said that when he was promoted to commissioner from the deputy's post in 1982, the Texas Savings and Loan Commission had a total of thirteen examiners to keep tabs on 254 state-chartered thrifts. "We finally got it up to eighteen," Bowman said, "but it was woefully inadequate. Every year we'd ask for more examiners and [every year] we got cut back." In any case, pay scales were so miserly that Bowman never was able to hire up to the authorized level. "We couldn't afford to hire accountants," he said. "The Big Eight [accounting and consulting firms] were paying $18,000 to $22,000 for entry-level people. We were paying $13,000 and requiring full-time travel. We got no takers. So we took the people we thought we could use. I tried to find people with degrees in finance, maybe accounting degrees but from the smaller colleges. People who hadn't passed the CPA exam, but who maybe had some knowledge of finance, maybe junior officers at small savings and loans. We took them anywhere we could find them. There just weren't that many candidates out there."

In 1987, after the Texas thrift industry had already crashed in flames and was approaching an insolvency of more than $25 billion, the Texas State Auditor's Office conducted an examination of the effectiveness of the State Savings and Loan Commission. Not surprisingly, its report was devastatingly critical.

Not only was the state thrift examination and supervision staff too small, the report noted, but many of the examiners were not qualified for their jobs when hired and then were not trained. "There are two field examiners who were hired without a college degree or prior work experience in the credit industry," the report said. "There are some examiners who have degrees in English, Biology, Religion and Music. These types of degrees normally do not have a curriculum which would prepare an individual for the complexity of the savings and loan industry."[27]

Moreover, the audit found that the Texas S&L Department didn't take full advantage of existing professional training programs. The report noted that although the FHLBB had offered free training courses to state examiners and supervisors since 1983, only twelve Texas examiners had been sent through the program between 1983 and the end of 1985. What's more, the Texas Savings and Loan Department had no written policies regarding training or training objectives, and "has not requested training funds for examiners in any of their legislative appropriations requests. . . . Some examiners, including senior and review examiners, have not had some of the more relevant training courses since 1982 and deregulation; that is, real estate appraisal and lending."[28]

Overall, the report revealed an ineffective, inadequately staffed and generally lethargic state supervisory system that couldn't have done its job properly even before deregulation—much less kept pace with a gang of rampaging cowboys and high-rolling speculators who were riding the industry into the ground. Among other things, the audit found that the Texas S&L Department had no written guidelines or a standardized format for working papers produced during a field examination, no criteria for determining when an institution needed to be placed under state supervision, and no policies on when examinations should be conducted. In short, the report found that the Texas Savings and Loan Department was a mess.

The inadequacy of the examination staff, in terms of both numbers and training, wasn't the only parallel between the federal and state regulatory systems. Political impotence was another point of similarity. Just as Ed Gray was outmaneuvered by lobbyists and administration opponents and found himself isolated as a re-regulator, the Texas S&L Commission's efforts to impose controls were confounded by politically savvy thrift owners.

In 1985, for example, Bowman went to the Texas legislature with a bill that would have strengthened his commission's supervisory powers. By that time, it was clear that the industry was in deep trouble and that the cowboys were running rampant. The bill he proposed had what was known as an emergency clause that would have made it law immediately upon passage; without an emergency clause, there's a ninety-day waiting period in Texas after the legislative session ends before a bill becomes law. However, a two-thirds vote rather than simple majority is required for approval of a bill with an emergency provision.

According to Bowman, a group of cowboy thrift owners from Houston and Dallas hired as their lobbyist a former parliamentarian of the Texas house of representatives. This lobbyist knew that certain members of the legislature wouldn't vote for a measure, even if they supported it in principle, unless they had a printed copy of the bill prior to the vote. So the lobbyist simply called in a favor owed by a typesetter in the state printing office, and the bill was "misplaced" and not printed before the vote.

In the end, the bill passed, but not by the two-thirds required for immediate enactment. Bowman believes the thrift owners used the ninety-day waiting period to shift bad loans among themselves—"a rolling loan gathers no loss"—at an ultimate cost to the federal deposit insurance fund of several million dollars.

In addition to being outmaneuvered politically, another factor that contributed to the ineffectiveness of the regulators was conflict between state and federal officials. Ed Gray's efforts to superimpose federal regulations over state-chartered thrifts didn't win him many friends in Austin, Sacramento, Tallahassee, and other state capitals where the rules had been relaxed. Gray basically was out of step with state regulatory officials, who tended to be "under the thumb" of the industry's lobbyists, in the words of FHLBB special supervisor Joe Selby.

"I became kind of an enemy because I was interfering with the states," Gray says. "I wasn't a good old boy. The state commissioners were saying 'Don't tread on us.' They said, 'You're trying to destroy the dual [charter] system.' They called the states laboratories for experimentation. Well, the experiment didn't turn out very well." [29]

Bowman saw it differently. "He [Gray] believed that the way you solved a problem was through regulation," Bowman says. "I believed that you first identified the problem, then you dealt with it through supervision. Ed Gray . . . didn't want to just walk in the front door of a problem shop with both guns blazing and say, 'Okay, now you're going to stop what you're doing or we're going to put you under some sort of restraint and you're going to straighten up and fly right.' Instead, Ed would write a regulation that covered the entire industry. . . . It was wrong, insane." [30]

As an example, Bowman cites Gray's 1985 regulation limiting the growth of thrifts, which Gray believed were on a feeding frenzy of brokered deposits. That regulation, Bowman said, was issued in response to the failure of Empire Savings and Loan Association of Mesquite, Texas, a Dallas suburb. When Empire was closed on March 14, 1984, at a cost to the FSLIC of $279 million—at the time, the largest insolvency to date in the thrift industry—Gray issued a rule that no thrift could expand its asset base more than 25 percent each year.

Declaring a blanket, industrywide regulation instead of zeroing in on a problem thrift with supervisors "was a mistake," Bowman believes. "While a lot of institutions shouldn't have grown more than 25 percent a year, some smaller ones had to grow more than that in order to get out of this gridlock of their loan portfolio being under water [providing less interest income than what had to be paid for deposits]. They had to make loans that were rate-sensitive and would move with the market. So some associations that were $100 million, $105 million, $110 million in size almost needed to double in size as quickly as they could in order to survive. But then you had a Vernon Savings, which was already almost $1 billion in size [by 1985]. To give Vernon Savings carte blanche to grow $250 million a year was wrong."[31] Ultimately, of course, it was not only wrong. It was also prodigiously expensive, since Vernon's failure in 1987 cost the insurance fund almost $1 billion.

Who was correct? The truth is that both Gray and Bowman were both right and wrong. The regulatory systems at both the federal and state levels were simply inadequate to the task of imposing new rules on an industry that had gone wildly out of control. Misperceptions—deregulating an industry that wasn't a free-market business to begin with—had clouded the view of the Reagan administration, the Congress, and the regulators in Washington and the state capitals. Add to those misperceptions an explosive mix of politics and federal-state jealousy over turf, and you come up with a formula for disaster.

Gray claims to have seen the collision coming as early as August 1983, when he received the FSLIC briefing about brokered funds. But the disaster was evident to everyone by 1985, when the industry was already as much as $15 billion insolvent. Of that total, probably $10 billion was in the Ninth District, most of it in Texas. "When Empire failed [in 1984], we knew that it was the beginning of something to come," said Rosemary Stewart. "What we didn't realize was how big that something was. Empire was the first big failure. It was the first real indication that things were so much worse than we knew." Stewart's office was notified only when problems with specific institutions had grown beyond the ability of the district banks to handle. And by 1985, she said, "the number of cases referred to us by the Dallas office just went up dramatically."[32]

So it was that in 1986 Gray dispatched Joe Selby and 260 special examiners to Texas to inspect the wreckage and control the damage. But by that time the battle was mostly over. The regulators' job in 1986 and 1987 had more to do with counting bodies than with dispensing first aid. Most of the seriously wounded could not be saved. In 1986, a total of forty-six thrifts either failed, merged, or came under federal supervision nationwide. Thirteen of them were in the Ninth District, eight in Texas. The next year another twenty-five went under nationwide. And in 1988, when the Federal Home Loan Bank Board began trying to make sense of what had happened and find a way out of the massive insolvency, another 233 either failed or were merged into other institutions, ninety of them in Texas.[33]

By early 1989, the regulatory process had moved to the courts, where officials began trying to recover as much money as they could find. But early indications were that once again, the regulators were bound to be disappointed —despite the Bush administration's commitment of $50 million to recover funds stolen or misappropriated by the cowboys and the gamblers.

"A lot of talk now in Congress is how do we get back all the millions of dollars that were lost," said Rosemary Stewart. "Well, I don't subscribe to the theory that this whole thing was concocted, that people were taking the money and running away. They wouldn't have put so many hundreds of millions of dollars into real estate and into those buildings if they were interested only in running away with it. Most of those millions didn't go into someone's pockets. The money didn't get put into banks offshore. The money got put into real estate, into empty buildings. It's all there, but it's gone. You'd better believe it's gone. It's not somewhere you can get it back by filing a lawsuit."[34]

If so, the government has been spending millions of dollars chasing a horse that's already been through the glue factory. In 1987 the Justice Department dispatched a task force of more than two hundred investigators and attorneys to Texas to find and punish the guilty. By early 1989, the task force had obtained more than a hundred convictions—but they were all minor players. No owner of a major thrift engaged in questionable or patently illegal activities had been convicted. The only major prosecution concluded by the Justice Department by the spring of 1989 was of Independent American's Tom Gaubert, Jim Wright's favorite fund-raiser. Gaubert was tried in late 1988 on charges of illegally pocketing $5.6 million of an $8 million loan from an Iowa thrift, Capitol Savings and Loan Association. After a three-week trial, he was found not guilty.

Even when the Justice Department successfully prosecutes thrift executives for illegal activities, the criminals usually get off with little more than token punishments. Consider, for example, the penalty imposed upon Beverly Haines, who was convicted of embezzling $2.8 million from Centennial Savings & Loan Association of Santa Rosa, California. Haines was executive vice president of the thrift and admitted taking the money. Sentenced to five years in prison, she served just sixty-seven days, then was assigned to a halfway house for three years. Most of the money she took, said a congressional investigating committee, was never recovered.[35] According to the committee, thrift fraud "has been one of the easiest crimes to get away with. . . . And with resources limited and cases complex, the odds of minimal investigation and no prosecution are greater than they should be. . . . The lack of severe and meaningful sentences also explains why the culprits are not deterred."[36]

According to the Justice Department's own guidelines for imposing sentences on persons convicted of defrauding thrifts, the recommended punishment for an insider who steals up to $500,000 is twelve to eighteen months' imprisonment. For a "sophisticated scheme" involving the theft of more than $5 million, the recommended punishment is thirty to thirty-seven months in prison.[37] In other words, if you own a thrift and manage to steal $5 million that can be safely hidden, you can admit to the crime, do the maximum time, and console yourself with the thought that you've "earned" more than $135,000 for every month you serve in prison.

The lessons taught by regulators and enforcers couldn't be clearer: When thrifts are involved, crime does indeed pay very nicely, thank you.

As Congress and the Bush administration struggle to clean up the carnage of the thrift industry, Ed Gray is laboriously working to keep from being labeled as the man who presided over the greatest financial disaster in the nation's modern history. Gray's concern for his reputation is understandable. And he is going to considerable lengths to protect it.

For example, the *Washington Post* published a relatively mild editorial on January 13, 1989, largely blaming the White House and Congress for permitting the S&L disaster to occur. Almost in passing, the editorial said "the regulators were late to see what was happening."[38]

Gray responded with a remarkable nine-and-a-half-page letter defending his stewardship of the FHLBB between 1983 and 1987. The single-spaced typewritten letter ran for more than five-thousand words—about fourteen times the length of the editorial it addressed. Gray appended to the letter some eighty pages of excerpts from speeches and congressional testimony he had given starting in 1983 warning of the problem.

Gray cannot be blamed for being defensive. And he makes a good case for his early warnings. "Hypocrisy does reign . . ." Gray argued in his letter to the *Post.* "[But] many seem to have forgotten what I was saying, and what I was trying to do back there when it really counted—back there when few were concerned about the growing, deepening thrift crisis, or even gave it much thought or attention . . . .

"It is difficult for me now . . . to read [about] a crisis, a huge bill the taxpayers must now pay. 'Gosh [people say], where were the regulators? There were regulators, weren't there? What the hell were they doing? They caused the problem, of course. Yes, it was them. They were there. It's somebody's fault. Must be the fault of the regulators. Pin it on the regulators. Where were they?' "

Ed Gray is an anguished man. He said he "yelled about the problems," even though no one would listen. "The fact is, few wanted to listen back then, to pay any attention," he wrote. "It was not the vogue of the day. If they had spent as much time then trying to help as they now spend seeking scapegoats, things might be much, much different today."[39]

Rosemary Stewart voiced the same lament, much more succinctly. "It's discouraging," she said, "to see yourself blamed every day for something you don't really feel you are responsible for."[40]

What Gray was saying, what Stewart was saying,

what Bowman was saying—indeed, what everyone was saying—is all the same. The regulators were guilty, yet they weren't. The Congress was guilty, yet it wasn't. The administration was guilty, but of what? Devotion to deregulation? The industry and its lobbyists were both perpetrators *and* victims. Real estate developers were saviors in 1982, villains in 1985. Where can the blame be assigned? It's all depressingly reminiscent of the postwar apologia of collective innocence that permitted the German people to avoid responsibility for Nazism:

When everybody is guilty, no one is guilty.

THE
POLITICIANS

V irtually no special-interest group in modern times has enjoyed the combination of moral virtue and political muscle wielded by the U.S. thrift industry and its principal lobbying organization, the U.S. League of Savings Institutions. Ever since the days of the New Deal, the thrift industry and its leaders have wrapped themselves in a politically potent cloak of righteousness, portraying themselves as defenders of America's economic and social stability.

Speaking at an S&L conference in 1983, Ed Gray summed up the thrift industry's view of itself. Reminding his audience that the savings and loan association, "through generations now, has been largely responsible for making us a nation of homeowners," Gray went on to explain how homeownership "is part and parcel of the American dream," how it "brings strength and stability to our economic and political heritage," how it "gives millions of Americans a stake in the system," how in short it "symbolizes the best of the concept of 'a man and his castle,' and represents a cornerstone to the family, the neighborhood and the community."

Lofty sentiments—and for many years not entirely unjustified ones. As the nation struggled out of the Great Depression and through a decade of global conflict, the newly revamped thrift industry—revamped by the Glass-Steagall Act of 1933—did indeed help to develop middle-class stability in the United States. It did so by promoting thrift among small savers and by making it possible for millions of Americans of modest means to purchase their own homes. Protected by Glass-Steagall, which permitted thrifts to pay savings interest up to half a percentage point higher than commercial banks, the nation's S&Ls did not have to scramble for funds. Nor, with interest rates low, did they chafe under the Glass-Steagall provisions that prohibited them from investing their federally insured deposits in anything riskier than good old-fashioned residential mortgages.

All that changed, of course, in the mid-'70s and early '80s, as the combination of runaway inflation, modern consumer needs, and deregulation fever turned the industry on its head. There was another factor, too, that helped to topple the industry from its once-lofty moral perch—the growing tendency of thrift institutions to be owned by stockholders rather than depositors. The trend was unmistakable. In 1980, for example, sixty of the sixty-eight new thrifts granted federal charters were stockholder-owned. Similarly, in 1981, thirty-nine out of forty-three newly chartered thrifts were stock associations.[1]

The trend was especially evident in the Ninth Federal Home Loan Bank District, the Sunbelt district where the cowboys were concentrated. As of the end of 1983, the district boasted a roughly equal number of stockholder-owned and depositor-owned thrifts—256 that operated under stock charters versus 242 mutual associations. A year later, the number of stock associations had risen to 266, while the number of mutual associations had dropped to 192. By the end of 1985, there were 283 stockholder-owned thrifts in the Ninth District, compared to just 164 mutual associations.[2]

The implications of this shift in the nature of thrift ownership were clear. Because they existed for the benefit of depositors, who were the recipients of any and all profits earned by the institution, mutual savings associations tended to be extremely prudent, if not actually stodgy, with their money. Stockholder-owned associations, on the other hand, operated for the benefit of their stockholders, who in many cases were also their senior managers. This type of ownership encouraged greed and speculation, since any and all profits could be taken out immediately in the form of dividends, while most of the burden for losses would be absorbed by the federal insurance fund.

And, indeed, in the early '80s, the increasingly stockholder-owned thrifts rushed to lend money to real estate speculators or invest in junk bonds and interest-rate futures. At the same time, they became less efficient at mortgage lending and thus less competitive. As a result, by the mid-'80s, S&Ls were no longer the dominant force in the residential mortgage business. Between 1976 and 1987, the thrift industry's share of the residential mortgage market declined from almost 55 percent to less than 39 percent.[3] Commercial banks and mortgage companies quickly filled the gap, offering better terms and lower rates. By 1987, they had captured nearly half the market.

Nonetheless, the powerful thrift lobby in Washington continued to act as if it represented institutions whose prime concern was the well-being of consumers rather than stockholders. Sometimes it presented itself as the savior of home buyers. BankWatch, a Washington-based consumer organization headed by Ralph Nader, noted in a 1989 report on the U.S. League of Savings Institutions: "What the League has done skillfully is to wrap itself in the mantle of housing and exploit the political appeal of housing to obtain a continuing series of special exemptions, privileges, waivers and indulgences."[4] And when it wasn't claiming to be protecting the American dream of home ownership, the thrift lobby was putting itself forward as the small saver's friend. When, for example, it began pushing Congress to remove the deposit interest caps imposed by Glass-Steagall, it insisted it was doing so not simply to make S&Ls more competitive in the marketplace, but for the protection of depositors who might otherwise be tempted to put their funds at risk in uninsured investments.

However self-serving such arguments may seem, the thrift lobby has long had the muscle to make them stick. To begin with, over the years the Federal Home Loan Bank Board has become a virtual captive of the U.S. League of Savings Institutions. "Not only does [the league] have easy access to the [FHLBB's] top officials," noted the *Wall Street Journal* in 1986, "but it also receives confidential agency briefings and internal drafts of regulations. And it has virtual veto power over many proposals by the independent agency. . . ." Former FSLIC director Peter Stearns told the newspaper: "The Bank Board doesn't regulate anything unless the U.S. League and the top S&Ls agree. . . . How in hell can you really be a tough regulator when you keep going back to the League [for instructions]?"[5]

Of course, the real power resides in Congress, and it

is on Capitol Hill that the thrift lobby has long concentrated its efforts. Its assets in this regard are awesome. To
begin with, congressmen tend to pay special attention to
industries with interests in their districts, and virtually
every community of any size has its own S&L. And the
larger the community, the more S&Ls it is bound to have.
In 1981, at the height of the deregulation frenzy, there
were about five thousand thrifts scattered throughout the
United States—an average of more than ten for each congressional district. What's more, the thrift industry has
some powerful allies—among them, the 150,000-member
National Association of Homebuilders, the 800,000-mem-
ber National Association of Realtors, and the 7,000-mem-
ber Independent Bankers Association of America. (Small
commercial banks usually have more in common with
thrifts than with the big money-center banks.) The result
of all this is a potent political bloc that Congress has found
difficult, if not impossible, to ignore.

When, in the mid-'80s, Ed Gray tried to impose new restraints on an industry running wild in the wake of massive deregulation he found himself on the wrong end of a
laughably one-sided battle. On one side was Gray, the
former California public relations man and self-described
"nice guy" who headed an agency that few Washington
insiders took seriously. On the other was the powerful
U.S. League of Savings Institutions, headed at the time
by William O'Connell, a veteran of four decades of Capitol Hill horse-trading. (O'Connell retired from the league
in 1988.)

Each year during his tenure as bank board chairman
(he lasted from 1983 to 1987), Gray would march dutifully
to the Hill to ask Congress for more supervisory powers,
for limitations on brokered deposits, for refinancing of the

FSLIC. "And each year," Gray told the Senate Banking Committee in 1988, "lobbyists from the thrift industry had [the proposals] killed. They whispered that we really didn't need the legislation, or that there weren't any real problems, certainly not major ones, and that the regulators were merely engaging in perhaps understandable but overzealous hype and exaggeration."[6] According to Gray, what the league did in each instance was to propose alternative legislation that effectively gutted the expanded powers proposed by the regulators. What's more, Gray says, the league didn't confine its efforts to public opposition to his proposals.

As an example of what Gray called "the considerable lengths" to which the League went "to bring strong back-door political pressure on the Bank Board," he cited a story that appeared on page 1 of the *Wall Street Journal* in July 1986. The story, which detailed the cozy ties between the League and thrift regulators, appeared at a time when Gray was trying to persuade Congress to recapitalize the FSLIC's dwindling insurance fund. The industry opposed the recapitalization, since it would have increased the FSLIC's ability to shut down insolvent S&Ls.

Under the headline "Friendly Terms: Thrifts' Trade Group and Its Regulators Get Along Just Fine," reporter Monica Langley recounted how Gray's visit to a thrift industry convention in the spring of 1986 had been subsidized by the league, which provided him with "chauffeurs and good meals" and "even a typewriter . . . in his $233 a night hotel suite." Though Langley noted that such subsidies were "an established precedent" enjoyed by previous bank board chairmen, she wrote that Gray's acceptance of the league's largess "may violate federal ethics rules" and that the federal Office of Government Ethics had begun a probe of his relationship with lobbyists.[7]

In fact, the league had picked up only $735 of Gray's expenses for the Montreal trip, and nothing ever came of the ethics office's investigation. But the political damage had been done, severely undermining Gray's influence with Congress at a critical time.

Gray is convinced that the league itself planted the story in order to cripple his efforts to persuade Congress to refinance the FSLIC and reimpose some regulatory control over an industry that was running amok. He insists that Langley, who has since left the *Journal*, told him that O'Connell and other industry lobbyists had cynically shopped her the information specifically to destroy his credibility. (For her part, Langley denies ever telling Gray anything of the kind.)

In one sense, it doesn't really matter whether the league planted the story or not. The fact is, as the story pointed out, the regulators didn't control the industry, the industry controlled them. And it didn't achieve this control merely by wrapping itself in the flag and reminding everyone how it had been the thrifts that made it possible for ordinary people to achieve the American dream of home ownership. It acquired its clout by distributing copious amounts of favors and money to some powerful friends in Washington.

Fernand St Germain—known to his friends as Freddy—is perhaps the best example of the kind of useful ally the thrift lobbyists cultivated in Congress. The longtime chairman of the House Banking Committee, and principal co-sponsor of the landmark Garn–St Germain deregulation bill, St Germain served his constituents loyally in the House for twenty-eight years. The problem was that by the time he was turned out of office in 1988, it had become clear that St Germain considered his primary constituency not the Rhode Island voters who had sent him to Washington for fourteen terms but the S&L executives who lavished him with campaign contributions and other perks.

The saga of St Germain's ties to owners of thrifts and other financial institutions within the jurisdiction of his committee has been chronicled several times, most recently in *Wall Street Journal* reporter Brooks Jackson's book *Honest Graft*, an examination of how the American political process is subverted by big money from political action committees.[8]

Jackson relates, for example, how St Germain pocketed more than $300,000 in a series of deals involving concealed ownership of five International House of Pancake restaurants in Rhode Island, Maryland, Texas, and New York. According to Jackson, St Germain bought the properties, which were valued at $1.3 million, without a penny of his own money; all of the funds were borrowed from "friendly Rhode Island institutions that loaned him the money despite some extraordinary risks." Because St Germain was chairman of the powerful House Banking Committee, "bankers were in no position to deny his insistent personal requests for financing."[9] Those "insistent personal requests" weren't limited to Rhode Island institutions. St Germain also put the arm on lenders in New York, Texas, and Florida. To conceal his ownership, Jackson reported, St Germain put the restaurants in an anonymous trust in which his interests remained concealed until 1978, when Congress began requiring more disclosure from its members. Even then, St Germain wasn't wholly candid, listing his holdings as having a value of slightly more than $236,000, a sum Jackson called a "gross undervaluation."[10]

But it was St Germain's ties to the thrift industry that eventually caught the serious attention of federal investigators. Those relationships began with a friendship St Germain struck up with Raleigh Greene, chief executive officer of Florida Federal Savings and Loan Association of St. Petersburg and a former president of the National Savings and Loan League, the trade group that represents the interests of large thrifts. In 1979, St Germain acquired a six-room condominium in Tampa for $4,000 less than the appraised market price of $110,000; the seller was Florida Federal. St Germain later became a partner with Greene in several Florida land deals, including the purchase of another condo, this one on the St. Petersburg beachfront, for which St Germain put up only $1,000 of the $174,000 purchase price. The balance was financed by Florida Federal. According to Jackson, neither St Germain's name nor Greene's was listed on real estate records.[11] Then St Germain got greedy and tried to turn a fast dollar speculating in Florida Federal stock following deregulation of the industry under the 1982 bill that bore his name as cosponsor.

In 1982, Florida Federal was a mutual association, legally owned by its depositors. Freddy's friend and business partner Greene wanted to convert the thrift to a stock association and was asking the Federal Home Loan Bank Board for its permission to make the conversion. At the time, the FHLBB looked favorably upon such changes, reasoning that the sale of stock was an excellent way to raise the fresh capital a rapidly expanding industry needed in order to grow. This sort of new capital might also, over the long run, relieve pressure on an increasingly inadequate thrift insurance fund.

Even so, the bank board denied Greene's first request. He reapplied for clearance, but after waiting several months, St Germain apparently got impatient. The Rhode Island representative was a depositor at Florida

Federal, and therefore a legal owner of the institution. He would thus be entitled to buy stock at the relatively low issuing price if and when the FHLBB granted Greene permission to convert the thrift from a mutual to a stock association. So St Germain's principal aide at the House Banking Committee, Paul Nelson, began calling Richard Pratt, the FHLBB chairman at the time, asking what was holding up the process. According to Jackson, Nelson called Pratt's office at least three times about the Florida Federal application and also made several calls to the district home loan bank in Atlanta, which would also have to approve the application. "Nelson's calls set off alarm bells within the Bank Board," Jackson reported. "Pratt said Florida Federal was the only institution St Germain's aide ever inquired about." [12]

The Florida Federal application eventually was approved, and St Germain got in on the ground floor, buying 1,500 shares in May 1983 at a price of $20 a share. During the two years he owned the Florida Federal shares, St Germain concealed his holding by reporting it only as an unspecified investment in Florida Federal. From the vague way he described it on disclosure forms, the investment could have been nothing more extraordinary than an insured savings account. St Germain filed a more explicit report only when he learned that reporters were inquiring into his financial affairs.

In addition to his ties with Greene, another relationship St Germain enjoyed until it drew the attention of ethics investigators was his friendship with James "Snake" Freeman, a Washington lobbyist for the U.S. League of Savings Institutions. *Washington Post* reporter Kathleen Day, writing in *The New Republic*, acidly commented: "No one seems to know for certain why Freeman is called 'Snake,' though one theory naturally suggests itself and seems to have occurred to almost everyone who knows him."[13] One of Freeman's principal duties apparently was the care and feeding—literally—of the House Banking Committee chairman. According to Brooks Jackson, Freeman and St Germain were seen together "night after night" at various Washington watering holes, eating and drinking and enjoying companionship of congenial women provided by Freeman. (St Germain's wife was back in Rhode Island at the time.) Justice Department records quoted by Jackson and other sources indicate that over the years Snake Freeman and the U.S. League of Savings Institutions spent between $1,000 and $2,000 a month entertaining St Germain.[14]

But dining, drinking, and carousing with agreeable women was a minor-league hustle compared with what St Germain attracted from the thrift industry in campaign contributions. According to a *Wall Street Journal* study of Federal Election Commission records, in the three election cycles from 1984 through 1988 St Germain received a total of $149,200 in cash from political action committees (PACs) sponsored by FSLIC-insured institutions. This made him "by far the most favored recipient" of thrifts' political giving, noted the *Journal*.[15] The figure didn't include personal donations by industry executives or other fund-raising activities by savings and loans. Nor did it include walking-around money such as the $4,000 in honoraria St Germain received from speaking at thrift-industry meetings just in 1987.[16]

Of course, St Germain wasn't alone in receiving the industry's bountiful gifts. Thrift PACs were carefully bipartisan in doling out their money. The *Journal* survey showed that of the ten representatives who received the most in thrift PAC contributions, three were Republicans (led by David Dreier of California, who received $49,528 in the three elections). More evenhandedly, of the ten senators who got the most in thrift contributions, five were Republicans (led by California's Pete Wilson, who received $105,409).[17] The *Journal* quoted Republican Rep. Jim Leach of Iowa, a member of the House Banking Committee who refused to accept PAC funds, as saying the industry's investment during the three election cycles certainly paid off. "What's impressive in some ways is not how much they gave, but how little they gave . . . for such an impressive return," Leach said.[18]

That's the point of making campaign contributions to congressmen, of course: to get Congress to act—or not act —on matters affecting your business. And it is pertinent that during the three election cycles starting in 1984 through 1988, the House Banking Committee led by St Germain held no hearings of substance on a thrift crisis that everyone acknowledged was getting out of control.

Unlike St Germain, another powerful friend the thrifts had in Congress didn't sit by quietly as the industry slid downhill toward destruction in the mid-'80s. That was House Majority Leader (later Speaker of the House) Jim Wright of Fort Worth, Texas.

Wright's ties to the thrift industry have long been public knowledge. When the scent of suspected fraud or mismanagement became strong, his thrift-owner friends would use the relationship to try to keep nosy regulators at bay. Wright's defense was that he was only providing responsive representation to his constituents. There's only one slight hitch to that apologia; none of the thrift owners Wright helped out happened to live in his district.

Whatever Wright's motivation, his influence did prevent timely passage of a 1987 bill that would have pumped $15 billion in recapitalization funds into the FSLIC. At the time, the Federal Home Loan Bank Board estimated that the FSLIC needed just under $20 billion to close down the most insolvent thrifts and take over other seriously troubled institutions. Had that bill been approved, the price tag for taxpayers wouldn't be as large as it is today. So Wright must shoulder a large portion of blame for the high cost of the thrift crisis. (So too must the U.S. League of Savings Institutions, which worked with Wright in keeping the infusion of new funds low enough to prevent the liquidation of insolvent S&Ls.)

The most prominent of Wright's friends in the thrift industry was Tom Gaubert, the Dallas developer-turned-thrift-owner who eventually was ousted by regulators from his insolvent Independent American Savings Association. Gaubert, who served as finance chairman of the Democratic Congressional Campaign Committee from 1985 until 1986, and who once held a fund-raiser for Wright and other Democratic congressional candidates that set a new record by raking in $1.6 million in a single evening, kept a signed picture of Wright posted prominently on the wall of his office at Independent American. The picture bore the inscription "To Tom—a good friend, transportation expediter, fund-raiser and all-around Good American." [19] Gaubert entertained hopes of someday being named national chairman of the Democratic Party. And through his friendship with Wright, Gaubert just might have gotten the job—if he hadn't gotten involved in some sticky thrift business.

But Gaubert wasn't the only thrift owner whose cause Wright adopted as his own. There were others, too, such as Don Dixon. Dixon, it will be recalled, was the thrift owner whose Vernon Savings was closed down by regulators in late 1987 at a cost of $1.3 billion. Dixon's services for Wright and other Democrats went beyond cash contributions. He also made his Potomac River–based yacht, the *High Spirits*, available to Democratic leaders for fund-raising affairs, and he put Vernon Savings' fleet of six airplanes at the disposal of Wright, Majority Whip Tony Coelho of California, and other congressional leaders.

Yet another thrift owner Wright helped out was Dallas real estate syndicator Craig Hall, owner of a large share of Resource Savings, a relatively small thrift based in Denison, Texas.

Wright's relationships with savings and loan executives was one of several potential ethical conflicts probed by the 1989 House Ethics Committee investigation into the Speaker's affairs, which ultimately led to his resignation. For the most part, that inquiry focused on two troubling allegations involving Wright's longtime friend George Mallick, a Fort Worth real estate developer and investor. For one thing, Mallick apparently had more than a passing interest in legislation dealing with the thrift industry, having guaranteed a $2.2 million loan from a thrift to his son at a time when he was "advising" Wright on thrift matters. The second allegation regarding Wright's ties with Mallick involved a separate incident in which Wright apparently gained about $50,000 on a Florida real estate deal arranged by Mallick with the chairman of a troubled Florida thrift, American Pioneer Savings Bank of Orlando. Reportedly, Mallick had invested $42,500 in a Florida development project through Mallightco, a closely held Texas company half owned by Wright and Wright's wife. When the project was completed it produced a profit of about $100,000 for Mallightco, half that sum going to the Wrights.[20]

However shabby the deal may have looked, there was no evidence that Wright ever interceded with federal regulators on behalf of his partner's thrift. As the *Wall Street Journal* reported, American Pioneer Savings might have been having profit problems but it was still solvent. In any case, its difficulties were "minor compared with those of two Texas thrifts aided by Mr. Wright, which collapsed at a cost to the government of hundreds of millions of dollars."[21] Those two thrifts were Gaubert's Independent American Savings and Dixon's Vernon Savings.

It wasn't that Wright acted illegally when he pressured Gray and other regulators to give special consideration to Gaubert and Dixon. Rather, the problem was simply that Wright was wrong. By defending thrift owners with problem institutions and delaying assistance to the FSLIC, Wright sent the wrong message to his congressional colleagues. The message Wright telegraphed was that the thrift industry wasn't in all that much trouble. By his actions, Wright signaled that it was perfectly proper to support multimillionaires who owned government-regulated institutions—even if that support might eventually cost the taxpayers billions of dollars.

During the period when Wright was putting the muscle on regulators on behalf of Dixon and Gaubert, the insolvency of their two institutions grew by $927 million. The negative net worth of Gaubert's Independent American Savings went from $316 million as of June 30, 1986, to $453.8 million when regulators closed it down in May 1987, while Dixon's Vernon Savings went from a positive net worth of $72.5 million in 1986 to a negative net worth of $716.9 million by 1987, a collapse of $789.4 million altogether. Thus, one could argue that Wright's personal intervention on behalf of Gaubert and Dixon cost the American taxpayer almost $1 billion.

Craig Hall's problems with the regulators began in 1986 when he sought to renegotiate about $600 million in loans from several thrifts, one of which, California-based West-

wood Savings, had gone bust and was under FSLIC supervision. A real estate syndicate Hall had put together
wasn't paying the interest, much less the principal, on the
loans. What Hall wanted was some relief on both the
interest rate and the repayment schedule. Without it, his
syndicate faced bankruptcy.

The conservator of Westwood Savings, Hall's primary lender, was Scott Schultz, a supervisory agent who
had been dispatched from the FHLBB's San Francisco office. According to Hall, Schultz and the FSLIC ignored his
repeated requests for a meeting to discuss his problems.
So Hall went to see Wright. They met in Washington on
September 3, 1986. As the two sipped grape juice, Wright
asked questions and took notes, never digressing from
the specific problem of what Hall described as the unre-
sponsiveness of the FSLIC, Scott Schultz, and Schultz's
boss, Ed Gray. Originally set for thirty minutes, the meeting wound up lasting an hour and a half.[22]

In all that time, Hall never volunteered and Wright
never asked the most important question of all: What
would be the effect on American taxpayers if regulators
were allowed freely to proceed with foreclosure on Westwood's loans to Hall? The answer is that the action would
have netted the federal government tens of millions of
dollars in recaptured income taxes from Hall's wealthy
investors in the real estate syndicate. (Had the FSLIC proceeded with foreclosure, the tax benefits to syndicate
investors would have been erased, and they would have
had to pay taxes on what otherwise would have been
sheltered income.)

In any case, Hall must have gotten Wright's sympa-
thy, for within a week Ed Gray's phone rang with a call
from the then Majority Leader. "He [Wright] knew all
about Scott Schultz and that kind of surprised me," Gray

later recalled. "The Majority Leader of the House of Representatives knows all about this little guy out in California?" Gray added that Wright "was really unhappy. I couldn't quite believe this. He wanted me by God to do something about it. He didn't tell me what to do. He just said it wasn't fair to Craig Hall."[23]

With the FSLIC recapitalization bill still pending in Congress, Gray wasn't about to offend the House Majority Leader. So Schultz was sent back to San Francisco and a new conservator was brought in from New York City to oversee Westwood. "I called Jim Wright and said I just wanted you to know that we have replaced Scott Schultz," Gray said. "Wright seemed very pleased by that. Then I was told that he [Wright] wanted to have a meeting with me and some of the members of my staff. I called Paul Nelson [of the House Banking Committee staff] and asked what the meeting was all about. Nelson said, 'Find out who Tom Gaubert is and find out everything you can about him.' "[24]

The meeting was held toward the end of September 1986. According to Gray, Wright barely participated. Most of the talking was done by four other Texas congressmen, principally Republican Steve Bartlett of Dallas. "For two hours these guys were hurling accusations, complaining about mistreatment of institutions. They wouldn't tell us who because they feared reprisals. They talked about Gestapo tactics." Wright left the meeting after about twenty-five minutes, Gray said, never having mentioned Gaubert's name.[25]

Yet that wasn't the end of Gray's problems with Gaubert or with Wright. After reviewing Gaubert's troubled stewardship of Independent American, the FHLBB closed the thrift. That prompted another irate call from Wright, complaining about "Gestapo" regulators. This

time, according to Gray, the conversation got ugly.
Wright reportedly accused a top regulatory official of homosexual conduct and claimed that a "ring of relationships with homosexual lawyers" had been established in
the Southwest. There was no reason to believe the accusations were true, nor were they generally accepted in the
financial community. It was a shabby performance for the
man who was soon to be second in the line of presidential
succession. "I was shocked," Gray later recalled. "I
couldn't believe what I was hearing."[26]

That was the penultimate time Gray ever talked with
Wright. The last time came shortly after Christmas 1986.
Gray was at home in San Diego when Wright phoned to
ask if it was true that the FSLIC intended to close Vernon
Savings. Wright "was really feisty" on behalf of Don
Dixon, Gray said. Though they didn't speak again directly, Wright didn't stop trying to block regulators' efforts to shut down the money hole Vernon Savings had
become by early 1987. Between Christmas 1986 and March
20, 1987, when the thrift finally was closed, Wright continued to harass regulators. According to William Black, a
former FSLIC attorney, Wright was "blackmailing" Gray
with the threat of killing the FSLIC recapitalization bill,
"saying that the only way to get any money at all for the
FSLIC is to promise to not go too hard on the insolvent
Texas S&Ls."[27]

In the end, Wright kept the FSLIC recapitalization bill
locked in committee for more than six months. Ostensi-
bly, Wright wanted the $15 billion appropriation cut to $5
billion, a wretchedly inadequate amount to solve the
problems that had been mounting. Wright eventually
agreed to increase the FSLIC authorization to $10.8 bil-
lion. But even here his intent apparently was to prevent
the FSLIC from getting the funds it needed to start shut-

ting down the most massively insolvent thrifts. For he agreed to support the bill only on the condition that the money be spent over a three-year period rather than all at once. Thus, at a critical juncture, when the FSLIC needed a minimum of $15 billion to stanch a major hemorrhage, it found itself hamstrung.

While Gray does not suggest that Wright's actions were motivated by anything more than his coziness with Texas thrift operators, he also believes that the former Majority Leader was a willing tool of the powerful thrift-industry lobby. With Wright's help, Gray says, the U.S. League of Savings Institutions "succeeded in delaying the recapitalization bill beyond their fondest hopes."[28]

How could the league have been so blind to what was happening to its members? As Gray tells it, the league was anything but blind. Rather, he says, it was pursuing a self-interested strategy of monumental cynicism. According to Gray, he was first clued in to the league's real agenda in April 1987 while visiting Capitol Hill with two of the industry's "most powerful trade-association people." Gray won't identify them by name, but he does say they were the principal executives of two of the three strongest state thrift associations—meaning they were from either Florida, California, or Texas. In any case, Gray claims that the two lobbyists "just told me flat out what their plan was. The plan was simply this: Keep the [recapitalization] bill down to $5 billion in bonding authority. We'll have a new administration in 1989—they were hopeful it would be Democratic, since Democrats have been better for thrifts. By that time it will be abundantly clear that $5 billion will not even begin to take care of the problem, and therefore the taxpayers will have to take care of it. They did this for their membership. So that the Treasury would have to pay the bill. It was a particularly brilliant piece of strategy on their part. And consider that they had on their side the Democratic Majority Leader, Jim Wright, and Steve Bartlett [a Republican] . . . this was not really a partisan matter."[29]

William O'Connell, the league president at the time, denies that the thrift industry wanted to delay recapitalization in order to throw the burden on the backs of taxpayers. "I was in charge, and I never recall ever saying anything like that," he insists. According to O'Connell, the industry opposed the $15 billion recapitalization proposal because the Treasury Department had said that it couldn't afford to give the FSLIC more than $5 billion a year in authorized funding. The league chose to side with the Treasury Department, O'Connell maintains, because Gray's estimates provided no reason to believe that the industry was in trouble. "If the bank board thought there was going to be a substantial loss, no one ever said that in 1987," O'Connell claims. "Ed [Gray] says now that he knew it was much more than that [$15 billion], but that's ridiculous. He never said that. If he had ever come and said it [the insolvency] would be $30 billion or $40 billion I think we would have just pulled back . . . right away."[30]

Whatever the truth, the thrift industry was certainly adroit in its lobbying to maintain the freedoms it had won under Garn–St Germain. O'Connell concedes that the industry supported "forbearance," the regulatory forgiveness of reckless operations, believing the economic problems faced by thrifts were temporary, particularly in Texas. And so the thrift lobbyists continued to wrap S&Ls in the flag of promoting home ownership—and to blame the regulators for all of their problems.

In the summer of 1988, Theo H. Pitt, Jr., chairman and president of Pioneer Savings Bank of Rocky Mount, North Carolina, and chairman of the U.S. League of Savings Institutions, addressed a conference on regulatory policy in Washington. Coming as they did in the middle of a year in which the industry would lose a record $12.1 billion even as it was sucking up $20 billion in government bailout funds, Pitt's remarks were a monument to cynical self-interest and revisionism.

"The savings and loan business is *not* in crisis, thank you," Pitt declared. Most of the nation's thrifts were profitable, he argued, and the problem rested with the FSLIC. Conceding that fraud and mismanagement played some part in the failure of some S&Ls, Pitt insisted that "most of the scoundrels and the bad managers have been driven out of the business." And who was to blame for their having been there in the first place? The Reagan administration, which "plunged headlong into deregulation . . . with a vengeance." Asking the industry to pay for the cleanup was "Vampire Economics," Pitt said. Attacking the thrift industry, Pitt concluded, is the same as assaulting "this nation's traditional commitment to home ownership."[31]

But Pitt was wrong if, as he said in his speech to the industry faithful, he thought that the American people still had faith in their neighborhood savings and loans. The thrift lobby may have won the battle over who would have to pay for the bailout. But the industry's excesses appear to have lost it the war for both the allegiance of the American people and its favored position in Congress.

Two developments reveal the extent to which the thrift industry's influence has declined as a result of its refusal to face up to its own inadequacies. The first was a March 1989 Media General–Associated Press poll showing that the industry no longer commanded the confidence of the American people it once served so faithfully.

According to the survey, only 53 percent of those polled believed S&Ls were a safe place to keep their money; fully one-third who had money in thrift accounts said they were afraid of losing their savings. What's more, almost half the people surveyed—48 percent in all—said blame for the thrift crisis resided with the industry itself.[32] This lack of confidence was reflected by hard reality. Between November 1988 and the end of April 1989, net withdrawals from FSLIC-insured thrifts reached a record $43.9 billion as worried depositors shifted their money to other investments.

The second indication of the thrift industry's diminished status came in the form of a blunt lecture delivered by Senator Phil Gramm—not only a Texan, but a conservative Republican and staunch advocate of deregulation to boot—to industry lobbyists during March 1989 hearings on how the debacle developed. "If anybody on earth has been irresponsible, it's the league," Gramm said. And he added that the untrustworthiness of the thrift industry's principal lobbying group is "rivaled only by members of Congress in terms of absolute irresponsibility." Concluded Gramm: "I'm sure you all have got lots of friends here—but less than you used to have."[33]

So the debacle was almost complete. It was a debacle permitted by an outdated system unfit for new freedoms, a regulatory framework wholly inadequate to police those freedoms, a greedy industry willing and able to misuse the political clout it had long since ceased to deserve, and congressional patrons who followed blindly behind campaign contributions and favors. But the last act had yet to be played. The final failure, the ultimate breakdown, would come when the FHLBB chairman who replaced Ed Gray frantically began what appeared to be an attempt to cover up the iniquities that had already been committed.

9.
THE
$40 BILLION
COVER-UP

In the 366 days beginning on January 1, 1988, the Federal Home Loan Bank Board committed almost $40 billion in public funds to clean up the mess it had helped create. Sixty percent of that amount—almost $25 billion altogether—went to salvage Texas thrifts. The commitments were called the "Southwest Plan." It was a plan that generally involved both tax breaks and promissory notes pledging public funds, which were never approved by Congress, to cover (or cover up) the bad loans of failed thrifts taken over by new investors.

Net net, as the bankers say, the Southwest Plan was the most colossal deception yet in a dreary history of incompetence on the part of elected officials, regulators, and the thrift industry. Democratic Representative Henry Gonzalez of Texas, who took over as the new chairman of the House Banking Committee following the defeat of Fernand St Germain in 1988, said the Southwest Plan set a new low in the annals of government cover-ups. "I think when this is over," Gonzalez told the *Wall Street Journal*, "It's going to make the Watergate people look like a Boy Scout troop of honor."[1] As the House and Senate began taking a detailed look at the Southwest Plan in March 1989, Gonzalez added that it was "obvious beyond any doubt that the Federal Home Loan Bank Board concealed the facts concerning the depth of the FSLIC's insolvency." The bank board, Gonzalez said, "misrepresented facts . . . denied reality, and, ultimately, destroyed the credibility of the entire Federal Home Loan Bank system."[2]

A review of the record indicates that the Federal Home Loan Bank Board either didn't know what size problem it had on its hands—a case of official negligence —or it did know and didn't tell the truth—a case of official deception. In the summer of 1987, the new chairman of the FHLBB, M. Danny Wall, estimated the thrift bailout cost at $10.8 billion. A year later, he reappraised the tab at $22.7 billion. In July 1988, Wall raised the figure again, to about $31 billion. But the number kept leaping upward. By December 1988, Wall was saying that bailing out the thrift industry would cost $50 billion.

Throughout the FHLBB's revisions of the price tag, independent analysts who followed the industry repeatedly said the bank board didn't know what it was saying. Wall retorted that the critics were wrong. But they weren't. We now know from studies done by the General Accounting Office that the minimum bailout tab will be more than $200 billion. In any event, without apparently knowing what they were doing, the regulators committed $40 billion in 1988 to the bankrupt savings industry.

Consider, for a moment, what $40 billion represents. It would take a stack of $1,000 bills about three-quarters the height of the Washington Monument—some 420 feet high—to total just $1 billion. Picture forty such piles. An expenditure of $40 billion could be used to give $5,633 to each of the 7.1 million American families earning less than the $11,611 annual income defined as the poverty benchmark by the federal government. A $40 billion fund could finance scholarships of $12,000 each for 3.3 million college students. It is easy to grow lyrical about how $40 billion could be usefully employed for the greater good of the public.

But the $40 billion committed by the Federal Home Loan Bank Board in 1988 wasn't used for such worthwhile purposes as helping to feed and house poor people, or to educate future leaders of business, education, and government. Instead, the money was pledged to pay for the extravagance, fraud, and mismanagement that bankrupted an industry. And the commitments were made without congressional approval.

I believe so much is wrong with the Southwest Plan that it's difficult to know where to begin the catalogue of its flaws. For one thing, the Southwest Plan represented bad business judgment and faulty economic reasoning, since it sought to delay rather than resolve a critical problem. Worse, it was reprehensible as public policy since it was accomplished through secret agreements to give away billions of dollars in assets and tax benefits to some of the nation's richest citizens without regard to the burdens that would be imposed on ordinary Americans. Hastily conceived and incompetently executed, the Southwest Plan stands as a monument to bureaucratic cynicism that borders on immorality, if not illegality. Indeed, several good arguments can be made that the Southwest Plan has little if any legal basis. In any case, about the best that can be said for the Southwest Plan is that it was a temporary fix inspired by less than noble motives. From all appearances, the Southwest Plan seemed primarily intended to cover up the mistakes that had been created by Congress, allowed by the regulators, ignored by the Reagan administration, and, most of all, abetted and encouraged by the industry itself.

When M. Danny Wall took command of the sinking thrift ship as chairman of the Federal Home Loan Bank Board on July 1, 1987, almost no one wanted to know how bad the industry's problems really were.

The lone exception might have been outgoing chairman Ed Gray. But Gray's credibility with both the industry and the administration had been worn threadbare by the summer of 1987. Gray's efforts to reimpose regulatory disciplines not only had earned him the antagonism of the powerful thrift lobby on Capitol Hill but had also provoked the hostility of the Democratic leadership in Congress and the disciples of deregulation in the Reagan administration, especially Donald Regan, who had moved over to the White House as Chief of Staff.

The industry certainly didn't want to force the issue of assessing the damage and cleaning up the mess. Every day that could be put off would mean one more day of grace for the still healthy S&Ls, who were legally obligated to make up any shortfall if the FSLIC found itself unable to cover fully the losses suffered by insolvent S&Ls protected by the umbrella of federal deposit guarantees. This was a powerful motivation, because if the full extent of the damage had been known, the resulting call for funds probably would have bankrupted the industry overnight. The fact was that at the end of June 1987, the industry rested uncomfortably upon a slender pillar of only $43.3 billion in equity capital. And of this amount, $27.5 billion—almost two-thirds—consisted of goodwill and other intangibles. This left only about $16 billion in solid equity to back up the thrifts' promise to repay the FSLIC in the event of a shortfall.[3] But this $10.6 billion in equity wasn't even enough to cover losses from insolvent thrifts still open at the end of 1987. And over the next twelve months unprofitable thrifts would suffer additional net losses totalling $16.4 billion.

So the industry's strategy was to be quiet and let things get worse. If the mess was left untouched, then it wouldn't be long before the price tag became so inflated that the only possible solution would be a taxpayer bailout. In other words, if the situation was allowed to get bad enough, the industry could get off the hook, contractual obligations to the FSLIC notwithstanding and the public be damned. In this sense, delay was most assuredly in the best interests of the industry.

So, too, was concealment in the best interests of many thrift executives. The motivation of some of these executives had to do with the nature of white-collar crime. It may not be equitable, but a painful fact of criminal justice is that you stand a much better chance of going to jail for robbing a 7-Eleven of a six-pack of beer and $12 in change than for owning a bank and flagrantly mismanaging or stealing millions of dollars through insider dealings and other questionable transactions. In part, this is because if you wave a Saturday-night special in the face of a 7-Eleven clerk and flee with the meager loot, the cops will come after you. But you can't be pursued if no one is aware that anything has been stolen. And the only way to know that a bank has been looted from the inside is to subject it to a thorough examination. So from the standpoint of many executives of high-flying thrifts in Texas (as well as quite a few in California), it would be much better to avoid inspection. As long as the problems could be concealed, there was always the chance that oil would soar back to $30 or more a barrel, which would revive the economy and breathe new life into all of the bad loans that were on the books. As former Texas S&L commissioner Linton Bowman put it, if oil had recovered quickly, the cowboys "probably would have gotten away with . . . the fraud that took place."[4]

Nor did Congress wish to have the thrift crisis laid bare and the enormous cost unveiled. Certainly the Democratic leadership could not be expected to see any profit in such an exercise. In the first place, Congress had always been the ultimate regulator of the thrift industry. It had set the rules for the Federal Home Loan Bank Board. It—or, rather, its Democratic majority—had allowed the crisis to develop. In particular, House leaders such as Jim Wright and Fernand St Germain would have a lot of embarrassing questions to answer if the true dimensions of the S&L mess became known. With an election coming up in November 1988, from the standpoint of the Democratic majority in Congress it would be best to defer any in-depth exploration of the thrift industry.

Of course, the Democratic leadership's vulnerability on the thrift issue wasn't a weakness that could be exploited by the Republicans. After all, it had been the Reagan White House that had blocked Ed Gray's efforts to increase the size of the FHLBB's regulatory police force. There was also the troubling matter of Vice President George Bush's involvement in overseeing the deregulation process that helped contribute to the crisis. Bush had served as chairman of the administration's task force on deregulation in 1984 and 1985. While the position was largely ceremonial like so many other vice presidential functions, it nonetheless gave the appearance of negligence at the very top.

The fact is that exposing the monstrous proportions the thrift crisis had reached by 1988 carried no political advantage for either party. Former Senator William Proxmire of Wisconsin, a longtime chairman of the Senate Banking Committee, told *Financial Planning* magazine in April 1989: "If [Democratic presidential candidate Michael] Dukakis had come forward and said, 'Look, this administration has put us into a hell of a jam and we're going to have to take 20 billion of your dollars to bail this out,' then the Republicans would have come back and said, 'Dukakis wants to take $20 billion of your money to bail out savings and loans.' . . . On the other hand, if Bush brings it up, he's discussing something for which he had responsibility. The administration itself was responsible for appointing all the members of the Federal Home Loan Bank Board over the last eight years."[5] Danny Wall himself concedes the point more succinctly. "There was complicity all around," he says. The fact that the S&L crisis didn't surface as a campaign issue in 1988 "was a clear acknowledgment of that."[6]

But regulators, politicians, and the industry weren't the only ones who benefited from a cover-up. The legal and accounting professions as well as the crippled real estate industry in the Southwest also had an interest in maintaining the status quo.

Lawyers stood to gain a lot of new business from failing thrifts, S&L consolidations and mergers, and government criminal prosecutions. As long as the problem went unsolved, thrifts would be suing borrowers for not repaying loans, borrowers would be countersuing thrifts with allegations of lender liability, and the FSLIC would be suing both. In 1987, the U.S. thrift industry spent $480 million on lawyers, and another $253 million in 1988—an average of almost $1.4 million in legal fees every day for two years. The legal business spawned by the debacle even had a ripple effect beyond just law firms. For example, one Dallas court-reporting and legal-copying company reported having to hire ninety temporary employees and lease seventy copying machines just to handle one thrift case that required duplicating 430,000 separate documents.[7]

For accountants, the issue wasn't one of new business. It was a matter of having to explain old work. As the crisis widened, the accounting profession found itself under increasing attack for its laxity in permitting the problem to develop. The Federal Home Loan Bank Board began to consider suing accountants who had audited the books of failed thrifts. Its potential targets included three of the nation's largest accounting firms—Deloitte Haskins & Sells, Coopers & Lybrand, and Touche Ross & Co. Noted *The New York Times:* "Many are wondering whether these hard-nosed pencil-pushing professionals lost what they valued the most: their cool logic. Critics are saying that while accountants could not have stopped the crisis, they could at least have sent up a warning shot."[8] Clearly, a thorough exploration of the thrift chaos wouldn't help the accounting profession.

Nor did real estate executives see any benefit in a solution that might require the federal government to address the S&L problem honestly—not if that meant disposing of real estate the FSLIC acquired from failed thrifts. The glut of empty commercial, retail, and warehouse space in Texas and the Southwest had already depressed the real estate market to its lowest point since the 1930s. As of December 31, 1987, thrifts had repossessed a total of $9.45 billion worth of Texas real estate; the figure would rise more than 46 percent, to $13.81 billion, over the next twelve months.[9] If the government began closing down thrifts and taking possession of that property, the threat to the real estate industry was that even more property would be dumped at fire-sale prices on an already reeling market.

The final beneficiary of the $40 billion cover-up was Melvin Danny Wall himself, Gray's beleaguered successor as chairman of the Federal Home Loan Bank Board. Wall, too, had a selfish reason to keep the depth of the crisis from becoming fully known.

Born in Watertown, South Dakota, in 1939, Wall had studied architecture, first at Northern State Teachers College in Aberdeen, South Dakota, then at North Dakota State University. For seven years in the '60s, he worked as a city planner and director of urban renewal in Fargo, North Dakota. In June 1971, Wall was appointed to organize the Salt Lake City Redevelopment Agency. It was there that he met Jake Garn, just a few months before the future U.S. senator was elected mayor of Salt Lake City.

Garn and Wall got on well, and when Garn was elected to the Senate in 1973, he asked Wall to come with him to Washington. By 1975 Wall was part of the Utah Mafia that Garn brought to Capitol Hill, a group that included Richard Pratt, the former finance professor who would precede Gray as FHLBB chairman and would engineer the deregulation express in the early 1980s.

Wall spent his first four years in Washington working in Garn's office. That was followed by two years as the ranking minority member of the Senate Banking Committee staff, and then six years as majority staff director when the Republicans controlled the Senate.

As Wall put it, he and Garn "shared quite a ride" in the Senate.[10] The Senate Banking Committee was not a high-profile place when Garn first joined it in 1974. But as public attention came to be centered on financial deregulation in the inflation-ridden Carter years, the Banking Committee became perhaps the Senate's most active and visible arena, equaled only by the Armed Services Committee. Thus Wall was thrust into the spotlight, especially after the Republicans gained control of the Senate in 1982 and he became the Banking Committee's senior staff member. It was a position that would propel Wall in 1987 to the chairmanship of the FHLBB.

Wall's contribution to the S&L mess was more than just casual. *U.S. News & World Report* likened him to Dr. Frankenstein. As the majority staff director of the Senate Banking Committee when the Garn–St Germain Act was written, the magazine said, Wall "stitched together the legislation that turned a moribund savings and loan industry into the debt-ridden monster now terrorizing the financial community [and] legislators. . . . "[11] For his part, Wall argues that Banking Committee Democrats were equally responsible for the bill. The only negligence Wall admits was in "not making the link," in failing to realize that along with deregulating the thrift industry, Congress should have also strengthened the FSLIC's oversight powers.

Whatever Wall's responsibility in creating the brutish creature the thrift industry had become by 1987, it was his job to put the monster in chains when he became FHLBB chairman. His solution was the Southwest Plan, which he unveiled in March 1988.

The big problem Wall faced when he took over the bank board in the summer of 1987 was the fact that the FSLIC insurance fund was virtually drained.[12] This made it impossible for the FSLIC to take direct action by shutting down insolvent thrifts. FSLIC could act only if it received more money from Congress. And Congress wasn't going to acknowledge a multibillion-dollar problem in an election year.

So Wall had to develop an alternative solution. That turned out to be the Southwest Plan, which Wall says originated with a proposal by the Texas Savings and Loan League—another case of the industry looking out for itself.[13] (Others reportedly involved in devising the plan included bank board member Roger Martin, a former accountant and real estate expert with Mortgage Guaranty Insurance Corporation,[14] and former Dallas bank board chairman Roy Green.)

The thrift industry's dilemma in the Southwest at the time was a knotty one. Many thrifts were having to pay deposit rates well above the market—in some cases a full percentage point higher—in order to attract the funds they needed just to stay afloat. But the higher rate—"the Texas premium," as it was known—merely made their problems worse, since it increased the thrifts' cost of doing business by millions of dollars each month. Another problem was the massive increase in foreclosures, which not only forced the thrifts to admit that loans were going bad at an alarming rate but also imposed on them an additional burden of expenses they could ill afford. In the first three months of 1987, Texas thrifts repossessed some $1.12 billion worth of properties, increasing their holdings of other real estate owned, or OREOs, as they were called, by almost 25 percent, to a total of $5.88 billion. And that was only the beginning; in the remaining nine months of 1987, Texas S&Ls would foreclose on another $3.57 billion in loans, meaning that in a single twelve-month period the Texas thrift industry had increased its holdings of money-losing OREOs by an incredible 98.5 percent.[15] As the thrifts fell deeper into insolvency, the FSLIC thus became the effective owner of golf-course condominiums, chains of hamburger stands, and a Houston home-building company that was the largest residential developer in Texas. And these unwanted acquisitions were in addition to the more predictable foreclosures, such as empty office buildings and shopping centers that had been financed with thrift loans. The Texas thrift industry was free-falling without a parachute.

That's what the Southwest Plan was intended to arrest. Basically, the Southwest Plan called for merging the most insolvent thrifts into marketable packages, then selling the new entities to outside investors who could provide new capital. In theory, at least, it appeared to be a workable remedy that would sidestep the inability of the FSLIC insurance fund to close insolvent thrifts and pay off depositors. In reality, though, what the Southwest Plan did was to repackage corpses. Said House Banking Committee chairman Gonzalez: "They've taken a lot of dead horses and stitched them together into one big horse that's just as dead and stinks even more." [16]

In practice, what happened was that the remedy broke down in two key, related areas. The first problem with the Southwest Plan was strategic: How could outside investors be persuaded to put fresh capital into institutions that were already billions of dollars insolvent? The second problem was tactical: Who should be assigned the task of executing the plan? In both cases, the government got it wrong. Begin with the tactical error: Wall gave the job of administering the Southwest Plan to a young and inexperienced political appointee who arbitrarily decided that the Texas economy would be fully recovered within ten years—and on that basis "solved" the strategic problem of how to lure investors by offering them incredibly generous incentives that amounted to a wholesale raid on the Treasury of the United States.

Tom J. Lykos, Jr., a Harvard graduate with a law degree from the University of Texas and no business experience whatsoever, was all of thirty-one when he started work at the FSLIC as deputy executive director for the Southwest Plan. His background was limited largely to Capitol Hill, where he had worked as a Republican staff member of the securities subcommittees of the Senate Banking Committee and the House Energy and Commerce Committee. He had also put in some time at a New York law firm and with the SEC.[17] He had never negotiated a deal of substance, much less a billion-dollar transaction.

Although he was responsible for committing billions of taxpayer dollars to rescue dying thrifts, Lykos kept a determinedly low profile while running the Southwest Plan, refusing to make himself available either to investors who wanted to get in on what many regarded as a giveaway or to reporters covering the S&L crisis. Danny Wall, who hired him, characterizes Lykos as having "a different personality . . . no one could ever intimidate him."[18]

Whatever his personality, Lykos did put together some unusual, secretly negotiated billion-dollar deals underwritten by insured deposits and government guarantees—deals that apparently have allowed some very rich people who were bargain-hunting for thrifts to put up very little capital and reap vast rewards, all of it with the government's promise that they wouldn't have to lose money.

Actually, the guidelines for Southwest Plan deals were set before Lykos moved over to the FSLIC from the Senate Banking Committee on April 7, 1988. The broad precedent was established in an earlier transaction negotiated by the FSLIC in which the lifeless remains of one of the nation's largest thrifts, the $30-billion-plus American Savings of Stockton, California, were handed over to billionaire investor Robert M. Bass of Fort Worth.

The Bass deal began in 1984 when federal regulators forced the resignation of Charles Knapp, chairman of Financial Corporation of America, the parent of American Savings. Knapp and William J. Popejoy, his successor as FCA chairman, it will be recalled, had bet wrong on interest-rate swings in addition to making several billion dollars' worth of risky commercial real estate loans. As a result, FCA was hemorrhaging. Regulators concluded that only a government-assisted sale of American Savings would stop the drain.

The bank board retained Salomon Brothers as its investment banker to seek a qualified buyer. Negotiations were held with a number of interested parties—chief among them, Ford Motor Co., which was seeking to expand its financial services operations, and a group headed by Bass, who was becoming one of the most visible corporate raiders on Wall Street through his friendly takeovers of Bell & Howell and Westin Hotels and unsuccessful hostile assault on Macmillan, Inc.

For months, Ford seemed to have the inside track. But then the company's auditors began to question the value of promissory notes the FSLIC proposed to issue to the buyer to cover American Savings' bad assets. The auditors contended that while FSLIC deposit insurance might have the backing of the U.S. government's "full faith and credit"—and even that was an arguable proposition—promissory notes backing bad loans did not enjoy that protection. The auditors' doubts deterred not only Ford but other large, publicly owned companies as well. The ultimate effect of this was to limit the pool of potential bidders for insolvent thrifts mainly to Wall Street sharks who scented the possibility of enormous profits combined with very little risk, since the FSLIC seemed willing to extend some unusual financial incentives in order to un-load money-losing S&Ls. As a result, the list of new own-ers of thrifts would come to be dominated by such names as Bass, Ronald O. Perelman of the Revlon Group, and the Pritzker family of Chicago.

In any case, by the middle of 1988, Ford had dropped out of contention and the Bass group had emerged as the leading candidate to acquire American Savings. From the outset, Bass's approach represented an ambush of the U.S. Treasury. In all, the Bass group proposed to put up $550 million to take over American Savings' $16.9 billion in healthy assets. (It would receive a hefty management fee to liquidate the thrift's $21.9 billion in bad assets.) That $550 million in new capital would not come out of Bass's own deep pockets. Instead, the capital infusion would be financed by a combination of junk bonds and borrowings from other banks, with American Savings stock serving as collateral. What's more, Bass requested permission to put as much as 10 percent of American Savings' good assets, or more than $1.5 billion, into an affiliated merchant bank that could be used to finance corporate takeovers. In ef-fect, what Bass sought was government backing to in-crease his already awesome ability to mount raids on other companies.

Federal regulators were willing to swallow most of the Bass package, although they had serious reservations about the way Bass intended to finance the deal. But Cal-ifornia officials balked at the idea of allowing Bass to use the reorganized bank to conduct corporate raids, and that was the rub—the American Savings charter was issued by the state, not the Federal Home Loan Bank Board. The *Wall Street Journal* reported: "William Crawford, the Cali-

fornia S&L Commissioner, got cold feet about the proposed $1.5 billion [for] the merchant bank and said he
wouldn't approve a state charter for what wags were calling Bass Bank." [19]

After intensive negotiations that began around
Thanksgiving 1988 and ended two days after Christmas,
a compromise was reached. The overall price of American
Savings was reduced to $500 million, only $350 million of
which Bass would have to put up at the start. (The remaining $150 million would be phased in over a three-
year period.) Bass would be permitted to borrow most of
the capital, but he would not be able to use American
Savings stock as collateral. Finally, he would be allowed
to form a merchant banking subsidiary that could be used
as a platform for future acquisitions, though not on the
terms he had originally demanded. Instead of being able
to put $1.5 billion of American Savings' good assets into
the subsidiary, he would be limited to a maximum of $500
million. In return, the FSLIC agreed to pay for any losses
resulting from American Savings' bad assets and to put
up an $8 billion ten-year note guaranteeing roughly half
of American Savings' good assets—a note that would pay
Bass a rate 2 percentage points higher than the average
cost of funds for California thrifts, thus not only guaranteeing Bass immediate profitability, but locking in that
profit for a full decade.

It was, in short, a no-lose deal for Bass. The *Wall
Street Journal* noted that the "larger message" of the deal
seemed to be "that the Bank Board is trapped in a virtually
impossible situation." Because the FSLIC was essentially
bankrupt and didn't have sufficient funds to close down
even a small thrift, much less one the size of American
Savings, the agency "had virtually no alternative to selling the thrift to a corporate buy-out artist." [20]

While the American Savings deal wasn't concluded until the end of 1988, the precedent it set provided the framework within which Tom Lykos would administer the Southwest Plan.

Altogether, the Southwest Plan had a brief life, only nine months. But those were nine very expensive months, during which Lykos supervised fifteen transactions that merged or closed eighty-eight Texas savings and loans, with a commitment of $24.5 billion in public funds through promissory notes or tax breaks.

Each of the deals was different. But they all fell within the guidelines that had been established by the American Savings transaction. The pattern seemed to include all of the unpleasant characteristics that had brought the thrift industry to its knees—among them, political pull and favoritism to industry insiders, sweetheart financial arrangements to guarantee that those people favored by the regulators wouldn't lose money, and wanton disregard of taxpayers' welfare.

Basically, it was done as follows. In return for all of a failed thrift's good, money-earning assets, a buyer would put up a minimum amount of new equity capital, usually no more than 1.5 percent—and sometimes not a penny of it in cash. The bad assets would be covered by a note from the FSLIC, which promised to pay for any and all bad loans plus a profit of up to 2.75 percentage points over the thrift's cost of funds over the ten-year life of the note. Of course, as the Ford Motor Co. auditors had pointed out, such FSLIC notes were of questionable value. In essence, the FSLIC was thus trading a questionable note for bad assets—in other words, exchanging a dead horse for a dead cow. Perhaps the regulators *had* learned something from the cowboys.

In addition, the FSLIC would agree to indemnify the

buyer from all lawsuits. This was no small thing. Already, one Dallas developer, T. F. Stone, has won a $62.9 million judgment in a lender-liability suit he brought against Sunbelt Savings, the propped-up corpse created from the ruins of Fast Eddie McBirney's Sunbelt Savings Association, Tom Gaubert's Independent American Savings, and several other failed thrifts. If that judgment is upheld on appeal, the FSLIC will have to pay the tab.

Even more worrisome, as a result of its penchant for secrecy and generosity, the FSLIC may have dug itself a legal grave. According to a novel legal argument devised by a Dallas developer accused of defaulting on a loan from an insolvent thrift that had been absorbed under the Southwest Plan, because the FSLIC has guaranteed the interest and principal of all the thrift's loans, he cannot be considered to be in default—hence, the thrift has no right to repossess his property. It's like having a rich uncle who has guaranteed your mortgage payments. Whether or not you are aware of the guarantee, as long as the principal and interest are being paid, the debt is good. What's more, the developer argued, the government has no right to take his property since the agreement was made without his knowledge or consent. Attorneys and judges alike are still scratching their heads over that one.

The first major Southwest Plan deal negotiated under Tom Lykos involved Dallas-based Southwest Savings Association, a privately held thrift with assets of nearly $1.5 billion. Ironically, until it got into trouble, Southwest Savings had enjoyed a well-earned reputation as one of the region's best-run institutions. Under the leadership of chairman C. Todd Miller, one of the industry's most respected executives, Southwest Savings had eschewed the shady tactics practiced by so many Texas thrifts. Nonetheless, by March of 1987, Southwest was sliding toward insolvency, caught in the vise of the "Texas premium"—the fact that it had to pay more for funds than it could earn from loans in a deteriorating economy.

Southwest Savings's slide toward insolvency was particularly embarrassing because Miller also happened to be vice chairman of the Federal Home Loan Bank of Dallas. He had been elected to the board in 1985, and was one of its most respected members. But image problems were the least of Miller's woes. Far more worrisome was the fact that Miller's employer was in potentially severe financial trouble because of an agreement signed in the early 1980s. The majority owner of Southwest Savings was the Caroline Hunt Trust Estate, which was set up on behalf of one of the richest people in the United States. According to *Forbes* magazine, in 1987 Caroline Hunt had a net worth of $900 million, making her "probably not" the wealthiest woman in America, but certainly one of the top three.[21]

Caroline Hunt's business acumen was keen. She had enough sense to avoid the silver deals and other market-cornering schemes devised by her better-known brothers, William Herbert Hunt and Nelson Bunker Hunt. Indeed, in 1983 she had her trust specifically split off from her brothers' operations. She thus managed to avoid becoming embroiled in their tangled legal difficulties, including the personal turmoil and business bankruptcies that plagued the Hunt brothers after the spectacular drop in oil prices in 1986.

But Caroline Hunt was still exposed, if not as vulnerable to financial ruin as her brothers, through her trust's 90 percent ownership of Southwest Savings. This was because she had signed what was known as a "net worth maintenance" agreement with the Federal Home Loan

Bank Board—in effect, a pledge that if Southwest Savings' net worth dropped below the legal minimums, her trust would make up the difference.

With a capital base of only $27.6 million as of March 31, 1988, and that diminishing at a rate of $3 million a month, Southwest Savings had already absorbed $22.9 million of Caroline Hunt's money under conditions of the net worth maintenance agreement. Indeed, at that point, the cash she had injected into Southwest Savings represented fully 83 percent of the thrift's required capital. If Southwest Savings continued downward, she might have to put up more. Of course, with a personal net worth of $900 million, Caroline Hunt had the resources to keep Southwest Savings afloat. In this respect, she was very different from many other thrift owners.

But then Uncle Sam, in the person of Tom Lykos and the FSLIC, came to her rescue. Shortly after Danny Wall announced the broad outlines of the Southwest Plan, Southwest Savings chairman Todd Miller submitted a proposal to Lykos that would boost Southwest Savings into the thrift industry's major leagues, restore its solvency with tax-backed dollars—and, most important of all, let the Caroline Hunt Trust Estate off the hook for its contractual obligations. The deal offered something for everyone. Miller needed it to save Southwest Savings, and the regulators needed it to keep up appearances that something positive was being done.

In broad outline, the deal called for Southwest Savings to put up $25 million in new capital to absorb four insolvent Texas thrifts—Stockton Savings Association, Lamar Savings Association, Briercroft Savings Association, and City Savings and Loan Association. For its part, the FSLIC would provide $483 million in promissory notes to cover the thrifts' bad assets (the loans or repossessed properties that were producing no interest or principal payments). The transaction would transform Southwest Savings from a thrift with almost $1.5 billion in assets to a $5.5 billion institution and swell its deposit base from just under $1 billion to $5.4 billion almost overnight.

Not everyone thought it was such a good idea. Southwest Savings wasn't exactly a financial powerhouse, pointed out Bert Ely, a Virginia thrift consultant. "Some people in the industry are looking at this deal and shaking their heads. The regulators are just building bigger warehouses for their problems."[22]

Indeed, the particulars of the transaction looked to be as remarkably sweet for Southwest Savings as they would be costly to the taxpayer, whose dollars were to back the commitments made by Lykos and his FSLIC negotiators. There may have been something in the deal for almost everyone—but that didn't include the taxpayer.

For one thing, the ten-year promissory note issued by the FSLIC would guarantee that Southwest Savings would receive a yield from its newly acquired bad assets starting at 2.75 percentage points above the thrift's cost of deposits. (The guarantee would be scaled down to 2.6 percentage points the second year and gradually drop to 2.0 percent as the note matured.) This meant that if the average cost of deposits was, say, 10 percent in the first year, the government would give Southwest Savings however much money it took to boost the return on its acquired bad assets to 12.75 percent. Not bad for a bad asset. And while the FSLIC shouldered the financial burden of the bad assets, Southwest Savings would get the ones that were earning money. The deal did call for Southwest Savings to pay the cost of leasing and managing money-losing properties. But that sticky and potentially costly problem could be avoided simply by letting those foreclosed buildings sit empty; there was little incentive for Southwest Savings to try to fill them.

At the end of ten years, the assets covered by the government IOUs would be sold, presumably at a profit, which would go to the FSLIC. If, however, the Texas economy hadn't improved enough to produce profits, the government would eat the loss. Also at the end of ten years the FSLIC would receive 90 percent of the first $60 million of Southwest's net worth, and 50 percent of all equity above that amount—that is, if there was any.

On paper, it looked like a good deal for the regulators. All that needed to happen was a recovery in the Texas economy and real estate market. And, indeed, the economic projections prepared by Lykos showed that within ten years the Texas economy would be back on its feet. By 1998, according to Lykos's estimates, the properties would have regained and actually increased their value and, hence, could be sold at a healthy profit. Thus taxpayers would be relieved of the obligations Lykos was distributing so generously on their behalf.

In reality, however, those economic projections had little foundation other than the regulators' optimism and the FHLBB's desire to rid itself of problem thrifts. They were predicated on stable interest and inflation rates, as well as some chancy assumptions about rising oil prices.

But the optimistic nature of Lykos's economic projections was hardly the only objectional feature of the deal. The agreement also contained a provision that allowed Southwest Savings to come back to the FSLIC if the government's initial estimates of the extent of the thrift's problems turned out to be faulty. And faulty they were. Within a year after the deal was signed, the FSLIC had to give Southwest Savings a second promissory note for another $200 million—boosting the total government commitment to nearly $700 million—to cover bad properties it had missed the first time around.

To make matters worse for the taxpayers, Lykos and his fellow negotiators agreed to cover Southwest Savings's legal costs in a way that seemed to guarantee that those expenses would be as high as possible. The agreement permitted Southwest Savings to capitalize legal expenses incurred in connection with bad loans made by the failed thrifts it was taking over. This meant that Southwest Savings could roll the cost of those legal fees onto the promissory note so generously extended by the FSLIC —and earn a 2.75 percent annual profit on the lawyers' bills. For example, on a specific $10 million bad loan, Southwest Savings might elect to spend $1 million in legal expenses pursuing the defaulted borrower. The agreement with FSLIC would allow the $1 million in legal fees to be added to the $10 million, raising the FSLIC note covering the bad asset to $11 million. The FSLIC would then pay the 2.75 percent premium over the thrift's cost of funds on the new $11 million figure rather than the original $10 million value, and the regulators would guarantee that at the end of ten years the loan would have a minimum liquidation value of $11 million. In short, this feature of the agreement made it profitable for the thrift to sue people regardless of whether the suits had any merit. Indeed, it gave Southwest Savings an incentive to file lawsuits even if the defendants were bankrupt and there existed no possibility of collecting if the suits were won. By collecting 2.75 percent profit per year for ten years on their covered-asset legal expenses, Southwest Savings could actually make a profit on the litigation even if it never received a penny from bankrupt borrowers it chased into court.

But from the standpoint of public policy, the most

odious provision of the Southwest Savings deal was the one that let the Caroline Hunt Trust Estate off the hook of its net worth maintenance agreement. Miller had made cancellation of the maintenance agreement a deal-breaker. As one negotiator involved in the transaction put it, there was "no way" Miller would agree to absorb the four failed thrifts unless the net worth maintenance agreement was voided by the FSLIC. "It wasn't even a matter of discussion," the negotiator said.

At first, the regulators resisted. But then Southwest Savings got tough. After six weeks of futile negotiations in the spring of 1988, the Southwest Savings bargaining team simply threw its documents on the table and said goodbye. We have an alternate plan, the Southwest Savings negotiators warned, and that is to circle the wagons and cut back. The threat was clear: Unless the FSLIC gave in to Miller's demands, Southwest Savings would reduce its own operations, lay off employees, and not give the regulators any assistance in rescuing the four insolvent thrifts. It even threatened to file a lawsuit charging the regulators with having caused Southwest Savings's troubles, on the ground that it had been the regulators' incompetence that created the problems that had taken Southwest Savings to the brink of insolvency.

Afraid of losing the deal—and afraid, too, of being sued by the Caroline Hunt Trust Estate (which, as Wall noted, was "an entity that could spend whatever it wanted" on legal fees)—Lykos and his team caved. Just four days after the Southwest Savings negotiators stalked out of Washington, the FSLIC called them back and said let's talk some more. Soon thereafter, the regulators agreed to cancel the maintenance agreement, thus bailing out a thrift owner whose net worth was almost $1 billion.

Why did the FSLIC cave in so easily? Why didn't the

agency negotiate with another party to get a better deal? According to Wall, the reason was that Southwest Savings was the "only qualified bidder." Technically, that may be true. After all, the qualifications were set by Lykos, who said in a statement prepared by the FSLIC that potential investors were identified through an exhaustive review conducted by the Dallas Federal Home Loan Bank, of which, perhaps not coincidentally, Miller was vice chairman. "The Bank Board and the Dallas Bank have the authority to reject any proposed managers if they are found unsuitable," the FSLIC statement noted.[23]

But technicalities aside, Miller and Southwest Savings were not the only potential bidders. For one thing, when the deal was first announced the majority stockholders of Lamar Savings Association, one of the four insolvent thrifts, cried foul. These owners said they had put together an investment group that would have injected $1.6 billion in fresh capital into Lamar, but were not permitted even to present their plan.

But even if the Lamar Savings group was not qualified, why weren't other potential investors sought by the FSLIC? There were certainly plenty of suitable candidates about. As early as the fall of 1987, interest in putting fresh capital into the thrift industry had been publicly expressed by such Texas heavyweights as Dallas billionaire H. Ross Perot, the founder of Electronic Data Systems; Mort Meyerson, Perot's handpicked successor at EDS and a millionaire in his own right; and Richard Rainwater, the reclusive Fort Worth millionaire who made himself a fortune (and earned his way onto *Forbes*'s list of the four hundred wealthiest Americans in 1987) negotiating deals for Sid Bass. Any of these three, and many others as well, would have certainly met the FSLIC's "major criteria," which included "management expertise . . . capable of analyzing, responding quickly, and demonstrating decision-making prowess."[24] (Then again, considering the good deal that Southwest Savings got, one can only wonder how much more could have been wrung out of the regulators by a veteran negotiator such as Rainwater or Perot.)

Once the Southwest Savings deal was announced on May 18, 1988, Wall says, "the floodgates opened and we had lots of interest" from outside investors in buying thrifts with FSLIC assistance.[25] A more appropriate analogy might be that of vultures circling a wounded animal. In any case, Lykos began cutting billion-dollar deals with clockwork regularity, committing the government to expenditures Congress never imagined. In fact, it is amusingly ironic that Southwest Savings complains today that its sweetheart deal wasn't quite as sweet as later transactions. "We didn't get any tax breaks," says one aggrieved Southwest Savings negotiator, adding that under subsequent Southwest Plan deals buyers received billions in tax benefits.

Yet the regulators insist that the FSLIC became more expert as 1988 wore on. Wall points out, for example, that negotiators learned to classify the risk potential of bad loans more specifically, rather than give blanket coverage to all of an acquired thrift's bad assets, as had been done in the deal with Southwest Savings.[26] Even so, the regulators were negotiating from a position of extreme weakness because they didn't have the money to close down insolvent thrifts. Thomas Vartanian, a Washington attorney and former bank board member who represented buyers in several deals, told the *Wall Street Journal*: "It was like they [the regulators] were playing tennis blindfolded and with one arm behind their back."[27]

Consequently, even if Lykos and the FSLIC negotiators did become more expert as time went by, the new investors still were able to find creative ways to suck money out of the government. Revlon Group's Ronald O. Perelman, for example, got $1.3 billion in tax benefits from the Southwest Plan deal he cut through a subsidiary, MacAndrews & Forbes Holdings, Inc. Even as he put $300 million into a group of failed Texas thrifts led by First Texas Savings, Perelman got an immediate tax deduction of $900 million. That apparently wasn't enough, because he also tried to get the FSLIC to pay a "finder's fee" of $1 million to Texas banker Gerald Ford (no relation to the former President), who negotiated the deal for MacAndrews & Forbes. To their credit, even the regulators were unable to swallow this blatant raid on the Treasury. But though they said no to the "finder's fee," the regulators did say it was okay for Perelman to pay Ford an annual salary of $400,000 to run the new bank. The *Wall Street Journal* concluded that Perelman's "virtually risk-free" transaction alone will cost each American taxpayer about $30 in additional payments to the IRS.[28]

Nonetheless, Wall and the regulators insist that the Southwest Plan was a success. A document produced by Lykos's office, entitled "Frequently Asked Questions and Answers About the Southwest Plan," claimed that consolidations and closings of S&L branch offices under the Southwest Plan resulted in an average decline of 36 percent in administrative expenses for institutions involved in the first five deals. The document also said that Southwest Plan deals had resulted in a reduction of the "Texas premium," and had thus helped to keep insolvent thrifts afloat. According to the document, in March 1988 the average cost of funds for Texas thrifts was 8.03 percent, compared with 7.38 percent for thrifts nationwide. Six months later, the document noted, the average cost of funds for Texas thrifts had actually dropped slightly, to 8.02 percent, while the national average had risen to 7.51 percent. In addition, the document asserted that the Southwest Plan had attracted $1.1 billion in new capital to the Texas S&L industry. (It did not point out that to lure that money, the FSLIC had to offer investors $24.5 billion in direct assistance and other guarantees against loss.)

More neutral observers are somewhat less enthusiastic about the deals cut by Lykos under the Southwest Plan. In February 1989, the Federal Home Loan Bank Board asked the Mid-America Institute, an academic think tank at the University of Michigan, to conduct a study of the Southwest Plan and other deals made in 1988 to dispose of ailing thrifts. The FHLBB didn't do so voluntarily; it authorized the study at the insistence of the Senate Banking Committee, which was beginning to have doubts about what was happening at the FSLIC, "specifically as it related to the controversy surrounding . . . the Southwest Plan."[29] The institute assembled a panel of nine academic experts—"world-renowned scholars"—from the fields of accounting, economics, finance, taxation, and business mergers and acquisitions. Their 103-page report (not counting overview summaries and addenda) was a model of academic restraint. It did not criticize the FHLBB or the FSLIC for making bad deals, for showing favoritism to certain investor groups, or for placing a monstrous burden on the taxpayers. That's what makes some of the study's findings so damning. In the cold, empirical language of academia, the experts concluded that the regulators simply got outnegotiated.

The report reviewed the causes of the thrift crisis, noting that a major culprit was deposit insurance, which increased thrift owners' incentive to take risks with government-guaranteed money. As those risks multiplied, regulators were not given sufficient resources to stay current with developing problems, the report said, suggesting that FSLIC information systems need improvement.

As for resolving insolvencies under the Southwest Plan, the report said several mistakes were made (although they weren't directly called mistakes). One of these was the nature of the yield maintenance agreements the FSLIC made to guarantee that new investors wouldn't lose money on bad loans for up to ten years. The yield maintenance guarantees given Southwest Savings and other acquirers, the report said, "have features similar to riskless securities, but usually pay higher interest than Treasury Bills. Moreover, the yield maintenance is [usually] tax-free, whereas interest on Treasury Bills is not. . . . " In other words, to the billions of dollars the taxpayers may lose as a result of Southwest Plan guarantees must be added billions more in lost tax revenues washed away because of the FSLIC's willingness to give the new investors tax breaks not available to the ordinary citizen. According to the report, the FSLIC should have required Southwest Plan buyers to rebate all tax benefits received under the plan.

The report also criticized the way the FSLIC estimated the costs of the buyout packages, calling its methods "subject to considerable error." The result of these errors was that the FSLIC made "imprecise comparisons" when deciding whether it would be more economical to liquidate or save an insolvent thrift. And the result of that was that the liquidation costs of more than a third of the assisted acquisitions in 1988 exceeded the agency's original estimates. For example, the study said, in the Bass group's deal to buy American Savings, the FSLIC underestimated the cost by $1.6 billion—an error that suggests that both past and projected future costs estimated by the FSLIC are "probably understated."[30]

In short, the Southwest Plan and other bailout deals negotiated by the FHLBB concealed how serious the problem really was. The cover-up may not have been deliberate or intentional, although there's plenty of evidence to suggest that a lot of people had reason enough to want the problems concealed, at least temporarily.

But that's almost beside the point now. The fact is that the problems were concealed and haven't yet been fully revealed. Any doubts about that were laid to rest when the FSLIC found it necessary to guarantee Southwest Savings another $200 million less than a year after the revived thrift had been given $483 million in promissory notes.

"The hole," says Danny Wall, "is bigger than we thought."[31]

10.
THE
SOLUTIONS

Danny Wall isn't alone in his ignorance of the problem's true dimensions. Indeed, it will be years before anyone can accurately gauge the depth of the crater left by the S&L debacle of the '80s.

By the summer of 1989, estimates of how much it would ultimately cost to bail out the industry ranged from a low of about $157 billion (suggested by the Bush administration shortly after it took office) to a high of $285 billion to $300 billion (which is what the General Accounting Office told Congress the tab could possibly reach).

The magnitude of the final cost depends on a number of factors—primary among them, the speed with which the federal government acts. If Washington moves relatively quickly, the taxpayers' ultimate burden will probably be at the lower end of the $157 billion-to-$300 billion range. That's because the faster the bill is paid, the lower the interest payments will be on the money the government will have to borrow to clean up the mess. In addition, the sooner the crisis is resolved, the sooner all that repossessed real estate will flow back onto the market—and the sooner depressed local economies (particularly in the Southwest) will begin to recover. Again, though, Congress plodded through the spring and summer of 1989 without taking action until nearly Labor Day, while the S&L matter ticked away at $10 million a day.

But perhaps the biggest uncertainty involves the hundreds of billions of dollars in junk bonds accumulated by thrifts over the past few years. If the national economy slips into recession any time between now and the end of the century, those bond portfolios could become worthless. And that would set off a new wave of insolvencies that would send the thrift industry plunging even further into the red.

Three elements are essential to any real solution of the massive crisis in the nation's savings and loan industry: reform of a system that has been misused and broken, justice for the ordinary people whose savings have been stolen, and reestablishment of the virtue of thrift as part of our national character.

The plan for rescuing the thrift industry offered by President Bush and substantively endorsed by Congress represented a beginning. But once again, as was the case in 1980 and 1982, the proposed solution dealt with only part of the problem. As well-meant as it was, the Bush plan attacked the symptoms of the crisis, not the disease itself.

The strength of the Bush plan was that it recognized reality. Stripped of rhetoric and reduced to simple economics, what the Bush plan called for was nothing less than the elimination of the thrift industry as it presently exists. It didn't make that proposal explicitly. But there is little question that if the plan's specifics are followed through to their logical conclusions, the nation's unhealthy S&Ls will be allowed to die, while its remaining healthy ones will be converted into commercial banks.

Those specifics were quite straightforward. First of all, the Bush plan called for S&L capital requirements to be raised over two years to the 6 percent level required of commercial banks. (This provision alone seemed to guarantee that two-thirds of the nation's S&Ls would be out of business by 1992.) Second, it would eliminate the Federal Home Loan Bank Board and the Federal Savings and Loan Insurance Corporation, transferring their responsibilities and functions to the Treasury Department and the FDIC. Finally, it would get rid of the gimmicky accounting rules that permitted—indeed, encouraged—so many of the thrift-industry abuses of the '80s.

Behind these specific reforms was a tacit and long-overdue acknowledgment of a fundamental fact of American economic life: the thrift industry has outlived its usefulness. Not only are its days numbered, but the number isn't a very large one.

In January 1989, net withdrawals from the nation's insured S&Ls exceeded $9.7 billion. On an annualized basis that represents an erosion of $116 billion—or fully 12 percent of the industry's deposit base. At that rate of decline, it will take only eight and a half years to eradicate a system that took 175 years to build.

And the fact is, that rate is not likely to abate. As of the beginning of 1989, at a time when the cost of funds was rising, nearly a third of the thrift industry's assets remained tied up in fixed-rate long-term loans. Sound familiar? It should, for that's just the squeeze in which S&Ls found themselves in the early '80s. Add to that problem the unknown level of liabilities resulting from a decade's worth of S&L speculation in mortgage-backed securities and junk bonds—a time bomb certain to explode if interest rates rise and the economy turns down. Add, too, the legal obligations of the remaining healthy thrifts to maintain the FSLIC's solvency and to pay off depositors who put their money in the many thrifts that caromed into the ditch. The net result is an accumulated burden several times larger than the industry's total capital.

According to data compiled by Veribanc, Inc., a Woburn, Massachusetts, firm that monitors the thrift industry, despite the $40 billion committed by the government in 1988, the nation's S&Ls were still nearly $100 billion in the hole in 1989. As of April 1989, Veribanc estimated, it would cost $75.1 billion to liquidate thrifts that had no real capital left, $15.3 billion to cover continuing losses, and another $8.1 billion to maintain repossessed real estate held by insolvent institutions.[1] That's $98.5 billion in all—and the figure is growing by $12 billion a year.

On the positive side of the ledger, as of December 31, 1988, the industry held a total of $49 billion in equity. But nearly 53 percent ($25.8 billion) of that amount consisted of goodwill and other intangibles—in other words, phony equity. This left the thrift industry with just $23.2 billion to fill a $98.5 billion hole that is growing at a rate of $12 billion a year according to Veribanc's estimate.[2]

The conclusion is therefore inescapable: The S&L industry is insolvent. To all intents and purposes, it has been eliminated as a viable part of the financial services sector.

To its credit, the Bush plan seemed to recognize this. Rather than propose some massive increase in government assistance—the sort of futile approach that the once-powerful thrift lobby continues to advocate—it took the opposite course, laying out a framework under which activities formerly reserved to S&Ls will be gradually assumed by the commercial banking industry.

But that was only a beginning. The question remains: Where do we go from there?

To truly solve the S&L mess, it will be necessary to attack the root cause of the problem, the cancer that has eaten away the vitals of the system. That cause is nothing less than the deposit insurance system established during the New Deal. The fact is, Franklin Roosevelt was absolutely right in his objections to broad deposit guarantees. Just as he predicted, they wound up encouraging speculation, greed, fraud, and mismanagement on the part of thrift owners.

Originally, of course, federal deposit insurance was intended to protect the savings of small depositors, ordinary people who accumulated modest sums of, say, $2,500 to $5,000, which they intended to use for their retirement, or to buy a home, or for their children's education. But over the years the system was twisted to become a haven for wealthy investors. Even though the government currently insures deposits only up to a maximum of $100,000, it is still possible—indeed, quite easy—for people with, say, $1 million to have the entire amount protected by federal guarantees; they simply deposit the money in ten different accounts in ten different thrifts.

This isn't what Roosevelt intended. Nor was it what Huey Long and his fellow populists had in mind when they forced deposit guarantees through a reluctant Congress.

The first step toward excising the root causes of the S&L mess should thus be a reform of the deposit insurance system. And the first phase of that reform should be to restrict federal protection to one insured account per person. Not only would this end the present multiple-deposit charade, it would also limit the dangerous practice of brokering funds—the fully insured "hot money" that financed so much of the fraud and irresponsibility of the last decade.

In addition to restricting guarantees on multiple deposits, the present system should be changed to reduce the size of deposit guarantees. Only the first $10,000 of a deposit should be fully insured, with deposits over that amount up to $100,000 receiving 90 percent protection. Under this plan, a person with $100,000 in savings would still have less than $10,000 at risk. (The first $10,000 would be fully insured, along with 90 percent of the remaining $90,000—that is, $81,000—for a total coverage of $91,000.) Such a scheme would fulfill the objective of protecting the modest wealth of small savers while preventing the more affluent from taking unfair advantage of the system.

At the same time, financial institutions could provide 100-percent-government-insured deposit accounts of unlimited size by offering accounts whose funds are invested solely in secure government instruments such as Treasury bills and Ginnie Mae bonds. Reflecting their lower risk, such accounts, of course, would probably pay lower interest rates than regular accounts.

The point is that adopting a plan for graduated deposit insurance doesn't mean that savers' money would be unprotected. All it means is that the government would not guarantee 100 percent protection. People would still have an opportunity to make investments backed by the full faith and credit of the U.S. government. Moreover, a system of limited deposit guarantees might encourage the private sector to enter the deposit insurance business. Private firms already provide a myriad of other types of insurance—life, health, automobile, even pet care. Why shouldn't they also offer deposit insurance?

Not only might that add to the nation's general economic well-being by creating a new industry, complete with additional jobs and new tax revenues, it would also provide another check on bankers, since private insurers would be certain to keep a close watch on how responsibly banks were acting.

Another essential prerequisite to solving the S&L crisis is justice—criminal and economic. Wrongs have been committed, and the system must seek some recompense from those who were responsible on behalf of those who were victimized.

It goes without saying that prosecuting the thrift executives who were most flagrantly to blame for fraud and mismanagement will be a long, costly, and frustrating process. In its first two years of work, the federal white-collar crime task force that descended on Texas in 1987 produced only about 120 indictments. And most of those indicted were conceded by prosecutors to be minor actors in the drama: friendly appraisers who jacked up their estimates of land values to accommodate land flips by thrift owners, or junior S&L officers who lent their names (as well as their banks' money) to illegal insider transactions. Only a handful of the most culpable—the thrift owners and senior executives who devised the schemes—have been brought to justice.

Of course, most of the money they squandered is gone. It was either spent on Las Vegas junkets, fleets of aircraft, and lavish parties or sunk into unnecessary and hence unprofitable real estate deals. Indeed, if you visit Dallas or Houston or Austin or San Antonio, you can see where much of the money wound up. It is visible in row upon row of empty office buildings and shopping centers.

But the fact that you can't get blood from a stone

doesn't mean the people responsible for the mess shouldn't be sought out and punished. The $50 million President Bush proposed to spend on recovering looted S&L funds was just a drop in the bucket. Not only is it a negligible amount compared to what was squandered, it is hardly enough even to begin the investigative process, much less follow it through to prosecutions and convictions. If the pump of justice were primed sufficiently, it could produce results that might at least begin to compensate the American people. Unlike crimes of violence, such as murder and armed robbery, which are often acts of impulse or passion, white-collar crime generally has a logic to it—a logic that makes white-collar criminals respond to the deterrent effect of vigorous prosecution and punishment. Going after the people responsible for the looting of the nation's S&L system might well have a positive impact throughout the entire financial services sector.

Along these lines, Congress should make the penalties for white-collar theft from a financial institution far more severe than they currently are. The maximum five-year prison term for stealing $5 million or more that existed when the thrift industry was looted is hardly enough to deter future thieves. Congress should also consider making recklessness by thrift managers a punishable offense. After all, if the owners of a savings bank or S&L use federally guaranteed funds to mismanage their way into insolvency, they are hurting not only their depositors, but also the general public whose tax dollars ultimately will have to pay for their mistakes.

The pursuit of justice, of course, should not be restricted to righting the criminal and civil wrongs. Economic justice is also necessary. And the first step toward achieving that goal would be to void the Southwest Plan and other welfare-for-the-wealthy giveaways. The financial sharks who mugged the FSLIC—and, by extension, the American taxpayer—in 1988 should be given back their money and told that their deals are off. (Alternatively, the government could permit the deals to stand, but force the sharks to go to court if they intend to collect on the dead-horse promissory notes issued by the FSLIC.)

Other than expediency, there was never any justification for the Southwest Plan. And though some may argue that the government must honor its commitments, the fact is that ample precedents exist for Congress to renege on deals that amount to bad public policy. A good example is the 1986 tax-reform bill, which retroactively revoked the real estate tax-shelter breaks given to wealthy investors some years before. Let the wealthy people who sought and received windfall profits from a corrupt and inequitable system earn their money the old-fashioned way—and that doesn't mean lifting it from inept regulators.

Another economic consideration is the question of what should be done with the billions of dollars in non-producing real estate that has been repossessed by insolvent S&Ls and, as a result, is now owned by the FSLIC. So far, with real estate values at rock-bottom levels in the Southwest, both thrift owners and the government have been encouraged to keep their huge inventories of unproductive property off the market. But all that does is put off the inevitable day of reckoning. Worse, it lets valuable assets waste away during what could be their most productive years.

The answer is painful but inescapable. The property should be put on the block. An empty building is not like a barrel of oil. Oil can be kept off the market until demand improves and prices rise; the oil won't spoil and the cost of the barrel is negligible. But an empty building cannot be withheld until the market revives, for unlike oil, an empty building can deteriorate and lose its value. The fact is, the value of improved real estate has a limited life. If you don't use it, you lose it. And that is precisely what is happening with all of those empty buildings across the Sunbelt that are being kept off the market, waiting for the unknown future date when conditions will be better. Their asset values are deteriorating daily, the result of neglect as well as improvements in real estate technology (better building-service systems, advances in energy efficiency, and so on), which will make them less competitive when the market does finally improve.

The best solution is one that somehow keeps getting overlooked: Let the free market decide the best possible use for the repossessed assets held by the thrifts and the FSLIC. These assets do have some value. It may not be the exaggerated value that was put into them; that premium has disappeared. But some value still exists, even if it is less than people would like.

It isn't necessary to dump all of the repossessed property on the market at once. Indeed, that would be as much of a mistake as keeping it all *off* the market. Rather, the property could be sold at open auctions held over a set period—say, five years. Disposing of the property in this way would have the salubrious side effect of adding the element of predictability to regional economies that are plagued as much by uncertainty as they are by empty buildings.

Needless to say, it's not likely that selling repossessed properties would raise nearly enough money to repay the unlucky depositors who put their savings into brain-dead thrifts now connected to the FSLIC's phony life-support system. So where will they find economic justice? The first place they should look to is the thrift industry's remaining capital base. After all, the still-healthy thrifts that enjoyed FSLIC protection signed contracts obligating themselves to repay losses at institutions that went under. Those obligations should now be honored. This is especially true of the many healthy thrifts, such as Columbia Savings & Loan, that prospered by gambling with depositors' insured funds. Like all gaming proceeds, these profits weren't earned in any real economic sense.

Even those healthy thrifts that remained true to their original purpose of helping ordinary people to save money and buy homes bear some culpability for the crimes committed by their less prudent colleagues. After all, the industry was supposed to regulate itself to a large degree. Where, then, were the industry, its responsible members, and its powerful lobby when less scrupulous thrift owners started scooping money out the back door to reckless developers or hiding cash in their own pockets? The industry's silence made it an accessory to the many crimes that were committed by the Texas cowboys and the California gamblers.

If the magnitude of the massive insolvency is such that liquidating dead institutions and repaying depositors from the capital base of healthy thrifts means the end of the S&L industry, then so be it. That, after all, is bound to be the ultimate effect of the Bush plan, however vague the administration's acknowledgment of that long-term goal may be.

What would be the human cost of dismantling the industry? Because of the wave of mergers, liquidations, and consolidations in recent years, it is hard to gauge precisely how many people are currently employed in the thrift industry. The most recent figures available from the U.S. League of Savings Institutions are for the end of 1987, when S&L employment totaled just over 406,000.[3] The toll in terms of human pain and suffering of dislocating so many people cannot be regarded lightly. Nonetheless, arguments both practical and economic suggest that the human cost should not deter us from dismantling the industry. For one thing, not all those 400,000 or so people would wind up jobless. Some thrifts would doubtless survive in a new, unified banking system. And there would be many additional jobs created in the commercial banking sector as it expanded to absorb the functions of closed thrifts.

To be sure, there will still be tens of thousands of current S&L employees who will not find new jobs in the financial services industry. What about them?

This is where the economic argument comes into play. The harsh truth is that the employees of insolvent thrifts are not making any contribution to the national commonweal. This is not to say that these employees are not themselves hardworking and productive. They come to the office daily, perform their assigned tasks responsibly and conscientiously, and earn the paychecks they receive. But the work they are doing—maintaining lifeless assets at the expense of depositors and, ultimately, the American taxpayer—diminishes the gross national product, rather than adding to it. What's needed here is an orderly, planned transition to other jobs that would include retraining, if necessary, and government-assisted relocation programs that would eventually equip these workers for truly productive employment—employment that would have the long-term effect of adding to the national wealth.

The third element necessary to solve the S&L mess is, in the long run, the most important one. The concept of thrift that built this nation must be restored to the American character.

In the broadest sense, the real tragedy of the destruction of the nation's thrift industry wasn't the fact that scores of billions of dollars went down the drain, but the corrosive impact it all had on the ordinary American's spirit of thriftiness. Thrift is, of course, a practical virtue, one that promotes social stability as well as financial security. It not only improves the individual's life, it strengthens his community and, ultimately, his nation. As we have seen, it was the small savings of millions of immigrants that provided much of the financing that transformed the U.S. economy into the most powerful and productive one the world has ever known. Today, similar saving by ordinary citizens could provide the capital to create new jobs, generate new resources, and ultimately reduce the nation's dependence on foreign investors.

In 1987, the rate of savings in the United States stood at a mere 3.2 percent of income, the lowest level in forty years. That low rate has placed the United States at a severe competitive disadvantage with nations such as Japan, where the 1987 savings rate was 16.8 percent of income, and West Germany, where the rate was 12.3 percent.

One reason why savings have declined in the United States is government policy. In recent years, tax benefits have generally been aimed at encouraging consumption rather than thrift. Take, for instance, the interest deduction permitted on mortgages for a second home. With millions of Americans unable to finance ownership of even a first home, such a deduction makes little sense as economic or social policy. The fact is, owning a second home is not saving; it is nonproductive asset accumulation.

Recent tax reforms, such as the gradual elimination

of the deductions for interest on consumer credit, represent a move in the right direction. But they are only a start —and a negative one at that, a stick rather than a carrot. What is needed is an affirmative program, one that encourages saving instead of discouraging consumption.

What might such a program consist of? Well, most solutions aren't the result of a miracle or even any special genius. More often, solutions to problems are based upon common sense—the kind of common sense demonstrated by the Reverend Henry Duncan back in 1810 when he was faced with the problem of how to protect the funds deposited by his humble parishioners in his fledgling Ruthwell savings society. He hit upon the simple device of a lockbox that required three keys to open.

So it is with a renewed national effort to encourage saving. Various methods have proved successful in the past; why not adapt them to the present? A good example is the individual retirement account. When the government first began allowing wage earners to defer taxes on up to $2,000 a year in income by putting the money into IRAs, applications for the accounts flooded into banks and S&Ls. When Congress started cutting back on the program in 1987, the river all but drained dry. The IRA example demonstrates that people will take advantage of a good program that works to their benefit as well as that of the nation at large.

The problem with IRAs, of course, was that they cut into federal tax revenues in a period of growing federal budget deficits. So what is needed now is a system that will encourage saving without having a sharp impact on federal receipts.

One solution that might have benefits beyond just bumping up the savings rate might be to allow people to defer taxes on increases in their income if they put the amount of the increase into U.S. Treasury instruments, either directly or through bank-administered programs. For example, someone who earned $50,000 last year and $55,000 this year could put the extra $5,000, or any portion of it, into what we might call a Treasury account. As with IRAs, taxes on that $5,000 and the interest it earned would not be due until it was withdrawn—presumably at some future date, such as retirement, when the saver found himself in a lower tax bracket.

Through such Treasury accounts, Americans could be encouraged to invest in their future as well as in the future of their government. The program could also have a significant impact on reducing the federal deficit. The tax-advantaged nature of a Treasury account might well result in a lower overall rate of interest on government debt—a reduction that could cut the government's annual interest costs by billions of dollars. What's more, in addition to fostering thrift, the plan could well result in an immediate increase in productivity. What better encouragement could people have to work harder in order to increase their income than the knowledge that 100 percent of that increase would be theirs to keep, that (for the time being at least) none of it need be eaten up by taxes?

Another significant benefit of this proposal would be the extent to which it might allow the government finally to get its hands on some of the estimated $500 billion in black-market earnings that currently go unreported. Some economists estimate that collecting taxes on this income alone would be enough to balance the federal budget. The Treasury account plan could amount to a kind of amnesty program for delinquent taxpayers, who would be able to take advantage of it by reporting their previously undeclared income as simply an increase over the previous year's earnings. They still wouldn't have to pay any taxes on the income (at least not right away), and they'd be able to stop worrying about getting caught.

In addition, this kind of program would provide the government with a new tool to encourage other kinds of economic behavior. For example, the government could permit first-time home buyers to make tax-free withdrawals of Treasury account funds for down payments. This would encourage home ownership by providing a direct subsidy to the consumer, instead of the indirect one resulting from the interest-rate limitations mandated by Glass-Steagall.

But beyond encouraging people to save more, the proposal's principal benefit would be to ease the nation's reliance on foreign investment. The savings of ordinary Americans—not the wealth of enormously powerful Japanese or European banks—could once again become the primary fuel powering the engine of American capitalism. Once again, Americans could take control of their own destiny.

The Treasury account program represents only one possible solution. The point is that the thrift crisis destroyed more than an industry. The S&L debacle also took a huge toll on the spirit of thrift that built a nation even as it strengthened the character of its people. Clearing away the wreckage of the industry will cost billions, but it can be done. True, the ultimate price tag may wind up soaring as high as $200 billion. But as bad as that may seem, that wouldn't be the worst thing to have come out of the crisis. What would be worse would be if the lessons of the thrift debacle were to go unheeded, if they didn't wind up providing the basis for the kind of positive action necessary to guarantee that such a catastrophe could never occur again.

NOTES

Chapter 1

1. Charles Dickens, "My Account with Her Majesty," *All the Year Round Magazine*, Vol. 2 (March 5, 1864), pp. 79–83.
2. "The Savings of the People," *Edinburgh Review*, Vol. 138 (July 1873), p. 101.
3. Ibid.
4. Franklin J. Sherman, *Modern Story of Mutual Savings Banks* (New York: J.J. Little & Ives, 1934), p. 21.
5. Ibid, pp. 21, 28–29.
6. *Quarterly Review*, Edinburgh, Scotland, Oct. 1816, p. 95.
7. Quoted in *Edinburgh Review*, June 1815, p. 141.
8. Ibid.
9. Prof. D. B. King, in *The Popular Science Monthly*, Vol. 28 (Nov. 1885), p. 161.
10. Ibid.
11. *Congressional Digest*, Vol. 10 (Nov. 1931), p. 296.
12. *Southern Bivouac Magazine*, Vol. 2, No. 1 (June 1886), pp. 25–27.
13. *1912 Annual Report of the U.S. Controller of the Currency*, quoted in *Literary Digest*, April 26, 1913.
14. Paul M. Warburg, address, reprinted in *Survey Magazine*, Vol. 44 (April 17, 1920), pp. 107–108.
15. Ernest Russell, "Humanity as the Bank Clerk Sees It," *World Today*, Vol. 14 (June 1908), p. 659.
16. Richard Boughton, "Humor and Pathos of the Savings Bank," *Century Magazine*, Vol. 61, No. 4 (February 1901), p. 483.
17. Estimate by W. A. Linn, "Building and Loan Associations," *Scribner's Magazine*, Vol. 5 (June 1889), p. 701.
18. D. A. Tompkins, "Working People's Homes: What Is Being Accomplished by American Building and Loan Associations," *Cassier's Magazine*, Vol. 23 (March 1903), pp. 600–14.
19. Ibid., p. 611.
20. Alan Teck, *Mutual Savings Banks and Savings and Loan Associations: Aspects of Growth* (New York: Columbia University Press, 1968), p. 121.
21. Susan Estabrook Kennedy, *The Banking Crisis of 1933* (Lexington, Ky.: University of Kentucky Press, 1973), p. 19.
22. Teck, p. 119.

Chapter 2

1. Sen. Thomas of Oklahoma, quoted in *Congressional Record*, Senate, Jan. 21, 1933; *New York Times*, March 1–10, 1933; Kennedy, p. 153.
2. Statistics from the Federal Reserve Board cited by Sen. Robert La

Follette of Wisconsin, *Congressional Record*, Senate, March 9, 1933, pp. 63–64.

3. Kennedy, p. 173.
4. Teck, p. 119.
5. Ibid.
6. *New York Times*, March 26, 1933, p. 7.
7. Kennedy, p. 215.
8. *New York Times*, June 4, 1933, p. 6.
9. Ray B. Westerfield, in *Journal of Political Economy*, Vol. 41, No. 6 (Dec. 1933), p. 746.
10. Bascom N. Timmons, *Garner of Texas* (New York: Harper & Brothers, 1948), pp. 178–80.
11. Ibid., p. 179.
12. Ibid.
13. *New York Times*, July 1, 1932, p. 15.
14. Ibid.
15. Timmons, p. 179.
16. *Congressional Record*, Senate, Jan. 5, 1933, p. 1332.
17. Ibid.
18. Ibid., Jan. 11, 1933, p. 1574.
19. Ibid., pp. 2262–66.
20. Ibid., p. 2508.
21. *Business Week*, April 26, 1933, p. 5.
22. Kennedy, p. 214.
23. *Business Week*, May 31, 1933, p. 20.
24. *Congressional Record*, Senate, March 11, 1933, p. 188.
25. *Business Week*, March 8, 1933, p. 32.
26. Ibid., April 12, 1933, p. 3.
27. T. Harry Williams, *Huey Long* (New York: Knopf, 1969), p. 634.
28. *Congressional Record*, Senate, March 11, 1933, p. 185.
29. Kennedy, p. 219.
30. *Business Week*, June 17, 1933, p. 19.
31. Ibid., p. 5085.
32. Ibid.
33. However, Roosevelt later in the month responded piquishly by calling Long to the White House for a "showdown" meeting. Roosevelt would tell Long that the administration was going to deny the Kingfish control over federal patronage in Louisiana. After the meeting, Long complained to Postmaster General James Farley: "What the hell is the use of coming down to see this fellow? I can't win any decision over him." Quoted in Williams, p. 637.
34. How it would repay that debt was a different matter, of course. If the insurance fund was depleted, options could range from selling off public land to the inflationary expedient of simply printing more money and thoroughly debasing the monetary system, as occurred in Germany in the early 1930s.

Chapter 3

1. *Time*, Jan. 15, 1973, p. 71.
2. Ibid.
3. Dwight B. Crane and Michael J. Riley, *NOW Accounts: Strategies for Financial Institutions* (Lexington, Mass.: Lexington Books/D.C. Heath, 1978), p. 3.
4. *Forbes*, Jan. 15, 1973, p. 17.
5. *U.S. News & World Report*, June 27, 1977, p. 68.
6. Statistics from William E. Donoghue, *The Complete Money Market Guide* (New York: Harper & Row, 1981), p. 8.
7. *Time*, June 8, 1981, p. 58.
8. Ibid., July 2, 1979, p. 57.
9. *New York*, April 21, 1980, p. 40.
10. *Newsweek*, Dec. 29, 1980, p. 56.
11. Frederick E. Balderston, *Thrifts in Crisis: Structural Transformation of the Savings and Loan Industry*

(Cambridge, Mass.: Ballinger, 1985), p. 4.

12. Quoted in *Federal Home Loan Bank Board Journal*, July 1979.

13. Quoted in *Changing Times*, Sept. 1980, pp. 25–26.

14. *Forbes*, Jan. 4, 1982, p. 83.

15. Hearing before the Committee on Banking, Housing and Urban Affairs, United States Senate, 97th Congress, First Session, April 6, 1981, Publication No. 97-10, U.S. Government Printing Office, Washington, D.C., p. 3.

16. Federal Home Loan Bank Board, *Annual Report, 1982*, April 1983, p. 4.

17. *Forbes*, Oct. 26, 1981, pp. 187–88.

18. Federal Home Loan Bank Board, *Annual Report, 1980, 1981, 1982*.

19. *Dallas Times Herald*, May 19, 1985, p. 1-G.

20. *U.S. News & World Report*, Jan. 23, 1989, p. 39.

Chapter 4

1. Office space data from Coldwell Banker Real Estate, retail space data from Henry S. Miller Co. Realtors.

2. Cushman & Wakefield, "Focus on Market Trends, 1989."

3. M. Danny Wall, interview with *Dallas Times Herald* editorial board, Dec. 14, 1988.

4. *Fortune*, May 11, 1987, p. 61.

5. Robert O. Anderson, *Fundamentals of the Petroleum Industry* (Norman, Okla.: University of Oklahoma Press, 1984), p. 276.

6. Data provided by U.S. Department of Labor, Bureau of Labor Statistics.

7. Ibid.

8. *Seventy-second Report of the Committee on Government Operations*, House Report 100-1088 (Barnard Committee Report), U.S. Government Printing Office, Washington, D.C. (1988), pp. 9–10.

9. Ibid., p. 55.

10. Ibid.

11. Edmond Taylor, *The Fall of Dynasties: The Collapse of the Old Order, 1905–1922* (New York: Doubleday, 1963), p. 137.

12. Byron Harris, in *Texas Monthly*, June 1987, pp. 11–13, 168–74, 182.

13. *Newsweek*, June 20, 1988, pp. 42–45.

14. Ibid.

15. Harris.

16. Federal Home Loan Bank Board data.

17. *Dallas Times Herald*, Aug. 16, 1987, p. A-15.

18. Authors' interview with confidential source, Feb. 8, 1988.

19. Harris.

20. *Dallas Times Herald*, July 17, 1988, pp. A-1, A-8.

21. Ibid.

22. Ibid.

23. Harris.

24. Bill Adler, "Jim Wright and Vernon S&L's High-Flying Honcho Don Dixon," *Texas Observer*, Dec. 4, 1987, pp. 1, 8–13. Reprinted in abridged form in *Regardie's Magazine*.

25. Ibid.

26. *Newsweek*, June 20, 1988.

27. *Time*, Feb. 20, 1989, p. 71.

28. *Dallas Morning News*, Dec. 4, 1988, pp. 1, 30–32.

29. *Newsweek*, June 20, 1988.

30. Ibid.

31. Byron Harris, in *Texas Monthly*

Magazine, Jan. 1988, pp. 88, 134–136, 143.

32. *Dallas Morning News,* Dec. 4, 1988, p. 29.
33. Adler, p. 13.
34. Marc Perkins of the Tampa, Fla., investment firm of Perkins Smith, quoted in *Fortune,* May 11, 1987, p. 64.
35. *New York Times,* April 29, 1987, pp. D-1, 15.
36. *Dallas Times Herald,* Sept. 20, 1987, p. A-17.
37. Ibid.
38. Ibid.
39. Ibid.
40. Adler, p. 10.
41. Ibid.
42. *Dallas Morning News.* Sept. 6, 1987, p. A-30.
43. *Business Week,* July 13, 1987, p. 96.
44. Ibid.
45. The 1983 Empire Savings exposé was the first scandal to strike the Texas S&L industry in the early 1980s. It took the government almost five years to come back with indictments against the thrift's principals, who included Empire president Spencer Blaine, Dallas developer D. L. Faulkner, and Mayor James Toler of the Dallas suburb of Garland, Texas. The three men went on trial in early 1989 on charges of racketeering, fraud, and conspiring to steal more than $100 million from five savings and loans in Texas and Arkansas. The indictments said Blaine received $22 million from fraudulent transactions, Toler $34 million, and Faulkner more than $40 million. Before the federal investigations of Empire Savings found their way to Blaine, Faulkner, and Toler, more than a hundred lesser Empire officials and business associates were convicted on various federal charges in connection with the investigation. Former FHLBB chairman Edwin Gray said in 1984 that Empire Savings records revealed "one of the most reckless and fraudulent land investment schemes this agency has ever seen." That statement was made, of course, before excesses at other Texas S&Ls were exposed.
46. *Dallas Morning News,* Sept. 6, 1987.
47. Ibid.
48. Ibid.
49. *Business Week,* July 13, 1987, p. 96.
50. *Dallas Morning News,* Sept. 6, 1987.
51. *Newsweek,* June 29, 1987, p. 45.
52. *Dallas Morning News,* September 6, 1987.
53. Bert Ely of Ely & Co., Alexandria, Va., quoted in *Dallas Times Herald,* Aug. 20, 1988, p. A-1.
54. "The Failure of the Citizens State Bank of Carrizo Springs, Texas, and Related Financial Problems," hearings before the Subcommittee on Financial Institutions, Supervision, Regulation and Insurance, of the Committee on Banking, Currency and Housing, House of Representatives, 94th Congress, Second Session, Part 1, Nov. 30–Dec. 1, 1976, Government Printing Office Publication No. 81-265-0, p. 581.
55. Ibid.
56. *Dallas Morning News,* Dec. 4, 1988, p. A-31.

Chapter 5

1. Rosemary Stewart, director of the Office of Enforcement, Federal

Home Loan Bank Board, interview with authors, Washington, D.C., Feb. 17, 1989.

2. *Wall Street Journal,* April 15, 1985, p. 3.
3. Ibid., Sept. 20, 1985, p. 54.
4. Ibid., Sept. 8, 1986, p. 7.
5. Ibid.
6. *New York Times,* Southwest Edition, Feb. 1, 1989, p. A-7.
7. *Forbes,* May 20, 1985, p. 194.
8. *American Banker,* Jan. 23, 1989, p. 1.
9. Sheshunoff Information Services, Austin, Texas, 1989.
10. Federal Home Loan Bank Board news release, FHLBB 89-29, Feb. 10, 1989, Table 1.
11. Jonathan E. Gray, "Financial Deregulation and the Savings and Loan Crisis," Sanford C. Bernstein & Co. research prepared for the Federal Deposit Insurance Corp. Office of Research and Strategic Planning, January 1989, p. 15.
12. Ibid.
13. *Business Week,* March 10, 1986, p. 34.
14. Financial Corporation of America, 10-K Report to the Securities and Exchange Commission, Dec. 31, 1987, p. 46.

Chapter 6

1. Federal Home Loan Bank Board, *Annual Report, 1982,* April 1983, p. 86.
2. Ibid.
3. Gray, p. 24.
4. Columbia Savings & Loan Association stock offering circular, March 29, 1984, p. 3.
5. Ibid.
6. Ibid., pp. 14, 27.
7. Ibid., p. 13.

8. *Forbes,* May 5, 1986, p. 37.
9. Ibid.
10. *Business Week,* June 29, 1987, p. 86.
11. Connie Bruck, *The Predators' Ball: The Junk Bond Raiders and the Man Who Staked Them* (New York: The American Lawyer/Simon & Schuster, 1988), p. 90.
12. *Forbes,* November 19, 1984, p. 209.
13. *Business Week,* June 29, 1987, p. 87.
14. Bruck, pp. 271–72.
15. Columbia Savings & Loan Association, *Annual Report to Shareholders, 1986,* p. 10.
16. Columbia Savings & Loan Association, 1987 10-K Report to the Securities and Exchange Commission, Dec. 31, 1987, p. 10.
17. Bruck, pp. 276–77.
18. *Business Week,* June 29, 1987, p. 87.
19. Bruck, pp. 310–11.
20. Ibid.
21. *Business Week,* June 29, 1987.
22. Ibid.
23. *Forbes,* Nov. 14, 1988, pp. 153–56.
24. Ibid.
25. Federal Home Loan Bank Board data, in *Dallas Morning News,* Feb. 14, 1989, p. D-1.

Chapter 7

1. *Wall Street Journal,* Dec. 27, 1985, p. 1, and July 16, 1986, pp. 1–15.
2. Edwin J. Gray, speech to the Annual Legislative Conference, U.S. League of Savings Institutions, Washington, D.C., March 6, 1984.
3. Edwin J. Gray, interview with authors, Miami, Fla., March 8, 1989. Subsequent quotations in this passage are from the same interview.
4. Edwin J. Gray, testimony before Financial Institutions

subcommittee of House Banking Committee (excerpt provided by Gray).

5. Edwin J. Gray, speech to the American Savings and Loan League, Albuquerque, N.M., Nov. 11, 1983.

6. Gray interview.

7. Letter from Edwin J. Gray to John W. Anderson, editorial page editor, *Washington Post*, Jan. 21, 1989. Copy provided by Edwin J. Gray.

8. *Barron's*, Feb. 27, 1989, pp. 14–15, 46–47.

9. Ibid.

10. Rosemary Stewart interview.

11. Gray interview.

12. Ibid.

13. Joe Selby, interview with authors, Dallas, Texas, March 3, 1989.

14. Ibid.

15. Ibid.

16. Edwin J. Gray, letter to Carol Crawford, Associate Director for Economics and Government, Office of Management and Budget, Feb. 3, 1986. Letter provided by Gray.

17. Edwin J. Gray, letter to Constance Horner, Director of the Office of Personnel Management, Feb. 18, 1986. Letter provided by Gray.

18. Ibid.

19. Gray letter to Anderson.

20. Gray interview.

21. Stewart interview.

22. Gray letter to Anderson.

23. Ibid.

24. Linton Bowman interview with authors, Austin, Texas, Feb. 14, 1989.

25. Stewart interview.

26. Bowman interview.

27. Audit of the Examination and Supervisor Agent Functions, Texas Savings and Loan Department, Texas State Auditor's Office Report No. 8–039, February 1988, p. 14.

28. Ibid., p. 18.

29. Gray interview.

30. Bowman interview.

31. Ibid.

32. Stewart interview.

33. Sheshunoff S&L Quarterly Ratings, Sept. 30, 1988, pp. I-32–36.

34. Stewart interview.

35. Barnard Committee Report, p. 38.

36. Ibid., p. 35.

37. Ibid., p. 40.

38. *Washington Post*, Jan. 13, 1989, p. A-20.

39. Gray letter to Anderson.

40. Stewart interview.

Chapter 8

1. Federal Home Loan Bank Board, *Annual Report, 1980, 1981.*

2. *Wall Street Journal*, Aug. 23, 1983, p. 35.

3. Data provided by the Mortgage Bankers Association of America, quoted in *Dallas Times Herald*, Dec. 8, 1989, p. C-1.

4. Ralph Nader and Jonathan Brown, *Report to U.S. Taxpayers on the Savings and Loan Crisis* (Washington, D.C.: BankWatch, 1989), p. 12.

5. *Wall Street Journal*, July 16, 1986, pp. 1, 15.

6. Edwin J. Gray, testimony before the Committee on Banking, Housing and Urban Affairs, U.S. Senate, Washington, D.C., August 3, 1988.

7. *Wall Street Journal*, July 16, 1986.

8. Brooks Jackson, *Honest Graft* (New York: Knopf, 1988).
9. Ibid., p. 172.
10. Ibid., p. 173.
11. Ibid., p. 175.
12. Ibid., p. 176.
13. *New Republic*, March 20, 1989, p. 26.
14. Jackson, p. 203.
15. *Wall Street Journal*, Feb. 7, 1989, p. A-18.
16. Common Cause press release, "Fee Speech: Truckers, Broadcasters, Securities and Tobacco Interests Are Top 1987 Honoraria Givers to Members of Congress: Common Cause Study Links Banking, Commerce Committee Members and Special Interest Honoria," August 3, 1988, p. 9.
17. *Wall Street Journal*, Feb. 7, 1989.
18. Ibid.
19. *Dallas Times Herald*, July 13, 1987, p. 3.
20. *Wall Street Journal*, March 21, 1989, p. A-26.
21. Ibid.
22. Craig Hall, interview with authors, Dallas, Texas, March 11, 1989.
23. Gray interview.
24. Ibid.
25. Ibid.
26. Ibid.
27. Adler, p. 8.
28. Gray interview.
29. Ibid.
30. William O'Connell, telephone interview with author, April 20, 1989.
31. Theo H. Pitt, Jr., speech delivered at the Third Regulatory Policy Conference of the U.S. League of Savings Institutions, Washington, D.C., June 28, 1988, in *Vital Speeches of the Day*, Vol. 54, No. 22 (Sept. 1, 1988), pp. 647–76.
32. Media General–Associated Press Poll, March 19, 1989.
33. *Dallas Morning News*, March 12, 1989, pp. H-1, H-12.

Chapter 9

1. *Wall Street Journal*, Jan. 13, 1989, p. 1.
2. Statement by U.S. Rep. Henry Gonzalez to the House Financial Institutions Caucus, March 14, 1989.
3. *Sheshunoff S&L Quarterly Ratings*, December 1987, p. I-7, December 1988, p. I-7.
4. Bowman interview.
5. *Financial Planning*, Vol. 18, No. 4 (April 1989), pp. 19–22.
6. M. Danny Wall, interview with authors, Washington, D.C., April 6, 1989.
7. *Dallas Times Herald*, Nov. 15, 1988, pp. C-1, C-8.
8. *New York Times*, March 12, 1989, Section 3, p. 1.
9. *Sheshunoff S&L Quarterly Ratings*, Dec. 31, 1988, p. I-12.
10. *Newsday*, April 9, 1989.
11. *U.S. News & World Report*, Dec. 12, 1988, pp. 67–69.
12. Ibid.
13. Wall interview with authors.
14. Martin resigned from the Federal Home Loan Bank Board on April 5, 1989.
15. *Sheshunoff S&L Quarterly Ratings*, March 1987.
16. *U.S. News & World Report*, Dec. 12, 1988.
17. Wall interview with authors.
18. Ibid.

19. *Wall Street Journal,* Dec. 30, 1988, pp. A-1, A-8.
20. Ibid.
21. *Forbes,* Oct. 26, 1987, pp. 146–48.
22. Quoted in *Dallas Times Herald,* May 20, 1988.
23. "Frequently Asked Questions and Answers About the Southwest Plan," FSLIC undated document, p. 4.
24. Ibid.
25. Wall interview.
26. Ibid.
27. *Wall Street Journal,* Jan. 13, 1989, pp. A-1, A-2.
28. Ibid.
29. Mid-America Institute Task Force, "Crisis Resolution in the Thrift Industry: Beyond the December Deals," Report on the Thrift Crisis, March 3, 1989, p. i.
30. Ibid., pp. ii-xi.
31. Wall interview with authors.

Chapter 10

1. Veribanc News Release 040489, Woburn, Mass., April 1989.
2. *Sheshunoff S&L Quarterly Ratings,* December 1988, pp. 1–7.
3. *Savings Institutions Sourcebook— 1988,* U.S. League of Savings Institutions, Chicago, Ill., April 1988, p. 57.

SELECTED
BIBLIOGRAPHY

Anderson, Robert O. *Fundamentals of the Petroleum Industry*. Norman, Okla.: University of Oklahoma Press, 1984.

Bruck, Connie. *The Predators' Ball: The Junk Bond Raiders and the Man Who Staked Them*. New York: Simon & Schuster/American Lawyer, 1988.

Cashin, Jack W. *History of Savings and Loans in Texas*. Austin, Texas: Bureau of Business Research, College of Business Administration, University of Texas, 1956.

Cooper, Kerry, and Fraser, Donald R. *Banking Deregulation and the New Competition in Financial Services*. Cambridge, Mass.: Ballinger, 1986.

Crane, Dwight D., and Riley, Michael J. *NOW Accounts: Strategies for Financial Institutions*. Lexington, Mass.: Lexington Books/D.C. Heath, 1978.

Donoghue, William E., with Tilling, Thomas. *William E. Donoghue's Complete Money Market Guide: The Simple Low-Risk Way You Can Profit From Inflation and Fluctuating Interest Rates*. New York: Harper & Row, 1981.

Ewalt, Josephine Hedges. *A Business Reborn: The Savings and Loan Story, 1930–1960*. Chicago: American Savings and Loan Institute Press, 1962.

Jackson, Brooks. *Honest Graft: Big Money and the American Political Process*. New York: Knopf, 1988.

Kennedy, Susan Estabrook. *The Banking Crisis of 1933*. Lexington, Ky.: University of Kentucky Press, 1973.

Melton, William C. *Inside the Fed: Making Monetary Policy*. Homewood, Ill.: Dow Jones/Irwin, 1985.

Meyers, Margaret G. *A Financial History of the United States.* New York: Columbia University Press, 1970.

Olmstead, Alan L. *New York City Mutual Savings Banks, 1819–1861.* Chapel Hill, N.C.: University of North Carolina Press, 1976.

Ornstein, Franklin H. *Savings Banking: An Industry in Change.* Reston, Va.: Reston Publishing/Prentice-Hall, 1985.

Schisgall, Oscar. *Out of One Small Chest: The Social and Financial History of the Bowery Savings Bank.* New York: ANACOM, a division of the American Management Associations, 1975.

Teck, Alan. *Mutual Savings Banks and Savings and Loan Associations: Aspects of Growth.* New York: Columbia University Press, 1968.

Timmons, Bascom. *Garner of Texas.* New York: Harper & Brothers, 1948.

Williams, T. Harry. *Huey Long.* New York: Knopf, 1969.

INDEX

ABOUT THE AUTHOR

PAUL ZANE PILZER, a graduate of Lehigh University and the Wharton Graduate Business School, made his first million when he was twenty-five. Now thirty-five, he is the managing partner of Zane May Interests, a $300 million national investment company that he cofounded. A former executive of Citibank, Pilzer currently serves as an adviser to the Bush administration and key congressional leaders, and as an adjunct professor of finance at New York University. He lives in Dallas.

ROBERT DEITZ, an award-winning journalist twice nominated for the Pulitzer prize, is executive business editor of the *Dallas Times Herald*. A former Neiman Fellow at Harvard University, he lives in Dallas.